CRAZY MAN, CRAZY

CRAZY

THE BILL HALEY STORY

BILL HALEY JR. AND PETER BENJAMINSON

Backbeat
Books
Guilford, Connecticut

Published by Backbeat Books
An imprint of The Rowman & Littlefield Publishing Group, Inc.
4501 Forbes Boulevard, Suite 200, Lanham, Maryland 20706
www.rowman.com

Distributed by NATIONAL BOOK NETWORK

Book design and composition by John J. Flannery

Library of Congress Cataloging-in-Publication Data is available

ISBN 978-1-61713-711-2

The paper used in this publication meets the minimum requirements of
American National Standard for Information Sciences—Permanence of
Paper for Printed Library Materials, ANSI/NISO Z39.48-1992.

Printed in the United States of America

No one cares for your tragedy
until you can sing about it.
–V. S. Naipaul

Contents

Introduction:
Bill's Three-Part Life

Rock 'n' roll by its very nature leads to
a breakdown in discipline.
–The Vice Principal Wolters character,
played by William H. Macy
in the 1995 movie Mr. Holland's Opus

NO ONE HIT the *Billboard* Top 20 with a rock 'n' roll song before
Bill Haley did with "Crazy Man, Crazy," in 1953, and no one rose to
No. 1 on the charts with a rock 'n' roll tune before Bill did in 1955 with
"(We're Gonna) Rock Around the Clock." By blending country and
western, rhythm and blues, elements of big band jazz, and a touch of
vaudeville, he became the world's first successful rock 'n' roller.

Bill Haley's achievement made him the idol of screaming crowds,
not only in the United States and Canada, but also throughout the
United Kingdom and continental Europe, Australia, New Zealand,
Mexico, Central America, South America, Japan, and almost everywhere else on earth where records were played, including Tunisia and
the Fiji Islands.

He has been largely ignored, overlooked, or dismissed, however, in
popular literature and discussions about the early days of rock 'n' roll.
While movies, documentaries, TV dramas, and stage musicals have
been made about Buddy Holly, Elvis Presley, Jerry Lee Lewis and other
rock 'n' roll pioneers, there's been barely a nod to Bill, who preceded
them all.

In part, this was Bill's own fault. Although he worked for years to
make himself famous and often told others how famous he hoped to
become, he was an intensely private man who often shunned the public eye and opposed others' attempts to tell his life story, even after he
became a worldwide celebrity.

This was partly because he had two skeletons in his closet. One was
his prolonged descent into chronic alcoholism. The other was that after
becoming the father of ten children with his three successive wives, he

abruptly abandoned and rejected his first two wives and the six surviving children he had with them, emotionally and financially.

Bill's musical and personal lives were closely linked. During his first marriage, he became the leader of a moderately successful hillbilly and western band. While divorcing his first wife and marrying his second, he started playing rock 'n' roll and became a rock 'n' roll superstar. While divorcing his second wife and marrying his third, he became Mexico's top pop music star. To do justice to a career so psychologically and musically fragmented, this book is divided, like Gaul in Julius Caesar's commentaries, into three parts.

This book is nonfiction. All the conversations and thoughts recounted within it have been vouched for directly by those involved in the conversations, or are statements made by Bill Sr. to Bill Jr. during telephone conversations. While conducting research, Bill Jr. also obtained and utilized hundreds of documents, contracts, letters, diaries, and other original sources maintained by family members and associates of his father.

Bill Jr.'s primary interview sources for part 1 included Dorothy Crowe Haley, Bill Sr.'s first wife; Amy Clark, who befriended Bill Sr. in her teen years, and original Saddlemen Johnny Grande and Al Rex.

Bill Jr.'s primary interview sources for part 2 were Joan Barbara "Cuppy" Haley-Hahn, Bill Sr.'s second wife and Bill Jr.'s mother; and Sam Sgro, business partner with James "Lord Jim" Ferguson and the band's business manager for most of the period covered by this book.

Bill Jr.'s primary sources for part 3 included Cuppy, as well as Bill Jr.'s sister Joan Haley Royce, and numerous late-night telephone conversations between Bill Jr. and his father from November 1979 until the day before Bill Sr.'s death on February 9, 1981.

In total, Cuppy contributed 20+ hours of formal taped interviews and engaged in innumerable casual conversations with Bill Jr. about her life with his father, providing a major source for this book beginning with part 2. All three parts are based on Bill Haley Jr.'s extensive and in-depth interviews, not only with Cuppy, but also with Bill Sr.'s first wife, children, business associates, and managers.

All three parts of the book are also based on Bill Jr.'s interviews with many of the original or early Saddlemen and Comets (with the exception of Billy Williamson). Those interviewed include Ralph Jones, Al Rex, Franny Beecher, Marshall Lytle, Johnny Grande, and Joey Ambrose. Bill Jr. also interviewed James Myers, credited as cowriter of the song "Rock Around the Clock"; and ex-Comet Bill Turner, who performed with Bill Haley Sr. in the 1970s.

Websites containing a wealth of information and photographs on the band's history were also consulted. Special thanks to Chris Gardner, Alex Frazer-Harrison, Bob Timmers, Rick Hull, and Denise Gregiore for creating and maintaining those websites. Frazer-Harrison and Gardner also moderate the International "Razor Bunnies," a Bill Haley online discussion group whose knowledgeable members contributed invaluable opinions and information.

Although this book explores Bill Sr.'s career in detail, it also touches upon larger issues against which Bill's life played itself out: institutional racism in America, teenage rebellion and the rise of juvenile delinquency in the 1950s, and the dark underbelly of the music business, including Bill's peripheral ties to the Mafia.

One

BILL GROWS UP, MARRIES HIS FIRST WIFE, AND BECOMES A COUNTRY AND WESTERN BAND LEADER

1

Out of Detroit

The only thing worse than being blind
is having sight but no vision.
–HELEN KELLER

William John Clifton Haley was born at 2:30 p.m. on July 6,
1925—right smack dab in the middle of the Roaring Twenties—
a portentous and appropriate beginning for a man who would go on to
initiate and popularize a revolutionary musical movement called rock
'n' roll. He would become world famous for his rendition of a timeless song titled "(We're Gonna) Rock Around the Clock," the ultimate
expression of *joie de vivre*, a symbol of an era, and one of the top-selling
singles of all time.

Bill's birth took place in a second-floor apartment in Highland Park,
Michigan, a city literally surrounded by Detroit. In 1959, Detroit would
become the home of the Motown Record Corporation, which produced music resembling Haley's, but by that time, Bill was long gone.
African Americans, who eventually became the majority of Detroit resi-
dents, later criticized Bill, who was white, for succeeding by imitating
black musicians or riding to the top of the charts by playing songs those
musicians already had recorded.

Although Bill, his parents Will and Maude, and his older sister
Peggy left the Motor City area early in Bill's life, Detroit left its mark on
him. Before he departed, a Detroit doctor performed a crude operation
to remove a mastoid behind four-year-old Bill's left ear in 1929 and
mistakenly severed the boy's optic nerve, leaving him blind in his left
eye for the rest of his days.

Initially unaware of their son's partial blindness, Bill's parents and
their two children left Detroit in the Spring of 1932, when Will, like
millions of others, lost his job to the Great Depression. The family
packed up their meager belongings, including Will's beloved banjo and
mandolin, loaded everything into their Ford Roadster, and headed east
to Marcus Hook, Pennsylvania. There Maude's father used his influ-

1

ence and connections to get Will a coveted job at the American Viscose factory, near the Sun Oil refinery on the Delaware River.

That job at American Viscose saved the family from destitution, but it became exactly the kind of fate that Bill struggled for the rest of his life to avoid—the timeless toil of factory life. Nevertheless, Will, who came from Firebrick, Kentucky, and suffered from a speech impediment, never complained. "He was just a little short guy who didn't have much to say," reported one of Bill's friends at the time, Amy Clark. "I didn't pay too much attention to him. He was a quiet person who kept to himself," Clark said, unlike Bill's Mom, who carried all the conversation.

A humble, steady man, Will Haley had been taught by his dad to always be a gentleman, reliable and trustworthy, and when his parents died prematurely, he'd postponed starting a family of his own in order to support and raise his brothers and sisters. His trusty mandolin and love of music sustained him during times of struggle, and his musical ability was part of what attracted him to Maude Green, his future wife, as well.

Maude was born in England, where she learned to play piano and read classical music as a young girl before coming to the US in her early teens. As an adult, she loved playing organ at the Methodist church she regularly attended, and she adored playing the piano at home while the rest of her family sang.

In 1932, shortly after the Haley family settled into their new surroundings in Pennsylvania, Will realized that his seven-year-old son was blind in one eye. He'd noticed that Bill, hearing an airplane passing overhead, shielded only his right eye from the sun when looking up at the bright daytime sky. He later realized that Bill also was nearsighted in his good eye.

The boy's vision problems made it impossible for him to do well in schoolyard baseball and football games; he was always the last one picked for any team. Also, because his eyes seemed to move independently of each other, some of the other kids called him "frog eyes." Perhaps Bill's memory of this slight caused him to write the line "I got legs like a rooster, eyes like a frog" in his later hit song "Hot Dog Buddy Buddy."

It wasn't long before Bill withdrew from all school sports and became a shy and awkward loner. To distract attention from his wandering left eye, he combed his hair into a big wavy bang over the right side of his forehead, an unusual hair style that would later evolve into his trademark spit curl. Although he was eventually prescribed glasses to correct his one-eyed nearsightedness, he wore them as rarely as possible and almost never in public. To further distract attention from his eyes, he began wearing a cowboy hat.

The hat soon became part of Bill's escape plan. The offspring of a musical family, he decided to become a singing cowboy like Gene Autry and others he saw in Saturday films at the local movie theater. His parents encouraged his ambition, giving him a guitar for his thirteenth birthday in the summer of 1938. His father taught him to play it by ear, and he was soon playing and singing in imitation of the tunes he heard on the radio (Bill never learned to read music). On weekends, the whole family would sing together, with Bill's mother and older sister Peggy taking turns playing the piano.

On June 5, 1941, Haley completed the tenth grade at Johnson's Corner School and soon went to work driving trucks and doing other manual jobs. Just sixteen years old, he was 6'1" and weighed 175 lbs., and he began telling his girlfriends he wanted to become someone important and not just a manual laborer. Bill flubbed his first attempt in that direction, however, when he entered a local talent contest after cracking his guitar in a bicycle accident earlier the same day. He did poorly, and was so embarrassed that he didn't perform in public again for close to two years, except to play with family and friends at private parties and get-togethers.

After the Japanese attack on Pearl Harbor in December 1941, Bill tried to join the military, lying about his age, but was rejected because of his poor eyesight. As the war dragged on and his friends served abroad, people at home looked at him strangely, wondering why such an apparently fit young man was not serving his country. Although he eventually adjusted to his situation, he still felt he was going nowhere — not physically qualified to serve, but too shy to sing in public.

In 1943, noting Bill's predicament, the manager of the Booth's Corner Sale, a local outdoor auction market near Bill's home, asked him to sing a couple of songs one night in the privacy of the manager's office. Bill did, not knowing that the manager had arranged for his songs to be broadcast on the market's public-address system. The resulting compliments convinced Bill that people liked to listen to him, and also inspired the manager to offer him a dollar for a half hour of singing intended to gather a crowd for the market's regular auctions. The response was so enthusiastic that Bill's playing time was expanded. His pay rate soon rose to five dollars a half hour, good money at the time on top of the thirty dollars a week he already was earning as a factory hand. His rise had begun.

2
The Singing Cowboy

Don't flatter yourself, cowboy.
I was looking at your horse.
—OLD SAYING

Although he'd never wanted to be a real cowboy, Bill was dead
serious about being a singing cowboy. By the summer of 1944,
he was wearing a white cowboy hat and a bright red cowboy suit with
white fringe to sing at Booth's Corner Sale, or wherever else he had the
opportunity to perform. (He'd ordered the outfit from a Philadelphia
tailor.) Bill also had learned to yodel, a top-rated skill for country music
singers of that era.

Fourteen-year-old Amy Clark had an adolescent crush on the tall,
handsome nineteen-year-old Bill Haley in the summer of '44. They'd
met that year at Radio Park, an open-air amusement park in nearby
Delaware featuring live Western entertainment on the weekends. Every
Sunday, Amy worked the spindle concession at the park, and Bill ran
the baseball throw booth, where you'd pay a nickel for three chances to
win a prize by toppling a row of lead-weighted milk bottles.

Bill and Amy would chat when things got slow during their 2 to 10
p.m. shift. Bill was shy at first but friendly, very charming and polite,
and they hit it off. It didn't take long for the conversation to turn
to music, and when Amy told Bill that her father had been paying
twenty-five cents an hour for her to take piano lessons since fourth
grade, he asked her to join him the following Saturday at his parents'
house, where he played guitar and sang with his friends each week.
His mom or sister Peggy usually sat in on piano, but they'd be happy
to let Amy play, he said.

Before long, Bill and Amy were "dating," although their relationship
would never progress beyond the petting stage. On one occasion, they
double dated with Bill's musician friend Bob Chandler and his girlfriend, Verna Wilgas, taking the bus to Chester and riding the ferry to
Riverview Amusement Park in New Jersey.

Amy Clark also worked at the Booth's Corner Sale, where Bill would appear in full cowboy attire every Friday night playing solo, singing, and yodeling on a makeshift stage set up under a string of light bulbs inside a huge barn with a dirt floor and loose hay hanging from the rafters overhead. Some of Amy's friends at the sale would make fun of Bill—out of jealousy, Amy thought—calling him a dandy and a phony cowboy. The way Amy saw it, Bill was way ahead of his time. People weren't ready for what he was ready to give them.

Amy loved to listen to Bill sing his western songs, not only the beautiful country ballads, but also the up-tempo numbers. One of the songs she and audience members asked him to sing again and again was "Paper of Pins." He performed the song, which begins "I'll give to you a paper of pins, and that's the way our love begins," with a female partner: Doris Chandler, Bob Chandler's sister.

Bill was occasionally accompanied on stage by "Pop" Guthrie, a joke-cracking fiddler who'd add cornball humor to Bill's musical act. Guthrie became such an attraction that even after Bill had become king of rock 'n' roll, Bill kept adding vaudeville-style slapstick humor to his and his band's performances. Many of Bill's big-time concerts were highlighted by band members who routinely split their pants on stage on purpose, rode their bass fiddles like horses in a perhaps unconscious reference to the cowboy singers they'd previously been, or somehow continued to play those huge, heavy instruments while carrying them above their heads or lying on their backs.

Bill's combination of music and onstage personality soon landed him an opportunity to perform for a huge audience at Radio Park in Delaware during amateur night, a highly publicized evening of entertainment topped off with the first East Coast appearance of Roy Rogers and the Sons of the Pioneers. It was a special event. Radio station WDEL, based in Wilmington, Delaware, was doing a remote broadcast of the two-hour show, a rarity for the time. Bill was excited about this opportunity and unfazed by the prospect of performing in front of ten thousand people plus a live radio audience. "Bill told me, 'I'm gonna make it someday,'" Amy later recalled. "He used to come to Radio Park with his suits on, all the glitter on them. He loved to dress up and get ready to go on stage. He was ready to be popular. There wasn't any doubt about that. He wasn't afraid to be different."

Bill's big-time debut was a success. "It was quite a show," Amy recalls. That led to an offer of full-time employment from a seven-member hillbilly and western band called Cousin Lee and His Boys, the house band at Radio Park. Cousin Lee also had one bad eye, which may have made him sympathetic to Bill, but Bill's appeal to Cousin Lee also was aided by support from one of Bill's most ardent local fans: promoter and record producer Jack Howard, owner of the Cowboy Record label.

Seeing Cousin Lee as his next step toward stardom, Bill immediately quit his factory job. He spent the next year and a half with his fellow half-blind music-maker, doing appearances at local fire companies, dances, theaters, and parks, and radio shows on station WDEL as a featured member of Cousin Lee and His Boys. (The name of his band may have been the inspiration for the name Bill later adopted for several of his later ones, including "Bill Haley and His Comets," as opposed to the more obvious "Bill Haley and the Comets.")

Young Bill Haley gained valuable experience working with Cousin Lee, both onstage and backstage. He got to meet and converse with a wide range of professional performers, including a man who would become something of a mentor and friend over the next several years: Hank Williams, the hillbilly Shakespeare. Some years later, Bill told an interviewer that Hank had taught him a few chords and influenced him. "He was a great blues singer and he stimulated my interest in R&B music, race music as it was called then," he said.

One evening, while performing with Cousin Lee at the Parish House on Fifth Street in Salem, New Jersey, Bill met a slender, dark-haired beauty with captivating eyes and a beautiful smile. She would become the first of his three wives.

Eighteen-year-old high school student Dorothy Crowe was in the audience with her friend Peggy White, and when the band went on break, Bill walked straight up to Dottie and started a conversation. Dottie, Peggy, and many other young girls in the audience thought Bill was very handsome in his white Stetson. "When he smiled at you, it made you feel good all over," Peggy said. "And how he could talk! He made his dreams become your dreams."

Dottie and Peggy thought Bill had great manners and a warm personality. Indeed, Bill had received two great gifts from his parents that would serve him well the rest of his personal and professional life. One was teaching him to always use proper manners and present himself as a gentleman. The second was the unconditional love and the frequent compliments and encouragement they bestowed on him. Bill confidently told the girls he was going to make it big one day and everyone would know his name. Peggy and her friends laughed behind Bill's back, but Dottie was smitten, and soon, she and Bill began dating.

As her last name implied, Dottie was half Crow Indian. Perhaps Bill was attracted by someone of his and his father's partial Native American ancestry, but her ethnicity aside, Dottie was an attractive and charming brunette. She was soon attending many of his appearances, traveling as far as fifty miles to see him play. When she didn't, Bill would call her from wherever he was performing.

In those performances, Cousin Lee was featuring Bill as "Silver Yodeling Bill," and Bill dreamed of becoming an even better yodeler. In pursuit of this version of his dream, he asked the advice of famous yodeler Elton Britt, an RCA Victor Records star known for his hit song "Chime Bells." Britt recommended drinking wine or whiskey instead of beer to avoid the urge to burp while yodeling. Unfortunately, Bill later followed Britt's advice with a vengeance.

Bill also picked up some valuable experience as an on-air radio personality while with Cousin Lee's band. At the invitation of the band's fiddle player, Wayne Wright, he served for a while as co-host on a half-hour country-western radio show Wayne honchoed on WSNJ in Bridgeton, New Jersey. Bill began doing solo performances in the Philadelphia area as well, and he eventually branched out from Cousin Lee and began sitting in with various other local outfits. He was appearing with the Blue Hen Ramblers in York, Pennsylvania, in November 1945 when his girlfriend Dottie told him about an ad in *Billboard* magazine for a lead singer and yodeler for a popular hillbilly and western band. This was a particularly interesting bit of information, because Bill knew that this band—the Down Homers, led by Shorty Cook—was a regular on the popular "Hoosier Hop" program, broadcast to the entire nation from radio station WOWO in Fort Wayne, Indiana, on the ABC radio network. Their lead singer and yodeler Kenny Roberts had taken a temporary leave of absence to serve in the United States Navy.

To Bill, an opening in such a well-known band looked like a chance to break out of his small-time career into national stardom. But with no money of his own, he needed a grubstake to make the move. Living close to the bone, he didn't even have the money to travel to Fort Wayne. Dottie, who had graduated high school and was now working in the office of a local factory, encouraged him and offered to lend him money. She was still living at home with her police officer father, John

Crowe, a decorated World War I veteran who strongly opposed her desire to lend Bill the money he needed. He disapproved of Dottie's relationship with an itinerant, guitar-playing musician, but Bill promised he would become rich and famous and have her join him once he got established and made a name for himself. Love overcame all, and Bill got the cash.

3
On the Road

You're on the road, the great American road!
—Voice-over from
a Chevrolet commercial

Bill's career with the Down Homers got off to an inauspicious start. Upon arrival, he waited in the Fort Wayne train station for three hours before calling Shorty Cook, only to find out that the boys Shorty sent to pick him up had walked right past him because they were looking for a much older man. It turns out there was another yodeling musician named Bill Haley, known in the Midwest, and that's whom they thought they'd hired when they interviewed Bill over the phone. Nevertheless, Shorty Cook was impressed by the younger, unknown Bill Haley's talent and enthusiasm, and even more so by the fact that to qualify for a spot in the band, Bill learned to play the bass fiddle in one week.

As a Down Homer, Bill cowrote his first published song with Cook, a cowboy ballad called "Four Leaf Clover Blues." Several of the "Four Leaf" verses show that in terms of their lyrics, there wasn't much difference between country and western tunes and the thousands of rock 'n' roll songs that would be produced a decade later, some of them by Bill himself. Rock 'n' roll rhythms and instrumentation would be much different, however. In "Four Leaf," Bill sang, "Want to roll them bones, and hear the losers moan, 'cause baby needs a new pair of shoes." Bill would write, or participate in writing more than 150 songs over the next thirty-five years, and this was the first.

Restless and rising, Bill spent only a few months with the Down Homers, traveling with them to Hartford, Connecticut, where they found a new home on station WTIC. When Kenny Roberts received an early discharge from the Navy with the end of the war, however, he resumed his role as lead singer and yodeler in the group, and Bill was relegated to a supporting role. Knowing he couldn't get rich playing in someone else's band, he hatched a plan to jump ship. After all, he'd promised Dottie he was going to be a star, not a hired band hand. Taking two other members of Shorty Cook's group with him (and thereby infuriating Shorty), he signed on a fourth musician. The new band then migrated to station WKNE in Keene, New Hampshire, where they appropriately dubbed themselves the Range Drifters.

After some initial success, including Bill's victory in the 1946 Indiana State Fair Yodeling Championship, the band headed for Chicago. Its progress there was hampered, however, when Shorty denounced its members as "band jumpers" to his many Chicago friends, severely restricting the group's Windy City employment opportunities.

Heading south to Oklahoma, the Range Drifters struggled through the brief but severe US postwar depression, which restricted their opportunities there as well. They continued on to San Antonio, Dallas, and New Orleans, working only sporadically. Although Bill may not have realized it at the time, this was a turning point in his career. In Chicago, New Orleans, St. Louis and East St. Louis, he heard a lot of sounds he'd never heard before: jazz music, Lena Horne tunes, and the music and melodies played by black Americans. As Bill's horizons expanded, he began to imagine the possibilities of combining styles and rhythms to achieve popular success in the music business. And he began nurturing another objective: to bring dance music back into vogue. He wouldn't be able to accomplish this until a few years later, however, when he began collaborating and experimenting with likeminded musicians.

Although Bill's musical education continued and his career plans solidified throughout the spring of 1946, his pockets were hurting. By then, the four young Range Drifters were living on canned beans and black coffee, often sleeping in their cars or in cheap hotel rooms. Inevitably, they started arguing. Bill quit the group and headed off on his own, appearing solo in pubs, honkytonks and open-air parks throughout the Midwest, Southern, and Eastern US. In Nebraska, he crossed paths with a patent medicine salesman named Doc Protheroe who hired him to sing and play his guitar to attract crowds to whom the doctor could pitch his "Miracle Tonic." This kept Bill in beans, but instead of becoming a star, as he'd hoped, he was back where he started, using his musical skills to attract crowds for an outdoor pitchman.

Soon afterward, Bill had to humble himself by hitching back to Fort Wayne and asking Shorty Cook to reinstate him in his old job with the Down Homers. His mood dropped into his boots when Shorty—overwhelmed with applications from talented country singers who were being discharged from the military as the war ended, and still angry at Bill for walking out on his band—told him no. Nevertheless, Bill looked so thin and downcast by then that Shorty lent him forty dollars to take a train back to his parents' house in southeast Pennsylvania, where he arrived in September 1946. He immediately climbed into bed and slept for thirty hours straight.

4
Recovery

*I'm always making a comeback but
nobody ever tells me where I've been.*
—BILLIE HOLIDAY

Bill Haley's first attempt at stardom had failed. It took a few weeks, and a lot of sympathetic murmuring from Bill's mom and his girlfriend Dottie, before he was able to fight off the depression that had settled on him. After all, he'd crawled home with little success to point to after a year on the road. His mood improved somewhat, however, when Wayne Wright, who'd taught Bill how to DJ in New Jersey and then moved to Keene, New Hampshire, told him that the radio station there was looking for a second disc jockey.

After borrowing the train fare from his parents, Bill moved to Keene and was hired as the No. 2 DJ at WKNE. For thirty dollars a week he spun tunes, played his guitar, sang solo, read news and commercials, and performed on air with the Range Drifters. At night, he slept on the living room couch in Wayne's apartment.

It soon became evident, however, that back in Pennsylvania, Dottie had helped Bill recover from his depression in nonverbal as well as verbal ways: he received a letter from his sister Peggy informing him that his girlfriend was pregnant. Deciding to do the right thing, Bill proposed to Dottie over the telephone. She took a bus to Brattleboro, Vermont, near Keene, where she and Bill were married by a justice of the peace on December 11, 1946. The newly married couple then moved into an apartment near the bus station.

Bill's new radio job paid better than his previous one, but his hours were long and the couple's budget was tight, even though he broadcast six evenings a week and Dottie worked part time at a local store. Their relationship wasn't helped by the fact that immediately after Dottie returned from her day job, Bill had to leave for his night job.

With a baby on the way, however, plus a job and a place to live, Bill's confidence and ambition returned. He devoted nearly all his extra time and most of his attention to furthering his career. "He was determined . . . ambitious. . . . He was going to make it to the top and nobody or nothing was going to stop him," Dottie said. He became determined to rise above the disc jockey level and move into radio management, where he would have some say in programming.

After a few months, searching for greater opportunity in a larger market, Bill reunited with the Range Drifters, and together they moved on to station WTIC in Hartford, Connecticut. In May 1947, he and the band relocated again, with a very pregnant Dottie in tow, to station WLBR in Lebanon, Pennsylvania.

Bill's first child, Sharyn, was born in June 1947, and as new babies are said to do, she brought him good luck. That October, Bill's father told him that a new station, run by a liberal businessman, was about to go on the air in Chester, Pennsylvania, not far from the family's home in Boothwyn.

Lou Pollar, the founder of radio station WPWA in Chester, was aware that the audience in this heavily industrial region surrounded by farmland was a mixed bag of first-generation Poles, Italians, Greeks, and Ukrainians, plus numerous whites and blacks who had migrated from the South. With the area crowded with larger radio stations, he wanted to attract immediate attention to his small start-up.

Pollar listened eagerly as Bill told him that if he was hired, he'd play live and recorded hillbilly and western music for the white Southerners; European folk music for the first-generation European immigrants; talk shows for housewives and sports enthusiasts; and "race" records, Dixieland, jazz and bebop for the blacks.

Aware that Bill had solid DJ experience and a sizeable following in the region from his frequent appearances at Radio Park, Sunset Park, and Rainbow Park, and also from WDEL, Pollar saw a real opportunity sitting in front of him. In November 1947, he hired Bill as not only the station DJ, but also its record librarian, custodian, ad salesman, newscaster, announcer, and host of the station's *Ladies Aid* program. It was a ground-floor opportunity, and Bill was determined to make the most of it. He was a new father, and what better place to put down roots than right back home in the Delaware Valley with the loving support of his mother, father, and sister.

Bill said goodbye to the Range Drifters for a second time, returned to Chester with his wife and daughter, and after a short while, he and Range Drifters bass player Julian "Barney" Barnard formed a new outfit to perform live twice a day as the house band at WPWA. They called themselves the Four Aces of Western Swing, soon to be known as the Western Aces.

5
Let's Try It Again

Nothing in the world can take the place
of persistence. Talent will not. . . . Genius will not. . . .
Education will not. . . . Persistence and
determination alone are omnipotent.
—CALVIN COOLIDGE

Bill moved his young family into a run-down, rodent-infested two-bedroom apartment on Rose Street in Chester, right next to some railroad tracks on which freight trains rumbled by at all hours of the day and night. Dedicated to his new job, he began spending six days a week, twelve to sixteen hours per day at WPWA, wearing a variety of hats and filling any programming gaps with live performances. On weekends, he'd scout nearby parks and local clubs, looking for talented musicians willing to play for free on the radio just for exposure.

"We had rough times, but they were good times," Dottie recalled wistfully, remembering that except for the baby, they lived on bread, peanut butter, and black coffee. Bill's goal from the day she met him was "going to the top, one way or another," Dottie said. "That's one thing I always respect him for . . . he got there."

Dottie insisted that Bill was "a very shy person who hated to go into a new place and meet new people." She said his fellow band members had to force him to come out of his dressing room when someone wanted to meet him. "Once he took that first step, though, things would go all right," she said.

Throughout 1948, Bill Haley and His Western Aces recorded hillbilly tunes released by the Cowboy Records company, owned by his friend and manager, Jack Howard. They didn't chart. Meanwhile, other groups began doing well with some of those same songs, including "Four Leaf Clover Blues" and "Candy and Women."

The fact that he seemed to be stalled only inspired Bill to work longer hours at the radio station. In April, he also took over management of the Radio Park amusement park in nearby Delaware with his musical partner Barney Barnard. (Cousin Lee, who had been managing Radio

Park, got into some trouble involving a young girl and needed to bow out.) Bill and the Western Aces played at Radio Park every weekend, and Bill spent the rest of his evenings running from gig to gig with his band. Their initial club dates were at dive bars like Luke's Musical Bar and the Maltone Melody Lounge, both in the seedy part of Chester.

Throughout the rest of 1948 and into the spring of 1949, the Western Aces kept on building their following with live appearances and performing on WPWA. On April 16, 1949, the group hosted the first nationwide "Hillbilly and Western Marathon" broadcast live from WPWA, raising $16,000 in pledged contributions for the American Cancer Society.

In May 1949, a program called *Judge Rhythm's Court*, hosted by "Shorty the Bailiff," moved over to WPWA from competing station WVCH. Although Shorty sounded black, he was a forty-year-old white man named James Reeves who was good at dialects. Reeves's two-hour show played "race" records, including Bill's later hit "Rock the Joint," which had been written and recorded by black musicians. Local black listeners in Chester and Wilmington loved listening to *Judge Rhythm's Court*, and Bill believed, although he couldn't prove it, that local whites loved it too. He certainly did, and although it might have been frowned upon by segregationists, he allowed himself to be influenced by what he heard.

On his *Western Swing Hour*, a show Bill created that followed *Judge Rhythm's Court*, he would introduce "cowboy jump" tunes, western songs with a beat. Few listeners appreciated this part of his effort, or realized that what Bill was doing was gradually trying to narrow the difference between country and western tunes and rhythm and blues music. Although Bill didn't know it, when that difference was finally bridged, rock 'n' roll would be born.

The twenty-four-year-old Bill told his musician friends that his ultimate plan was to "mix Dixieland, hillbilly, and western swing." And for a while, he thought he saw a way forward. His friend Slim Allsman bought an electric guitar that fascinated Bill. It was a real beauty—a golden maple Gibson "Premier" with a Bigsby vibrato tailpiece—and Bill compared using it to "holding thunder and lightning" in his hands. He managed to find time to go to Allsman's apartment to play the Premier, even when Allsman wasn't there, but he only went home to catch three or four hours of sleep between his late-night band performances and his 6 a.m. radio shows.

Although Bill gave all his attention to furthering his career, he did seem to love his wife and child. With Jack Howard, he wrote a song titled "Rose of My Heart" for his new daughter, and he later recorded it for Howard's Cowboy Records. "Now I've got a gal, as sweet as a rose," Bill sang, "I call her the rose of my heart."

Nevertheless, Bill often ignored Dottie and Sharyn, even though they frequently went hungry. His first priority was his career, which trumped playing an active role in raising his daughter. By contrast, Dottie, the product of divorced parents, wanted a stable, emotionally involved family, not one headed by a husband driven to work endless hours in pursuit of money and fame.

To make matters worse, working late nights in the clubs came with temptations that Bill couldn't resist. Occasionally Dottie, waiting by their open apartment window for Bill to come home late at night, would see him pull his car up to the curb, turn out the lights, and cut the engine. Then, if the night was still, she could hear him speaking in hushed tones and the giggles of one of his girlfriends. Sometimes what she heard was almost more than she could endure. Although she wept bitterly, she never confronted her husband later on when he'd slip into bed beside her. She felt vulnerable and lacked the courage to confront Bill, fearing that if she did so, he might leave her and their daughter to fend for themselves.

By mid-1949, however, Dottie was tired of heartbreak and long, lonely nights, and also worried that the occasional rat she heard in the apartment late at night would climb into Sharyn's crib. She moved back in with her father in Salem, New Jersey, and Bill began spending some nights in the basement of the radio station, sleeping on a cot near the coal bin. Often, however, he stayed with his parents instead in the house he'd grown up in. His mother, Maude, always listened to Bill's radio show, and if he'd be coming home that evening, he'd send her a signal by singing the song "Put a Light in the Window."

Not wanting to totally abandon his young family, Bill still would occasionally drive to Salem on Mondays to spend time with Dottie and Sharyn. Perhaps out of guilt, and frustrated at his lack of progress in his search for a new sound that would rocket him to fame, Bill turned to alcohol as an escape. It was the first but not the last time he would do so.

One night in the fall of 1949, while was playing at Luke's in Chester, half-drunk on port wine and with his shirt covered with cigarette ashes, Bill, on a dare, punched his fist through the wall of the men's room. This misguided act of bravado put his hand in a cast and ended his musical career for the next six weeks. Coincidentally, a few months earlier, three of Bill's band mates had been arrested at 3:30 in the morning for disorderly conduct, and one of them, Barney Barnard, had brandished a .32-caliber automatic pistol during a confrontation. Then, in September 1949, an indictment had been handed down charging Barnard with a violation of the Firearms Act for pointing the weapon. These incidents effectively spelled the end of the Western Aces. With only his day job at WPWA to occupy him, Bill moved back in with Dottie and their daughter.

6

The Birth
of the Saddlemen

We stole more records than anybody.
—FORMER OWNER OF A
WHITE-OWNED RECORD COMPANY

By late December 1949, Bill's hand had healed enough to let him go back to Luke's Musical Bar, this time performing solo. Luke's was a classic "dive" bar, known among the locals as "Bucket of Blood." Fights there were often settled in the parking lot out back, next to the graveyard. Chicken wire lined the crudely constructed stage to protect performers from thrown debris, and dim bulbs seemed to float in the smoky haze clinging to the cracked ceiling. The joint reeked of cigarettes, sweat, and stale beer.

At this second low point in Bill's adult life, he was approached by Billy Williamson and Johnny Grande, two young Philadelphia-area musicians looking for work because their temporary job—backing musician Jesse Stone in Newark, New Jersey—had come to an end. Before that they'd played in a band called the Southern Swingsters, led by Slim Allsman. From Allsman they'd heard about Haley's remarkable ability to remember the words and melodies to hundreds of songs, and his quixotic quest to combine hillbilly with other forms of music. Intrigued, they approached Bill at Luke's and asked him to let them be part of a collective effort to come up with a new, fresh sound.

It took a while for the two musicians to convince Haley to join them. He knew Billy Williamson, a superb instrumentalist with a fine Irish tenor voice, by reputation. Williamson specialized in lap steel guitar and also was an accomplished fiddler and rhythm guitar player. His nineteen-year-old sidekick Johnny Grande was still a little green, but he exuded a quiet confidence, and Billy vouched for him as a talented pianist/accordionist who could actually read music. Williamson and

Grande were persistent and passionate, and eventually Bill agreed to form a new group with them named Bill Haley and the Saddlemen. (By now, Bill had been performing for years in bars frequented by on-the-make men and women, and the double-entendre quality of the word *saddlemen* may have added to the name's appeal.)

Throughout that winter and into the spring of 1950, the three men each committed to daily two-hour rehearsals. Attempting to create a completely new format for popular music, they tried playing popular tunes in many different styles. Williamson in particular encouraged them to emulate the sounds and rhythms heard on "race" records, such as the big-band sounds of Count Basie. They also experimented with emphasizing the second and fourth beats in traditional monotonous four-beat measures, realizing that doing so pushed the songs forward and added energy and excitement.

In one low-tech move meant to compensate for the group's lack of percussion instruments, Bill and the Saddlemen started back-slapping the strings on their bass fiddle to add rhythm to the hillbilly tunes they were playing. They also hired four-hundred-pound Al Thompson as the group's initial bass player. Al, a crowd favorite, wore cut-off jeans, a shirt several sizes too small, and a floppy hat, and he threw his bull fiddle around the stage while cracking corny jokes. Thompson eventually quit because the long stage performance was too hard on his feet, and a skinnier musician—Al Piccirilli, who used the stage name Al Rex—took his place in the group.

Throughout 1950, the band experimented privately with hybrid beats and styles, and publicly performed hillbilly and western standards and favorites. In the meantime, they built a following with their regular radio appearances on WPWA and frequent performances at open air parks, dance halls, and small clubs throughout the Delaware Valley. By late 1950, the band had increased its popularity by recording some tunes for small record companies. Its attempt to combine R&B and country and western and add a beat had apparently made some headway: a *Billboard* magazine reviewer complimented the group's "zippy western rhythm tunes."

At this auspicious moment, on Dec. 1, 1950, Bill's first son was born. Bill and Dottie named him John William (Jack) Haley after Bill's close friend and business associate Jack Howard. Jack was Bill's second child with Dottie, conceived during a period of reconciliation between the two of them in the spring of that year. Now that he sensed himself on the rise once more, however, Bill once again lost interest in the relationship. For that reason, he chose to name the baby Jack, instead of Bill Jr. as Bill's mom had wished.

Meanwhile, songs Bill had written that were performed by others were making enough money to motivate Bill and Jack Howard, his longtime informal promoter, to form Haley-Howard Publications to handle the royalties the songs produced. This form of payback is known in the business as a song's copyright, its publishing royalties, or simply "the publishing." It can be a major source of income for whomever owns the rights involved. Every time someone records or sings the song on which you own the publishing rights, he or she must pay you royalties based on the number of records produced or the number of times the song is sung or performed.

Sometimes this requirement is enforced above and beyond the dictates of common sense. Various companies that have owned the publishing for the song "Happy Birthday to You" have employed agents to crash birthday parties at private homes where the song was being sung and demand immediate payment of the publishing. The struggle over "Happy Birthday," composed around 1893 and quite possibly the most popular song ever written, continued for more than a century. In 2008, Warner/Chappell Music collected two million dollars in royalties for its use. Finally, in 2016, a federal judge declared "Happy Birthday" to be in the public domain, meaning it could be sung anywhere for free.

Due to their potential immense monetary value, publishing rights for popular songs have long been disputed, bargained for, and outright stolen. Often people including agents, music company owners, record producers, and romantic partners of naïve song composers or recording artists have insinuated themselves into partial ownership of those rights merely by having themselves added to the song's list of composers. Sometimes they've paid the artist a small sum for this privilege. Other times, they've just added their names to the appropriate documents, hoping the artist wouldn't notice or, if he or she did, there'd be no objection.

There's no indication Bill ever engaged in shady publishing practices. He seems to have made the appropriate payments to the people who owned the publishing rights to songs he'd recorded but hadn't written. What he really wanted was to write songs himself, retain their publishing rights, and then record them, hoping they'd become popular enough for other musicians to want to record them themselves and pay him the publishing royalties.

In January 1951, Jack Howard renewed and reinforced his contract as Bill's personal manager and publicist and began aggressively advertising and promoting "Yodeling Bill Haley and the Saddlemen" as "The Most Versatile Band in the Land."

The group's up-tempo performances increased their local popularity, and soon the band was earning a total of $281.25 a week for performing six nights at the Spigot Bar in Philadelphia, a hangout for workers at the bustling Philadelphia Navy Yard and sailors returning from or heading into service in the Korean War, which had begun in mid-1950. Their reputation soon spread across the Delaware River to Gloucester, New Jersey; in February 1951, the owner of that city's Twin Bar hired them away from the Spigot by offering them a weekly salary of $350 to perform there every night but Monday.

A few months into their engagement at the Twin, the Saddlemen felt comfortable and playful enough to add a new wrinkle to their act. Although they'd already inserted swing- and back-beat-laden rhythms into the country and western tunes they were playing, the songs remained predominantly country and western. One night, however, Bill decided to ignore the unwritten rule and sing a "race" record tune in a white hillbilly joint. In a way it was a natural consequence, and the ultimate culmination, of his attempt to unite country and western, jive, popular, and rhythm and blues tunes: just go ahead and play black music and see what happened.

"All you sausages out there gotta go home now," Bill told the audience, "'cause we're gonna play a little something we call 'Cowboy Jive.'" He and the all-white Saddlemen then immediately ripped into a slam-bam version of "Rock the Joint," a tune that had been written and recorded by African Americans.

Bill and his band started by singing the song's startlingly violent opening verse: "We're gonna tear down the mailbox, rip up the floor, smash out the windows and knock down the door." People in the audience immediately jumped out of their seats and started to dance, hoot, and holler. Bill looked at the other band members and asked, "What did I do?" They all started laughing hysterically, but none of them stopped playing.

"Rock the Joint" had been written by Doc Bagby, Harry Crafton, and Wendell Keane and recorded by Jimmy Preston and His Prestonians. The composers and the singers were all African Americans. The Preston recording had been released in July 1949 on the Gotham label and had risen to No. 6 on the rhythm and blues chart, where black songs were listed. (White songs were listed on the popular music or pop chart.)

Back in Chester, Pennsylvania, Bill had listened to "Rock the Joint" every single day when Shorty the Bailiff had played it as his theme song on WPWA. Now Bill was using it to get ahead. It would rock his world, and the worlds of millions of others.

7

Once You Go Black, You'll Never Go Back

If I could find a white man who had
the Negro sound and the Negro feeling,
I could make a million dollars.
—SAM PHILLIPS, WHO WENT ON
TO DISCOVER ELVIS PRESLEY

Bill's realization in 1950 that black tunes would appeal to white audiences, and to young white people with money to spend, was starting to dawn on others in the record business. The changing market was soon brought forcefully to the attention of millions when "Sixty Minute Man"—sung by a black group, Billy Ward and his Dominoes—became the first "race" record to cross over onto the national pop charts in the spring of 1951.

This phenomenon was powered not only by money jingling in the pockets of white teenagers and the low cost of the newly invented 45 rpm records, but also by another interest of teenagers of all eras: sex. The phrase "rock 'n' roll," which soon would describe many tunes written and played by both blacks and whites, had long been understood by many as a euphemism for sex.

The lyrics of "Sixty Minute Man," a song about a man who could have sex for sixty minutes, made this connection explicit. The singer proclaims that girls call him "Lovin' Dan," because he kisses them for fifteen minutes, teases them for fifteen minutes, squeezes them for fifteen minutes, and "blows his top" for the final quarter hour. Its composition was credited to Billy Ward, a black musician, and Rose Marks, a white talent agent.

Sexual allusion wasn't rock's only appeal. White popular music was wearing thin and new input was needed. Record producer Sam Phillips of Memphis was only slightly behind Bill in arriving at this realization. Although he later produced records by such noted white vocalists as

Jerry Lee Lewis, Johnny Cash, and Elvis Presley, in 1951 Phillips made "Rocket 88," featuring African American vocalist Jackie Brenston and His Delta Cats. (Actually, the Cats were Ike Turner's backup group, the Kings of Rhythm.) "Rocket 88," ostensibly about a new high-powered Oldsmobile called the Rocket Hydra-Matic 88, rose quickly to No. 1 on the R&B chart, and many music historians now consider it the first rock 'n' roll song ever recorded. But because Brenston was black, none of the stores in white neighborhoods in the South would carry the record, and it never entered the pop music (or "white") chart. (Ike Turner, however, went on to marry another well-known African American artist, who, as Tina Turner, became one of the best-selling rock 'n' roll artists of all time and was known as the "Queen of Rock 'n' Roll.")

One year after producing "Rocket 88," Sam Phillips would start the Sun Records label. To distribute and promote "Rocket 88," he leased the tracks to a nascent company out of Chicago, Chess Records. "Rocket 88" was a smash in African American record stores in Southern cities, but Chess Records' East Coast sales rep couldn't convince white record store owners to carry it. He vented his frustration to Dave Miller, a young independent record producer from Philadelphia with whom he crossed paths at a diner in Richmond, Virginia. Miller, who owned a new label, Holiday Records, was intrigued when the rep facetiously told him he ought to find a white act to re-record them for the white market.

Miller returned to Philadelphia with a plan: find a white artist to re-record "Rocket 88" and to release the record with no photos on its sleeve, so he could place it in record stores in both white and African American neighborhoods. After making a few calls he was referred to Bill, already known as a white vocalist who was singing black songs. Miller offered Bill twenty-five dollars, and his bandmates fifteen dollars each, if they'd re-record "Rocket 88." He also promised them royalty payments if the record sold.

Surprisingly, considering how much effort he'd put into combining rhythm and blues with country and western, Bill was reluctant to take what he saw as a big step. Playing "race" tunes in a bar late at night was one thing, but doing so in a recording studio was another. He and the Saddlemen had achieved recognition as country and western performers, and Bill didn't want to alienate his hillbilly supporters.

In one sense he was right. To the unbiased listener, Bill's vocal performances of country and western tunes, such as Bill Trader's "(Now and Then There's) A Fool Such as I," were much more melodic and attractive than his renditions of many rock 'n' roll tunes, which he sometimes shouted rather than sang. Playing and singing country ballads was Bill's first love, and country and western tunes would remain his personal favorites for his entire life.

In the long run, Bill's insistence on keeping one foot in country music would turn out to be a fruitless endeavor. Having launched himself so boldly and creatively into the new rock 'n' roll musical style, he never was able to make a final break with his past. For the rest of his life, he'd try and fail to make records that would appeal to both country music fans and rock 'n' rollers. This time, however, Jack Howard and his fellow Saddlemen Billy Williamson and Johnny Grande were so enthusiastic about Dave Miller's proposal that they were able to talk Bill into re-recording "Rocket 88."

After listening to the Brenston recording a half a dozen times, the group decided to imitate it in its entirety. Bill, however, decided to improve the song's rhyming scheme by changing one of Brenston's verses, which was about getting a fifth and taking a little nip, to "Goin' 'round the corner and havin' some fun, takin' my Rocket on a long hot run." It's possible that he was trying to avoid any accusations that he was encouraging drinking while driving, which was, of course, illegal. He may also have been communicating his own personal enthusiasm for cars and driving. Bill loved cars, and as soon as he could afford to do so, he bought himself a series of big, flashy Cadillacs and drove them long distances to band gigs and on vacations.

When Bill wasn't driving himself, he regularly employed the chauffeur services of a red-headed pal of his, Harry "Reds" Broomall. On the flip side of "Rocket 88," Bill and the Saddlemen recorded a hillbilly ballad written by Broomall and Bill called "Tearstains on My Heart."

In the Saddlemen's version of "Rocket," released in 1951, musician Al Rex slaps his bass fiddle rather than plucking it, lending a percussive punch to the song. (The Saddlemen had no drummer.) Johnny Grande's boogie-woogie piano accompaniment sounds like Turner's playing on the original version. Adding to the record's aural pizazz as the song begins is the sound of a car's horn blowing and brakes screeching. And as the song ends, listeners hear the Rocket's engine starting, revving up, and fading away as the featured automobile takes off for places unknown.

Bill's imitation of Brenston's "Rocket 88" was far from total in other ways as well. Brenston's vocals, and the Kings of Rhythm's hard-driving dual saxophones, make it obvious that the Brenston-Turner tune was the African American original. In comparison, Saddleman Billy Williamson's lap steel guitar playing makes the Haley version sound something like a hepped-up hillbilly and western swing tune.

Nevertheless, Bill's version of the song was very appealing, and it became popular with white listeners, partly because Miller took Bill on a promo tour of radio stations in Pennsylvania, New Jersey, Delaware, and Ohio. With what came to be called "payola" not yet known to be illegal, at each station the two men handed out fifty-dollar US war bonds to DJs who agreed to play the record. "Rocket" sold ten thousand copies in two months' time in the East Coast regional markets, doing especially well in Richmond, Baltimore, and Philadelphia, and eventually sold close to seventy thousand records. Although it wasn't a major hit and didn't appear on any national chart, Miller was pleased enough with "Rocket" to sign the Saddlemen to a recording contract.

Two

CUPPY'S STORY: BILL MARRIES AGAIN AND BECOMES A ROCK 'N' ROLL SUPERSTAR

8
It's a Sin

While hoping for another hit, even a modest one, the Saddlemen, their popularity growing, continued to play six nights a week at the Twin. Nearby, nineteen-year-old Joan Barbara "Cuppy" Cupchak was living at home in Camden, New Jersey, with her parents, Steve and Sadie. She spent her days packing chocolates and performing other factory chores at the Whitman's Candy factory, and her nights listening to country music. The Hank Williams song "I'm So Lonesome I Could Cry" was one of her favorites.

(During twenty hours of interviews with her son, Bill Haley Jr., Cuppy described in great detail her life prior to meeting Bill Sr. and the dramatic ups and downs of her life after meeting him. Cuppy's thoughts and quotes throughout the rest of this book are taken directly from these interviews.)

Cuppy's social life before meeting Bill Sr. had consisted mostly of skating at a roller rink near her home. There she'd met Billy Joe Waldren, who was stationed at the US Army's nearby Fort Dix, and felt her first pangs of love. When Billy Joe's service ended, however, he returned home to Old Hickory, Tennessee, and their courtship was over. Cuppy was heartbroken and melancholy, so when her friends invited her to join them in listening to Bill Haley and the Saddlemen at the Twin, she allowed herself to be convinced, even though she'd never been near a bar.

When Cuppy arrived at the Twin, she felt she'd entered a new, grown-up world: dark, smoky, crowded, and exciting. The band was on a break, and when the bartender asked Cuppy what she'd like to drink, she froze. A confused, frightened look came over her face, and the bartender recommended a sloe gin and 7 Up. She paid him one dollar, fishing a dollar bill from her purse to pay for it, following her friends' lead and masking her anxiety as best she could. Her heart was racing. Cuppy's associations with drinking were unpleasant ones. When she was a child, her alcoholic father had often come home drunk late at night, and she'd hidden in her closet to avoid him.

She gazed nervously at the sea of faces all around her, soaking in this strange, new world. Suddenly, up stepped the Saddlemen in their fancy Western outfits and wide-brimmed hats. As they began to play and Bill Haley started singing, the audience erupted. Cuppy saw people dancing and rocking on their stools. Some of the guys were pulling girls out of their chairs and onto the dance floor. The band's sound was country, but with a beat Cuppy had never heard on any hillbilly records.

A few guys came up and asked Cuppy to dance, but she wasn't interested. None of them looked anything like Billy Joe. And tonight, although she tried not to show it, Cuppy could not keep her eyes off the tall, handsome cowboy singing on the stage, with his big white hat, sideburns, white-fringed shirt with shiny buttons, black string tie, tight black pants, and flashy cowboy belt buckle. He reminded her of Hank Williams and her other country and western heroes. To her, he sounded as good as any of them.

That night, before she left to catch the last bus home, Cuppy convinced herself that she'd made eye contact with Bill Haley. She didn't know if he'd felt anything, but she certainly had. As she sat on the bus, she played the scene over and over in her head. Then she walked from the corner to her front door, let herself in, and quietly slipped into bed, not wanting her mother to know how late she'd been out.

Cuppy returned to the Twin Bar the next week (a very long week for her). She met her friends there again, and soon they were regulars on Thursdays and weekends. Cuppy took up smoking and started feeling more comfortable and welcome at the Twin.

She and her teenage coworkers who frequented the bar feared its owner, John Anthony, however. Sporting a constant scowl, the intense, dark-featured Anthony, with his prominent nose and beady eyes, weaved like an angry shark through the barroom, barking orders at employees and demanding ID from many of the bar's younger patrons. The third time Cuppy came to see the band, John called her into his office and asked her, gruffly, "How old are you?" Trembling with fear, she fumbled through her purse for a driver's license she'd borrowed from an older friend and showed it to him. John let her go, even though she was certain he didn't believe her.

During the Saddlemen's performances, Cuppy would sit as close to the bandstand as she could and silently flirt with Bill every time she thought he looked her way. Soon, she was sure he'd seen her. He would give her a little smile, she noticed, and seemed to sing songs directly to her. Johnny Grande, one of the band members, began visiting Cuppy between sets and introducing her to some of the other musicians. Soon Johnny introduced her to Bill.

"Hello," Bill said. "I like your name. Cute. Just like you." Cuppy blushed, her knees went limp, and she became light-headed as the air was sucked from her lungs. Gathering her wits, she finally managed a shy smile and said hi. "I can see that you like our band," Bill said, and he asked what song she'd like him to sing.

"'It's a Sin,'" Cuppy said without hesitation. "Sin" was a favorite Eddy Arnold record she'd played countless times at home.

"It probably will be," Bill said with a broad, lingering smile before he turned and ascended the stage.

After the band first performed three or four of their prearranged songs, Bill told the audience he was going to sing a special song for a special lady. Looking directly at Cuppy, he began to sing, "It's a sin, my darling, how I love you . . ."

Cuppy floated home on a cloud that night, oblivious to everything but the sweet sound of a handsome cowboy singing his heart out to her. She was amazed that he'd singled her out, and she felt like a fairy-tale princess.

The following morning, Bill's parents later told Cuppy, as Bill joined them for breakfast in the kitchen of their home, he threw his cowboy hat in the air, poured himself a cup of coffee, and said, "Mom, I met the cutest little blonde. She's a doll. I can't wait to see her again. She's the prettiest little blonde I've ever seen in my life, and I'm gonna marry her."

Cuppy's friends at the Twin were surprised and a little jealous when Cuppy told them later that week that Bill had asked her for a song request. They teased her, saying she must have cast a spell on him. They all thought he was painfully shy. He always dashed directly to the dressing room during breaks, rarely mingled with fans, and looked uncomfortable when approached by strangers.

Nevertheless, during Cuppy's next several visits to the Twin Bar, Bill came over to talk to her during his breaks, asking questions and making conversation. "How did you like that song?" he'd ask. After a while, he asked her to have coffee with him at the diner across the street, where he'd order a turkey and mayonnaise sandwich every night after work. She said she'd love to, and somewhat to her chagrin, they were joined by Bill's close friend, chauffeur, and bodyguard, Harry Broomall. It soon became clear to Cuppy that Broomall considered Bill his best friend and was eager to carry instruments, get coffee, run errands, or assist Bill and the band in any way.

As it turned out, except when Bill and Cuppy went to the drive-in movies, either Broomall or Jack Howard accompanied them on most of their early dates. Very soon, Cuppy realized that Bill needed the comfort and security of having at least one close friend near him practically all the time. Even so, Broomall grew jealous of the time and attention Bill began to show Cuppy, and he wrote a song about it to express his disappointment. "You think a guy is your friend, then he meets some blonde and forgets all about you," the lyric went. Bill and Cuppy feigned sympathy with Harry but laughed about it privately.

The first night that Bill drove Cuppy home, he walked her to the door. He was wearing a wide-brimmed Stetson hat, with his forelock spilling out onto his forehead. As they embraced, Cuppy sensed that her mother was watching through the window. After thanking her for a fun evening, Bill bent down and kissed Cuppy good night—not a long, soul-searching kiss, just a nice good-night one. Peeking through the window, Cuppy's mother, Sadie, was stunned, and when Cuppy came in, Sadie was at a loss for words. Gathering herself, she cried, "My God, who was that? What is going on with you?"

"He's the most wonderful man in the world, Mom," Cuppy said, "and he's the man I'm going to marry."

Her mother looked at her, shook her head, started up the stairs to go back to bed, stopped, turned to face her daughter, and said emphatically, "I give up!" She soon dropped her opposition, however.

Bill began calling Cuppy constantly during the day and dropping by Cuppy's place after he finished his performance for the night. They'd kiss and cuddle in his spacious Plymouth, which he parked in front of the little row house. After a few weeks, Cuppy mustered the courage to bring Bill inside to meet her parents. He immediately charmed them. Before long he was coming in for coffee and something to eat at 2 a.m., and Cuppy, whose culinary skills were as yet undeveloped, would put cabbage instead of lettuce on his sandwiches, not knowing the difference. Bill politely ate the sandwiches and didn't mention the cabbage to Cuppy for fear of embarrassing her.

Eventually Bill and Cuppy needed a place to be alone together. So after dinner or coffee, they'd drop Jack Howard off at his second-floor office on 12th Street in Philadelphia and then drive over to his cozy little apartment on Cherry Street. Waiting for them to return, Howard would listen to the radio and read newspapers and magazines.

At Howard's apartment, Bill and Cuppy would drink coffee, smoke cigarettes, and listen to records on Howard's portable record player, mostly disks by Hank Williams, Hank Thompson, and Lefty Frissel. Bill told Cuppy that Lefty really played right-handed but was called Lefty because he had a mean left hook. After playing another record, Bill would say he was going to be as big as Hank and Lefty someday, and Cuppy believed him.

They both loved Hank Williams and would talk for hours about each of the songs he sang and how he might have written them. Sometimes Bill would pick up the acoustic guitar Howard kept in the apartment and play the songs for Cuppy, then sing some of his own songs. As the evening came to an end, Bill and Cuppy would hop in Bill's dark green Plymouth, pick up Howard, and drop him off at the apartment. Then Bill would drive Cuppy home.

9

The Rock in Rock 'n' Roll

On this rock, I will build my church.
—JESUS TO ST. PETER, *MATTHEW 16:18*

By the time Bill told Cuppy he was married but separated, she'd already sensed it and was too much in love for it to make a difference. A hopeless romantic, she saw Bill, seven years her senior, as the man who would take care of her forever. To her, he was the smartest person in the world. She adored and admired him, and he loved it. Bill told her his wife lived in Salem, New Jersey, with their two children, Sharyn and Jackie. He claimed Dottie had tricked him into getting her pregnant with Jackie after they'd separated, and that's why he hadn't named his son Bill Jr. He said he wanted a divorce and was waiting for an opportunity to ask Dottie not to contest it, but that if Dottie knew he was serious about someone else she probably wouldn't consent to it. Therefore, it was better, for now, for Cuppy to stop going to shows with him or make it obvious in other ways that they were a couple. Cuppy believed everything Bill said, although part of her was wondering if she'd gotten herself in a little over her head.

Nevertheless, the relationship grew, and it wasn't long before Bill asked Cuppy to meet his folks. Monday was Bill's regular day off, when his mother Maude always made a large family meal. Cuppy finished work the next Monday in time to catch the 4:14 p.m. train from Camden, New Jersey, to Marcus Hook, Pennsylvania, where Bill picked her up at the station in his Plymouth. She tried to ignore the butterflies in her stomach as they drove together through the bucolic countryside of Bethel Township. Anxiously looking around at the trees and open farmland, she thought to herself, "This is nothing like Camden."

Bill did his best to put Cuppy's mind at ease. "They're really going to love you," he said. "I've been telling them about you for so long."

Still, Cuppy was nervous and kept thinking, "What am I getting myself into? Are they *really* going to like me?" Looking over at Bill, she realized it didn't matter. She knew she could do this because it was so important to him.

Bill crossed the intersection of Faulk and Bethel Roads, pulled past a mailbox marked 345 and a weathered, hand-painted sign that said, "Mums for Sale, Eggs, Fresh Vegetables," and drove up a gravel drive-way. "Dad grows the mums," Bill said to Cuppy. "Mom grows the herbs and vegetables."

Looking over at the four apple trees his father had planted on cleared land to the left, Bill reminisced about the trip he and his sister and their parents had taken in the Spring of '32, when he was almost seven, in their Ford Roadster. Having just moved out of their second-floor Florence Street apartment in Highland Park, Michigan, they'd chug-a-lugged their way across the Appalachians, barely making it without breaking down. On every steep incline, they'd all sing, "I would if I could, I would if I could, oh, oh, I would if I could" to the tired motor to help it muster enough power to pull them to the top of each incline.

Past the four apple trees and a little creek running through the property, there was a garden. Chickens and roosters roamed in the house's yard. The senior Haleys' house was a tiny but cozy-looking bungalow with a low, slanted roof, a tiny side porch, and a well with a rope and bucket outside. Made of wood, the house was grayish colored and sat on the eastern end of a heavily wooded six-and-a-half-acre tract of land. As Cuppy remembered it, the front door led directly into a large kitchen equipped with a propane stove and small refrigerator. The small living room was full of old furniture bordering on shabby, but Maude had done a good job of making the room cozy and comfortable. An upright piano stood against one of the walls, and there was a small black-and-white television set on a stand in one corner of the living room, with a radio nearby. The house also contained a small dining room, two narrow adjacent bedrooms, a small sitting room, and a single bathroom off the kitchen with a bathtub but no shower. A dilapidated storage shed stood in back of the house, and a raised chicken coop was off to one side.

Maude Haley came outside to greet her son and his new girlfriend, drying her hands on her red-and-white-checked apron. "Welcome to our home," she said with a broad, toothy grin, revealing a slight British accent. Cuppy saw right away that Bill's mother was a talker who told her story to everyone, no matter who they were or where they came from.

Maude immediately put Cuppy at ease, taking her out to the garden to pick mint for her leg of lamb dinner, and then inside, where she showed Cuppy her house and proudly explained that she'd sewn the brown slip covers on the sofa and chairs. There were books and family photos scattered about, and fresh flowers from the garden in colorful pots. Delicious smells of home cooking filled the cottage, and Cuppy could see a freshly baked pie sitting on the counter in the kitchen. Bill had told Cuppy that Maude had spent much of her childhood in her father's bakery shop in Ulverston, Lancashire, England, and as a result was an excellent cook and baker.

Bill's somewhat thin and frail-looking father also was inside the house, and he too greeted Cuppy warmly. "A true Kentucky gentleman," Cuppy thought, observing that Will's shoulders were hunched slightly forward, making him seem much older than Maude. Will was just beginning to show signs of early-stage dementia. He smoked constantly and found it hard to sit down or keep still for any length of time. Nevertheless, he'd still smile and listen, and speak ardently when he had something to say. In the evenings after dinner, he'd pull out his banjo or mandolin and have a hootin', hollerin' good time playing hymns and country music with his son on guitar and Maude, or Bill's sister Peggy, at the piano.

The kitchen table was beautifully set with candles and flowers that night, and they all had a wonderful dinner together. Peggy, her husband George Gray, and their young daughter Sylvia also were there, and after that, the scene was repeated nearly every Monday. Soon Maude was filling Cuppy in on Bill's prior relationships and events from his childhood, and teaching her to make Bill's favorite pies and other foods. Bill was the apple of her eye, and it became very clear to Cuppy that Maude was enormously proud of him.

Maude also became very fond of Cuppy, who was different from the other girls Bill had brought home. She was from the city. She wasn't afraid to stand up for herself, and Bill admired and needed that. Moreover, Maude knew Cuppy loved Bill as much as she did. His dream was their dream, and there was an obvious understanding between them.

Initially, however, Maude didn't share everything she knew about her son with Cuppy. About a month after that first dinner, the younger couple's relationship nearly ended when Bill failed to show for a date, causing Cuppy to wait in front of the Metro restaurant in Camden for what seemed like forever. Finally, at 2 a.m., Cuppy took the last bus home. The next day, one of her Twin Bar friends suggested that Bill might still be seeing someone named Jean—a divorced woman with a small child— whom he'd hung out with before. Cuppy hadn't known about Jean and was furious. She called Bill at his parents' house. He denied seeing Jean and offered a lame excuse for failing to pick up Cuppy, but Cuppy told him to go to hell. "You make your choice!" she screamed. "That's it. Her or me!" and slammed down the phone.

Bill was shocked and humbled by Cuppy's indignation. He was used to being involved with docile, compliant women. Cuppy's feistiness was attractive, and the challenge she presented intrigued him. The next morning, he called her at her parents' house and apologized profusely, turning on the charm. By the next Monday at dinner, Maude and Cuppy were laughing as though the air had been cleared. Cuppy commented about an article she'd just read in *Seventeen* magazine. Maude said, "Jean buys that magazine, but she's much older than you, and you're more *Seventeen* than she is."

The mention of Jean's name made Bill defensive, and the tension escalated into a heated argument between Bill and Cuppy at the dinner table, in front of Bill's parents. Frustrated and angry, Bill picked up a bowl of potato salad and heaved it against the kitchen wall before storming outside. Cuppy watched as Maude got up from the table and began picking up the pieces of the broken bowl. Furious with Bill, Cuppy thought to herself, "If he were my kid, he'd be wearing that potato salad!"

"I wouldn't clean up after him if I were you," Cuppy said to Maude.

"But I love him," Maude replied, and Cuppy realized that in Maude's eyes, Bill could never be wrong.

Cuppy walked out through the kitchen door and found Bill sitting quietly on a large log with his guitar. It was an unusually warm evening. When Bill saw her coming, he began to sing "Cotton Haired Gal," a song he'd written a few years earlier with his friend Eddie Mallie. He then smiled and apologized for being angry and told Cuppy how much he loved her. He said he appreciated a gal who stood up to him and wasn't afraid to talk back to him, and that he was sorry he'd hurt her.

Looking down, Cuppy noticed that a three-and-a-half-inch jagged scar on Bill's exposed left ankle had been illuminated by the last rays of sunlight. She asked how it had happened. Bill told her that one night he'd heard a noise outside and confronted a man with a knife who apparently was going to rob the house. The guy slashed him on the ankle, Bill said, but Bill overpowered him and the man ran away.

Cuppy thought about that story and imagined the fear Bill must have felt. It sounded far-fetched, but she believed him. She fell silent as they sat together enjoying the evening air, looking out at the property. Suddenly, Bill pointed to a large, flat gray slate rock sticking out of the ground, about a hundred yards away.

"You see that rock?" Bill said.

"Yes."

"We're going to build our house on that rock. And we're going to raise our family on that foundation, that rock. And that's where we're going to grow old together, raising our family. Just like mom and dad."

Pausing, he looked up at the stars beginning to appear in the early evening sky. "You know, I'm going to make it in this business," he said forcefully, "and we're going to build an empire, and our sons will take after me and be musicians too."

"That would be wonderful," Cuppy said. Bill began to strum his guitar and softly sing his favorite Tex Ritter song, "You're Always Brand New."

"You're always brand new to me," Bill sang. " . . . you make life one happy day."

As he strummed the final chord, Bill laughed, and said the stars made him think of Trigger's glittering rhinestone saddle when Roy Rogers first performed at Cousin Lee's Radio Park near Bill's parents' house in 1944. That was the same night as Bill's first big performance there, in front of ten thousand people, right before he first started playing there with Cousin Lee. Roy took Trigger up on the stage, Bill said, and the horse did all the tricks, counting with his hoof and picking out the different colored handkerchiefs. Growing pensive, Bill told Cuppy how he'd met singer Hank Williams there, and Gene Autry.

"I'm going to make it big in this business," Bill said again.

"I know you will," Cuppy said softly, smiling, as Bill leaned in and kissed her. They joined hands and walked back to the house, where they both helped Maude finish cleaning up Bill's mess. Bill kissed his mother on the cheek and told her he was sorry and that he loved her. Maude smiled broadly. Once again, all was well with her Billy and her world.

Cuppy could not help feeling angry all over again, however. Bill had behaved like a spoiled child. She resolved that, unlike Maude, she wasn't going to stand for his temper tantrums—ever.

10

"Rock the Joint"

We're gonna . . . tear down the mailbox,
rip up the floor, smash out the windows,
and knock down the door.
–First verse of "Rock the Joint,"
written by Harry Craft, Wendell "Don" Keane,
and Harry "Doc" Bagby, and
performed by Bill Haley and His Saddlemen

Bill and the Saddlemen kept on broadcasting, practicing, performing and recording disc after disc, most of them country and western, but none of the records hit it big. Their breakthrough with "Rocket 88" hadn't been big enough to overcome Bill's business conservatism and the attraction of recording the music they knew best.

Musically they were living a double life. They recorded the tunes they thought most appropriate for an established western band, but still had fun playing their unique, cowboy-jive "race" music. Then, in 1951, David Miller, who had produced and distributed Bill's version of "Rocket 88," started a new label, Essex Records. He signed the Saddlemen to record "Icy Heart," a vocally engaging country and western tale of lost love that he thought could ride the coattails of Hank Williams's hit "Cold, Cold Heart." After all, Tony Bennett, backed by Percy Faith and His Orchestra, had had a smash hit the year before with his version of "Cold." Since childhood, Bill had aspired to appear on the Grand Ole Opry, the summit of country and western fame, and this record, he thought, might be his shot.

The night before the recording session, the band still hadn't decided what to put on the record's flip side. Although "Rock the Joint," wasn't anything like "Icy Heart," Jack Howard suggested putting "Rock the Joint" on the B-side simply because Twin Bar audiences loved it.

When the band finally recorded "Rock the Joint," the result sounded much more like rock 'n' roll than "Rocket 88" had. Marshall Lytle's bass slaps and Johnny Grande's pounding piano rhythm set an energetic pace, and Danny Cedrone's soaring guitar solo, along with alternate instrumental breaks by Grande and Billy Williamson's lap steel guitars, sustained the excitement. Also, Bill's vocal was much more powerful and direct on "Rock the Joint" than it had been on his "Rocket" vocal, producing an energy more melodic and energetic than Preston's original.

It shouldn't have surprised anyone that some DJs began to ignore the "Icy Heart" side of the record and play "Rock the Joint" instead. Bags of fan mail for the Saddlemen began to arrive at WPWA, although some of it was fake. Cuppy wrote piles of postcards at the dining room table in her parents' Camden home and mailed them to local radio stations, altering her handwriting, using fake names, and asking them to play more Bill Haley songs. She and Bill, or Bill's buddy Harry Broomall, were careful to mail the cards from different postmark locations.

"Rock the Joint" soon picked up momentum and caught the attention of record reviewers, as well as radio stations. One reviewer said it was "a fast-moving boogie beat item" with "novelty lyrics," "potent vocalizing," and a "dynamic arrangement." *Billboard* called it "an odd mixture of C&W and R&B" with which the Saddlemen "manage[d] to generate a sense of excitement." And a DJ in Waterloo, Iowa wrote that "With the record business and the music business crying out for something new . . . something really hot, 'Rock the Joint' *is it!*"

Still not convinced that the song was a breakthrough, Miller sent Bill and Jack Howard on a ten-day, three-thousand-mile tour to support "Icy Heart," not "Rock the Joint," with twenty-five-dollar US Savings Bonds to give DJs who played "Icy Heart." Often sleeping in Bill's Plymouth because they couldn't afford hotel rooms, they visited DJs in Detroit and many other cities.

The two men were leaving Nashville to go to Richmond, Virginia, when Miller called their motel to tell them that "Rock the Joint" was going to be a hit, not "Icy Heart." Sensing a big opportunity, Miller sent the rest of the band to join Bill and Jack as they traveled to Chicago, Washington, Baltimore, and Cleveland, where they visited rising DJ Alan Freed.

Two months previously, Freed, who also thought black music would sell well no matter who performed it, had produced his first Moondog Coronation Ball at the Cleveland Arena. It had featured Bill Ward and the Dominoes, the black group that had recorded "Sixty Minute Man," plus numerous other acts. More than eleven thousand tickets were sold for the nine-thousand-seat arena, and sixteen thousand fans showed up. Only one group was able to perform before the show was cancelled due to crowd-safety concerns.

Freed, who called himself "King of the Moondoggers," had created the Moondog persona from a song by African American bandleader Todd Rhodes called "Blues for Red Boy." Referring to the tune as "Blues for Moondog," Freed always played it as the opening theme of his R&B radio show while he screamed and howled into the microphone, occasionally guzzling scotch after introducing each song, as he pounded on a phonebook to the beat of the music and shouted, "Go! Go! Go!"

During their on-air visit with Freed, the Saddlemen sat around a large round table in the studio with a boom microphone suspended above them. Freed played "Rock the Joint" over and over, turning on the mike while the song was playing, banging on the table, and yelling, "Rock and roll everybody, rock and roll." The record sold two hundred thousand copies in the next few months, including thirteen thousand that one Philadelphia record store sold in just five weeks.

Because the band still wasn't sure they had a rock 'n' roll future, however, the next record they made featured the country and western classic "Dance with the Dolly (With the Hole in her Stocking)" on one side, and "Rocking Chair on the Moon," co-written by Bill, on the other. The record sold only moderately well and didn't chart. Nevertheless, for the rest of his career, Bill, remembering his poverty-stricken days as a penniless musical drifter, kept recording songs he'd written or cowritten, whatever their likely popularity, because there was more money in it for him if he did that rather than serving as the performer only. The problem with this strategy was that the songs he recorded that were written by others, especially by African Americans, were usually more popular than his own compositions.

It would take the combined efforts of a local entertainment booking agent, Sam Sgro, and his friend and associate James "Lord Jim" Ferguson, a WPWA radio personality, to move the conservative Saddlemen into the rock 'n' roll future.

During the 1930s, the burly Ferguson, then promoting amateur boxing, had been called a "nigger lover" in Philadelphia because he recruited black fighters for matches he arranged. This was unconventional at the time, and so was his later habit of wearing suit-and-tie outfits without socks and with a food-stained tie he refused to change. Ferguson's originality had been evident in an earlier life as a cadet on a large sailing ship before World War II, when he'd written numerous short stories about the sea. He'd mailed them to friends in the US, reminding them of Joseph Conrad, author of the famous sea novel *Lord Jim*, and inspiring them to nickname Ferguson "Lord Jim." During

World War II, Ferguson had served as the Lieutenant Commander of a Navy salvage vessel in the Pacific.

Lord Jim was invited to become a fourth partner in the Saddlemen, in the role of personal director and promoter. As a first order of business, knowing that teenagers now dominated the record-buying market, he urged Bill and his band to play free shows at area high school assemblies and record hops, partly to learn what kind of music the kids preferred.

Although initially reluctant to add free appearances to their crowded schedule, the Saddlemen eventually performed a total of 183 times at local schools. Soon they realized that watching teenagers react to their performances would help them perfect their act, as well as produce and record more chart-topping records. As the band built up or changed the beat, they'd watch the kids' reactions, noting when shoulders started moving, feet began tapping, and hands began clapping. With this data, they were able to whittle down their set lists and decide if a certain tune or style was worth keeping.

In both the short and long run, these free appearances, an early form of music-business market research, paid off big time. The band members quickly realized that kids wanted music that gave them a chance to participate, and that they were interested in a driving, easy-to-dance-to beat with simple, easy-to-remember lyrics. After each high school appearance, the musicians asked the kids what they thought of the band's performance and invited suggestions. Bill started keeping notes on how the teens talked and their favorite expressions.

Soon, at Lord Jim's suggestion, the Saddlemen had a new arranger. Juilliard-trained trumpet player Frank Pingatore brought in the hottest records on the "race" charts for the band to listen to and learn from. Seeking even more progress, Lord Jim asked his friend Sam Sgro, a booking agent, for advice on how to improve the Saddlemen even more. Sgro told Lord Jim to get them out of their cowboy suits so they could be booked into nightclubs. At that time, the band members were wearing tilted-back, white-and-beige-colored hats, white shirts, cowboy boots, and solid red neckerchiefs. Because they spent a lot of time performing on the Jersey shore, they also had deep tans, making their outfits look almost fluorescent.

Bill was aghast when Sgro told him he should drop that look. "What do you mean? That's my trade! That's my living! That's what I do!" he said. Sgro told Bill he'd never book a band with a cowboy look into a nightclub, but Bill only glared back at him. Nevertheless, the Saddlemen soon started toning down their Western look, occasionally wearing blazers, and by the fall of 1952, they'd ditched their boots and hats and began wearing suits and ties.

This left Bill with a problem, since he'd been using his hat to deflect attention from his wandering left eye. He decided to take advantage of the natural cowlick on his forehead and form a hanging curl, coaxed with pomade, as a gimmick and a diversion. It would soon become his trademark.

11

Bill and Cuppy Marry, and Bill's Father Attempts Suicide

During the summer of 1952, Bill and Cuppy had been spending weekends together in a rented house on the Jersey Shore. Bill tried to teach Cuppy to drive, but it didn't go well. She couldn't get the hang of using a clutch and shifting gears. She was nervous, and Bill became impatient and exasperated. When Cuppy ran over a toad in the road that he'd instructed her to avoid, he hired a driving instructor referred by his friend Lord Jim, but the man turned out to be lecherous. During one lesson, he put his arm around Cuppy when they were alone together and attempted to kiss her. She pushed him away, but he persisted and started groping her breasts, finally backing off when she screamed. When Bill came back later that evening and she told him what had happened, he blew up. He called Lord Jim, screaming and demanding to know where the driving instructor could be found, then grabbed a sharp kitchen knife and raced out the door, intent on exacting revenge. Lord Jim intervened and prevented Bill from doing something he would regret, but from that point forward, Bill's right-hand man Harry Broomall provided Cuppy's driving lessons.

By September, Cuppy had learned that she was pregnant. Bill was playing at the Twin at the time, and when he met Cuppy at her parents' house after a show, she nervously delivered the news at the kitchen table over coffee and sandwiches. At this point in their lives, neither Cuppy nor Bill wanted to have a child. Bill was still married. Cuppy, just twenty years old, was still single and not ready to be a mother, and it would disgrace her family if she had a child out of wedlock.

They tried to think of what they could do. Abortion was illegal and out of the question as far as Cuppy was concerned. But while Cuppy was scared to death by the situation she was in, Bill was very supportive. He pledged his devotion and said he'd press Dottie for a divorce so he and Cuppy could marry.

Bill then told Dottie he'd gotten Cuppy pregnant. That should have been the end of his relationship with Dottie, but she must have said something that caused him to suggest Cuppy have an abortion. The next evening, he came to see Cuppy, bearing an envelope containing a half-dozen red capsules, presumably intended to cause a miscarriage.

"Dottie said these are going to help us," Bill said. Cuppy knew Dottie a bit, liked her, and felt that Dottie liked her as well.

"Okay. I'll try it," Cuppy said. She took one of the pills, but the next morning, she was remorseful. "I just can't do this," she thought. She threw the remaining pills in the trash and told herself that whatever happened, she'd just live with it.

Cuppy was still confounded by her situation, and it showed on her face. Her mother Sadie kept asking what was wrong and dispatched Cuppy's older sister Catherine to meet her in a local restaurant and try to find out the truth. Catherine did, and shared the news with Sadie. Cuppy's parents were furious and exasperated, but Bill's mother Maude was ecstatic when Bill told her the news. She'd wanted a grandson named Bill Jr. more than anything, and had been disappointed when Bill had named his first son John William (Jack).

By early November 1952, Cuppy was five months pregnant, still single, and starting to show. Quitting her job at Whitman's Chocolates, she moved in with Bill and his parents with her parents' reluctant approval. Observing 1950s prenuptial protocol, she took Bill's bedroom while Bill slept on the couch in the living room.

By this time Dottie had been forced to accept that her marriage to Bill had been over for some time. Knowing Cuppy was pregnant and had decided to remain so, and that Bill was in a bind, she agreed to divorce him if he accepted financial responsibility for their two children. Bill agreed to do so, but in later years he would only make the required regular payments to Dottie if her father marched into Bill's office and demanded them. Nevertheless, Bill applied for a divorce, which was granted on November 14, 1952.

Bill was grinning from ear to ear when he hung up the phone in his parents' house the day Dottie called him to say she had the papers and the divorce was final. He and Cuppy immediately applied for a marriage license in Elkton, Maryland, where the waiting period was short and no blood test was required.

The wedding was set for November 18, the same day the license was due to be granted, before a justice of the peace. The night before, Cuppy slept at her parents' house in Camden, because it was considered bad luck to see one's future spouse on the eve of a wedding. She'd bought a pretty, pale blue satin dress for the occasion, with a long-sleeved bolero jacket. Hardly able to sleep, she was up and ready too early the next morning, and to make matters worse, Bill was late.

While Sadie was getting ready upstairs, Cuppy waited anxiously on the enclosed front porch, pacing and occasionally going into the living room to look at the hands on the grandfather clock. She kept worrying that Bill wouldn't show up and that her pregnant and unmarried condition would bring terrible shame upon her parents.

Finally, to her great relief, Cuppy spotted Bill behind the wheel of his Plymouth, speeding down Morton Street with Lord Jim Ferguson beside him in the passenger seat. Both men were smiling broadly. Her throat tightened and she choked back tears. The car screeched to a halt in front of the house, and Bill and Lord Jim popped out and rushed inside after Sadie greeted them at the door. Cuppy looked over at her father, Steve, who gave his daughter a rare and awkward smile that confused her. Bill walked over and pinned a pink and white corsage on her dress.

Cuppy blushed, smiled, and felt relieved but nervous as she, Bill, Lord Jim, and Sadie said goodbye to Steve and headed to the cottage to pick up Maude. Shortly after they left, Cuppy's old flame Billy Joe Waldren showed up and rang the doorbell. He'd heard Cuppy was getting married and had impulsively come all the way back from Tennessee to try to change her mind. Steve told him he was too late.

Harry Broomall, who would serve as Bill's best man, had shown up at the Haley cottage before the rest of the wedding party, and was attempting to comfort Maude when the others arrived. Maude was worried about leaving Will home alone, because he was having what she called one of his "bad" days: restless, agitated, and mumbling angrily, he was smoking one cigarette after another and pacing around in tight little circles.

When Bill and the others arrived, Will calmed down, and they wished him goodbye and rushed off to Elkton. They were running late. The clerk's office with the marriage license was supposed to close soon, but with Bill exceeding the speed limit, they got there without a minute to spare. By then, everyone's nerves were frazzled. Bill's mother Maude and Harry Broomall signed the marriage certificate as witnesses before the brief ceremony in the adjoining courthouse. After Bill and Cuppy were pronounced man and wife, Bill hugged and kissed Cuppy so forcefully that the corsage on her dress came loose and landed on the floor, prompting a collective nervous laugh from the small wedding party. Cuppy remarked that it was a bad omen, but Bill reassured her and reattached the corsage with a smile and a kiss.

The small wedding party celebrated over dinner at a nearby diner. Afterward they dropped off Maude and Sadie and drove off for a New York City honeymoon, which included a scheduled recording session. Meanwhile, Maude entered the house she shared with Bill's father to find that Will had apparently tried to shoot himself with an old revolver he kept in the bedroom, lost his nerve, and shot out the living room windows instead. She cleaned up the mess and removed Will's guns from the house.

Around 11 p.m., the newlyweds and Lord Jim reached the city. The other band members drove up separately with their instruments. A recording session was scheduled at Coastal Studios on 40th Street the next day to record two new songs: "Stop Beatin' Round the Mulberry Bush," written by WDRF DJ Bix Reichner, and "Real Rock Drive," Bill's latest creation, based on Tani Allen's "Tennessee Drive."

Cuppy was thrilled to be in New York for the first time, to go into a recording studio, and to be around "important" people. She tried to hide her nervousness and naiveté, only to have Bill scold her in the morning for making the bed in their hotel room while he was in the shower. He told her the maid would think they were dumb country yokels. After meeting Lord Jim for breakfast in the hotel coffee shop and spending many hours recording, Bill took Cuppy out to dinner—just the two of them for a change—at Jack Dempsey's Restaurant on Broadway.

Treating the meal as their special, romantic wedding celebration, Bill and his bride each ordered a cocktail before dinner and drank champagne with their meal instead of their usual coffee. Cuppy was as happy as she'd ever been in her life. She was finally married to the man she loved, and she would be recognized openly as his wife. No more hiding.

Cuppy felt that Bill was very proud of her and anxious to show her off. Bill told Cuppy he was happy they were finally married and that he now had his little "cupcake." They talked about their future together—about Bill's future, that is, because as far as Cuppy was concerned, Bill's future was hers. She couldn't imagine any role other than being "the woman behind the man" and thought her life path was now set. She'd have the baby, make a good home for Bill, go with him when she could, listen to him and encourage him, and always be available and there for him.

Bill spoke confidently to Cuppy about making it big and building a home for his family. He also talked about wanting to buy things for his parents and sister—and for her—with a fur coat at the top of his gift list. It had to be mink, to demonstrate that he was a huge success.

After dinner, Bill and Cuppy went to Radio City Music Hall, where they met up with Lord Jim, Mr. "Man About Town." After the Radio City show, Ferguson escorted them to jazz clubs and other hot spots in the city.

After they returned from New York, Bill and Cuppy rented a furnished third-floor, one-bedroom apartment for twelve dollars per week in Collingdale, Pennsylvania. Their first home together, it was relatively spacious, with a bedroom, bath, kitchen, and living room, and they settled into a domestic routine. Cuppy fixed Bill's favorite meals and constantly scrubbed the wooden floors. She washed and ironed Bill's two dozen white shirts and ran them out on a clothesline with a pulley that extended off the third-floor porch. Soon the two of them began planning for the baby, who was expected in March, shopping together for a bassinette and other baby items. By then Cuppy had transformed all her early worry and shame about her pregnancy into hope and anticipation of good things to come.

12

"Crazy Man, Crazy"

They play it wild, and they play it long.
–from "Crazy Man, Crazy,"
WRITTEN BY BILL HALEY AND PERFORMED BY
BILL HALEY AND HIS COMETS

Completing their ongoing transition from country and western singers to a rock 'n' roll band, the Saddlemen, hoping to become internationally known, changed their name from Bill Haley and His Saddlemen to Bill Haley and His Comets. The name was a riff on the worldwide fame of astronomer Edmund Halley, who had discovered Halley's Comet more than two hundred years previously and whose last name was often pronounced like Bill Haley's. The Comets bought new tan-colored suits with matching ties to celebrate the name change, and they began playing in more upscale clubs. As their popularity increased, they switched to tuxes and bow ties and added to their lineup an athletic young drummer named Dick Richards. Their last record release featured the session drumming of Julliard-trained jazz drummer Billy Gussak, and they would now need to add drums at live performances as well.

With Cuppy about to give birth to their first child, and thinking about the teens he'd encountered during his numerous high school performances, Bill began trying to write the ultimate song for and about kids having a good time. The first one he came up with was based on the teenage slang words and phrases he'd heard while performing at high schools.

To the teens, everything was "crazy": a "crazy tie," a "crazy pair of shoes." After their shows, Bill and the Comets would hear kids say things like "dig that crazy rhythm" and "that music's gone, man." The kids would tell the Comets that the "hep cats," not the "cubes" or "squares," got the "chicks" and that once you were "jacketed" it was off to the "submarine races." *Jacketed* had two meanings: "wearing a straight-jacket," or "crazy" as in "crazy to make out." "Submarine races" was a euphemism for making out in a car.

After one high school performance, a small group of youngsters gathered around while the Comets loaded their instruments into their cars. "How did you like our music?" Bill asked.

One tall boy with a ducktail haircut, wearing blue jeans and two-toned white and tan suede bucks, shook his head, snapped his fingers, and said, "Crazy man, crazy!" Bill wrote the phrase in pen on the palm of his hand.

As Bill and bass player Marshall Lytle drove to Bill's apartment to have lunch with Cuppy after the show, Bill started thinking about a song they could build around the phrase "crazy man, crazy." While Cuppy prepared food, Bill and Lytle sat at the kitchen table and shouted out ideas for lyrics. Bill grabbed his acoustic guitar, which always stood in the corner, and an opening verse spilled out of him describing a dance band with a "solid" beat. "When they start rockin,' boy, we start to shout 'crazy man, crazy' and man that music's gone!" he sang, spontaneously adding several more verses and a chorus ending using the popular football cheer, "Go! Go! Go!"

The next day, at a recording studio, the Comets ran through several versions of the song with the whole band working out the arrangement, including an infectious call and response between the vocal and guitars. The record was highlighted by a screaming vocal chorus of Comets, supplemented by some record execs and promo men who were visiting the studio, and the building's porter. They transformed the song into something cool yet crazy, wild, raucous, and joyful. Overseeing the whole process was studio engineer Tom Dowd, later a legendary record producer.

Essex Records released "Crazy Man, Crazy," backed by "Whatcha Gonna Do," another Bill composition, which he'd written after a minor argument with Cuppy in early April 1953. The record took off, selling one hundred thousand copies in its first weeks.

Soon "Crazy" was getting national airplay, and the band flew to the West Coast to support it with appearances there. The record soon rose to No. 12 on the *Billboard* pop charts, eventually reaching sales of 750,000 copies, and entered the R&B charts in Chicago as well. A follow-up song, "Fractured," cowritten by Bill and the Comet's bass player Marshall Lytle (mistakenly attributed to steel guitarist Billy Williamson on the label), rose to No. 24 on the *Billboard* pop chart.

It was a good couple of months for Bill Haley. On Thursday, March 26, Cuppy gave birth to their first child, Joan Patricia Haley, soon known as Joanie. As "Crazy" roared up the charts, Bill bought a used 1952 white and silver Cadillac Seville and went on the road again with the band, driving "Crazy" to No. 11 on the *Cashbox* pop chart. It was the first of many hits for him, and the first of Bill's many Cadillacs. That fall, "Crazy" became the first rock 'n' roll song ever heard on a nationwide TV network, CBS. It was played on the soundtrack of "Glory in the Flower," an episode in a series called *Omnibus* that featured future superstar James Dean. *Billboard* eventually ranked "Crazy" as the eighteenth most popular record of 1953.

Later that same year, after adding a sax player to the lineup, the Comets followed "Crazy" with a two-minute, fifty-three-second song called "Straight Jacket." The song title was a logical follow-up to "Crazy," and its lyrics made it doubly appropriate, since they consisted entirely of the song's title repeated fifty-eight times. "Straight Jacket" had a jazzy instrumental background, but with lyrics like these, it wasn't surprising that the song failed to chart.

While performing at clubs such as the Hofbrau on the Jersey Shore, Bill relaxed at a house he'd rented nearby with his mother and father, Cuppy, Joanie, and his two children from his first marriage, seven-year-old Sharyn and Jackie, now three.

Later that season at the Hofbrau, the Comets tried out a new song, "(We're Gonna) Rock Around the Clock Tonight." (Its title was later shortened.) They were greeted with an enthusiastic response. Written by Max C. Freedman and James E. Myers, who used the pseudonym Jimmy DeKnight, it had originally been recorded a few months earlier by the Italian American group Sonny Dae and the Knights. The Saddlemen had brought it into the recording studio several times, but producer Dave Miller had an ongoing feud with writer James Myers and refused to let them record it.

Due to that obstacle, the Comets decided to record two songs written by Bill: "Live It Up" and "Farewell, So Long, Goodbye," which had been inspired by another one of Bill and Cuppy's arguments. Even in this early stage of their marriage, their relationship had pretty serious ups and downs, evidenced by the fact that the second of the two songs contained ominous lyrics, such as "I'm gonna say to you these three little words and they mean that we are through, Farewell, so long, goodbye." Ironically, one of the things that had attracted Bill to Cuppy was her willingness to give back as good as she got, and the satisfaction of making up afterward made the arguing well worth it for both of them.

On days off, Bill and his band members would visit the Riptide Club, across the street from the Hofbrau. A black group, the Treniers, were playing songs there such as "Rocking on Sunday Night," "Rockin' Is Our Business," and "It Rocks! It Rolls! It Swings!" Later Bill's group would imitate some of the Treniers' stage moves. In return, Bill gave the group a song he'd recently written, "Rock-A-Beatin' Boogie," which the Treniers recorded for Okeh Records at the end of the summer. (The Comets' recording of the same song became a hit in 1955.)

With the playing of a baritone sax featured on one of their records in September, the Comets had added a sax player to their lineup, Joey Ambrose, who soon revolutionized the band's onstage performance. Seeing the young people in the audience reacting vigorously to his playing, and hearing and seeing girls his age scream after he soloed, Ambrose would go into his "walking the bar" routine, dropping to his knees and walking forward on them while leaning backwards and continuing to play his instrument. While he performed a second solo, he'd waddle out into the audience on his knees, wagging his sax back and forth.

Bass player Marshall Lytle, joining in the fun, would lie flat on his back, turn his bass fiddle on its back as well, prop it up on his feet, and play it by reaching around its huge body to pluck its strings. Then he'd turn the instrument on its side and keep playing it while riding it like a horse. After a short time, Lytle would then jump up, grab the bass by the neck, throw it over his head, rest the upper curve of the unwieldy instrument on his shoulder, and play away.

Bill always reacted to such behavior by bobbing his head and smiling, or rolling his eyes, or acting surprised at the appropriate moment, perpetually engaging the audience. By early 1954, the Comets were more popular than ever, although mostly in the Philadelphia-Baltimore area, and Cuppy was pregnant again.

13

"Rock Around the Clock" Hits the Top, and Guitarist Danny Cedrone Dies a Mysterious Death

When the chimes ring five, six, and seven,
we'll be right in seventh heaven.
—FROM "ROCK AROUND THE CLOCK,"
WRITTEN BY MAX C. FREEDMAN AND JAMES E. MEYERS
AND PERFORMED BY BILL HALEY AND HIS COMETS.

The Comets' growing popularity as performers, coupled with their failed attempts so far to reach the Top 10 on any chart, inspired them to end their association with Essex Records and move to Decca. Their new producer, the legendary Milt Gabler, decided that the A-side on their first record for Decca would feature an R&B tune called "Thirteen Women (and Only One Man in Town)." Gabler, who'd recently ended a fruitful seven-year stint producing the sensational Louis Jordan and his Tympany Five, owned a piece of the publishing rights for "Thirteen Women."

The B-side of the Decca record, by agreement, would be at the discretion of music publisher James Myers, who had negotiated the deal on behalf of Bill and his partners. Myers chose "(We're Gonna) Rock Around the Clock." In a later deposition, he admitted under oath that he'd added a writing credit for himself when he bought the tune from its actual author, Max Freedman, a veteran Tin Pan Alley composer. Myers had high hopes for this song and thought it was perfect for Bill, but no one at the time could have known that it would one day shake the world.

Although scheduled to start recording at 11 a.m. on April 12, 1954, at the Pythian Temple, a Decca studio in Manhattan, the Comets didn't get there until after 1 p.m. The ferry they'd taken from Chester got stuck on a sand bar, and they'd had to wait for a tugboat and the rising tide to set them free. Gabler thought about cancelling the session, but because the studio was booked for the whole day, he decided to take an early lunch and then wait for the band to arrive.

Gabler thought "Thirteen Women" might become popular because it was extremely topical. Written by Dickie Thompson, a former member of the Tympany Five, the song played on the idea of how many people would remain in a town and what they would do after a nuclear blast, and nuclear war was a major preoccupation of the day. Sex also was an obsession in the repressed 1950s, and "Thirteen Women" celebrated the possible life of a male nuclear survivor with such verses as "I had three gals dancing the mambo, three gals ballin' the jack…" "Dancing the mambo?" "Ballin' the jack?" Only the fact that this song never became popular stood in the way of parents protesting the effect such lyrics might have on their children.

Starting at 1:20 p.m. the band rehearsed "Thirteen Women" for nearly an hour, then recorded six takes before Gabler was finally satisfied he had a useable version. By then, less than an hour of studio time remained for the B-side, "(We're Gonna) Rock Around the Clock." Fortunately, the Comets were very familiar with the tune and had rehearsed and worked out the final arrangement the previous afternoon. At 4:45 p.m. the band did a first take, but the drummer, Billy Gussak, felt he could do a better job on the ending, so they did a second run-through, nailed it, and wrapped up the session by 5:40 p.m. Each musician was paid union scale— a total of $47.50—for his day's work. The next morning, Gabler listened to the two takes of "Rock Around the Clock" and decided he liked the vocal on the first take and the instrumentation on the second. So he spliced the ending of the second tape onto the first tape and cut a final two-minute, eight-second master that would eventually come to be considered a recording masterpiece.

The new record, featuring "Thirteen Women" on the A-side, sold seventy-five thousand copies in the first month following its release, rising to No. 23 on the pop chart. The strong initial sales were due mostly to Comets fans waiting for a new record. Few DJs flipped it over and played the B-side on air, however.

One young Comet fan in Beverly Hills, California, bought a 78 rpm copy of "Thirteen Women" as soon as it came out. Fifth-grader Peter Ford, son of actor Glenn Ford and actress Eleanor Powell, was a music lover and hobbyist. He was fascinated with "race" records in particular and had amassed a small collection of R&B discs during his frequent visits to the Beverly Hills Music Shop. He'd picked up a copy of "Crazy Man, Crazy" the previous year, and it had knocked his socks off. Peter couldn't wait for the next Haley record to come out, but when he gave "Thirteen Women" its first spin on the family record player in their spacious home, he didn't like it. Naturally he flipped the disk over, dropped the needle, and pow, that's what he was hoping for! For the better part of the next year, young Peter nearly wore out the grooves playing the B-side of the record. The Haley fans got it, but the DJs didn't.

After Easter, the Comets played a brief engagement at the popular Iacona's Broomall Café and Nite Spot close to home. Ads for their appearance at the café and a local country fair referred to the band as "Bill 'Rock Around the Clock' Haley and His Comets—Decca Recording Artists." By the time of their next appearance, on May 29 at the Hofbrau, "Rock Around the Clock" had become one of the regular songs in their act. And on the next day, Memorial Day 1954, Bill's second child with Cuppy—a daughter, Doreen Debra Haley—was born.

Although Bill and Cuppy were still living in their one-bedroom apartment in Collingdale, Pennsylvania, they believed that Doreen had been conceived one romantic evening the previous fall on "the rock" near Bill's parents' cottage, which they thought of as "their rock." The couple drew up plans for a new home to be called Melody Manor, a name inspired by Gene Autry's "Melody Ranch." It would be built on the site of that rock, just as Bill had envisioned. While it was under construction they moved back into Bill's parents' two-bedroom house, with Maude and Will in one bedroom and Bill and Cuppy in the second with their two young children.

In June 1954, at their second Decca studio session, the band recorded "Shake, Rattle and Roll," written by black songsmith Jesse Stone (under the name Charles E. Calhoun) for black musician Big Joe Turner. Turner, known as the "Boss of the Blues," had needed an up-tempo number for a recording session, and Bill was happy for the opportunity to record the tune. By now he was big fan of Turner, Ruth Brown, and many of the up-and-coming black artists, and he'd listened to Turner's version of "Shake" many times before the Comets recorded it. Turner's version of the song had been released by Atlantic Records in February 1954 and hit the R&B charts that April, where it would remain for nearly seven months.

The Comets did everything they could to make their version of this song work, adding a powerful instrumental chorus, hand claps, and a "Go!" cheer to make their version stand out. On the B-side of the disc they recorded "ABC Boogie," another tune that James Myers had acquired from an obscure black songwriter named Jimmy for $500. That completed their obligation to use Myers' tunes on the B-sides of their records.

The Comets' version of "Shake" was released late in June and became a smash hit, rising quickly on the pop chart. "Shake" rose to No. 7 there in August and was an instant hit in many traditional R&B markets, including Louisville, Cleveland, Kansas City, Harlem, and Chicago's South Side.

The four Comets partners equally divided their first royalty payment from Decca in July 1954, with each individual receiving a check for $5,000, the equivalent of the average annual salary in the US at the time. Bill was very, very generous with his new-found riches. Attempting to buy affection and loyalty, he would invariably pick up the tab and give money and gifts to those around him. Those in his inner circle quickly began to regard him as a soft touch.

The Comets seemed to be on a roll, and everyone's spirits were high. So on June 17, 1954, they were shocked to hear that the band's recording session guitar player, thirty-three-year-old Danny Cedrone, had been found dead with a broken neck at the bottom of a flight of stairs in South Philadelphia. The stairs led up to the second-floor dining room above the 819 Bar on Snyder Avenue. Cedrone fronted a popular Philadelphia-based guitar duo called the Esquire Boys. After he'd returned home from an early engagement at a nearby nightclub, his wife had asked him to run out to pick up something to eat. He never made it back, and a bag of roast beef sandwiches lay on the ground near his lifeless body.

Although Cedrone's death appeared to have been an accident, Bill was stunned and recalled some things Danny had told him about the darker side of the record industry. Cedrone was not a mob associate, but he had worked in clubs controlled and frequented by members of the Philadelphia organized crime family. He knew that the local family owned the jukeboxes in all the Philadelphia joints and insisted that the first five thousand records of every new song go directly to the mob's jukeboxes, with no payment to the artist. Cedrone—a big, powerful man who'd recorded the instrumental song "Caravan" and had received little financial return for his efforts—didn't like this situation, didn't like the enforced arrangements involved, was tired of getting taken, and wasn't shy about letting those around him know how he felt. Bill was solemn, quiet, and lost in his thoughts for days after attending Cedrone's funeral.

On July 5, 1954, on the eve of his 29th birthday, another major event took place in Bill's universe, although he didn't yet understand its significance. An unknown nineteen-year-old electric company truck driver from Memphis, Tennessee—a fan of Bill's named Elvis Presley—made his first recording. The song Elvis recorded for Sam Phillips at Sun Records, "Blue Moon Over Kentucky," was backed on the other side of the disk with "That's All Right, Mama." Elvis later told Bill that "Crazy Man, Crazy" had inspired him.

14

The Comets Play, Little Doreen Haley Dies in her Crib, and Bill's Father Turns on the Gas

On the evening of July 20, 1954, Cuppy—who'd spent the whole day taking care of her new baby Doreen and her older daughter Joanie—eagerly accepted Bill's offer that she accompany him, the Comets, and their wives to a local performance by the band. The show went well, the applause was resounding, and the Comets returned to the stage for two encores.

Afterwards, Bill and Cuppy were exhausted and anxious to get home. They parked the car, and oddly, the neighbor's dog greeted them with an eerie howl that gave Cuppy a chill as she walked into the house. They were careful to be quiet, but once inside they could hear Doreen crying, and they saw Bill's mother Maude heating up a bottle of baby formula in the kitchen. After greeting the returning pair, Maude handed the bottle to Cuppy and went to bed.

Cuppy picked the baby up from her bassinet, hoping her cries wouldn't wake little Joanie. She changed Doreen's diaper and put fresh nightclothes on her, then wrapped her in a light blanket and carried her into the kitchen to hold and rock her as she sucked from her bottle. It didn't take long for Doreen to finish, and Cuppy walked back to their family bedroom, placed the baby in her bassinet, and kissed her. "Sleep tight, little girl," Cuppy murmured into Doreen's tiny ear. By now, Bill was asleep in their bed, so Cuppy joined him and drifted off.

At daybreak Cuppy awoke, feeling startled. A breeze fluttered the sheer white curtains at the open window and birds were chirping. But something was wrong. Doreen wasn't crying for her morning bottle as she usually did.

Cuppy sprang out of bed and over to Doreen's bassinet, which was in the couple's bedroom. The infant was lying on her back in an awkward position with her head thrown back. Her tiny mouth was open, but she wasn't breathing. When Cuppy snatched her up, Doreen was cold and stiff, and Cuppy screamed, "Something's wrong with the baby! Something's wrong!"

Bill jumped out of bed, grabbed Doreen from Cuppy's arms, and started blowing into her little mouth, trying to force his breath into her tiny lungs. "Call the doctor!" he yelled between breaths. Cuppy raced to the rotary telephone on the table in their sitting room, stumbling and nearly falling. Somehow she remembered her family doctor's number. When Dr. Grey answered his phone, she cried, "Help, please, something's wrong with my baby!" She was sobbing and confused.

"Who is this?" Dr. Grey calmly asked. Hearing his kind voice, Cuppy was able to calm down enough to stop shaking and tell him who she was and what had happened. She kept saying, "She's not breathing!" causing Dr. Grey to wonder if Cuppy was talking about Bill's mother. He had been to the house many times over the years to treat Maude for her heart condition. (Maude's heart had been weakened by a childhood bout with rheumatic fever, and she required a daily dose of digitalis.) Dr. Grey knew exactly where they lived and told Cuppy to "just sit down and wait for me." He called an ambulance before leaving. By now, fourteen-month-old Joanie was awake. She stood up her in her crib, gurgled, "Hey, Mommy! Hey Daddy!" and threw her empty bottle at them.

Bill and Cuppy were frantic but didn't want to wake Maude, fearful of aggravating her damaged heart. In a matter of minutes that seemed like hours, the house was filled with medical responders. Paramedics examined Doreen, then sadly looked at each other and shook their heads. "But she's only a baby," Cuppy thought. "This has to be a nightmare. I'll wake up soon."

When Dr. Grey arrived, Cuppy walked over to the bassinet, picked up Doreen's little body, and held it close. One of the responders took Doreen's lifeless form out of Cuppy's arms and placed it on the sofa in the adjacent sitting room. Cuppy ran back into the bedroom to get Doreen's blanket and covered her daughter's body to keep her warm, not fully comprehending that her baby was dead. Having just turned twenty-two, she was in some respects still a child herself. Bill sobbed in the corner, and Dr. Grey quietly talked to someone on the phone.

Maude emerged from her bedroom, wide eyed, mouth open, seemingly dazed. She stared in horror and disbelief at the scene playing out before her eyes. Cuppy thought, "Dear God, she's going to have a heart attack." Dr. Grey hung up the phone, came over to Cuppy, reached into his black bag, and took out a syringe. He asked Bill to hold her arm gently, she felt a tiny sting, and soon she was drifting. In her dream, everything seemed to slow down. She looked toward the sofa, saw a house fly land on Doreen's forehead, walked over, and angrily swatted it away. The fly tried to return and she swatted it again, this time connecting in mid-air. Looking at the piano, she found it hard to believe that a couple of days before, this same room had been full of joy while Maude played and sang hymns for Joanie and Doreen, and Will accompanied her on his banjo. They'd all been so happy.

A paramedic walked over, picked up Doreen gently, and took her away. Bill and Cuppy looked at one another in disbelief, held each other, and cried. Thinking about the awkward way Doreen's head was tilted when she found her, Cuppy sobbed, "She must have been screaming during the night," and once again burst into tears.

Relatives were called and began arriving at the house. Bill's sister Peggy and her husband picked up Joanie and took her away from the scene. Cuppy was inconsolable. Dr. Grey asked Cuppy if she'd like to have an autopsy performed, but at that point, all Cuppy could think of was someone cutting her baby open, so she said no.

Bill and Cuppy then went to the funeral home, where they chose a tiny white casket. Peggy and Maude bought a little white dress and a pink blanket to cover Doreen. Cuppy was almost catatonic with grief. People kept asking her questions and she answered as best she could, but inside her a voice was screaming, "I'm numb! I don't want to feel anything anymore. Please leave me alone." Out loud she said, "I can't understand what is happening. I only want my baby back. Please somebody bring her back to me." Bill didn't know what to do but cry with her. Quietly, he told her no one could ever bring Doreen back.

That night, when Bill again tried to comfort Cuppy, she pushed him away, sobbing uncontrollably. She still felt guilty for not waking up and hearing Doreen's cries, and she told Bill to leave her alone. "She's gone, and tomorrow they're going to put her in the ground," Cuppy said. She was so consumed with her own grief that she couldn't see Bill's, and he quietly turned away. Before they both fell into an exhausted sleep, she heard him crying.

Cuppy woke up the next morning to another hot and humid day. Bill was in the kitchen having coffee with Maude and Will. At first it seemed like any other day, but reality returned quickly: today they would bury their baby. The funeral service, attended only by the immediate family, was a blur. Bill held Cuppy tightly as they kneeled before the open coffin. Doreen looked as if she were peacefully sleeping.

She looked like a little angel, they thought. Cuppy now looked at the top of the coffin and saw a large spray of Baby's Breath. "How ironic," she thought. "My baby will never breathe again."

As Doreen's casket was lowered into a deep, dark hole at the foot of Maude's parents' graves, Cuppy noticed a weeping willow tree growing nearby, and somehow it gave her a small measure of comfort. The final prayers were said, and Bill led Cuppy away from the grave. Glancing over her shoulder, she saw men quickly shoveling dirt into the hole, and she knew that a piece of her heart was being buried with Doreen.

One day ran into another. Soon Joanie was back from Bill's sister's house and Cuppy found some comfort and relief in staying busy and taking care of her. She began hovering over Joanie, however, fearful that she would die as well. When she put Joanie into her crib each night, she read the child a story until she fell asleep. Then, unable to fall asleep herself, Cuppy would wander around the house, drinking coffee and waiting for Bill come home from another late night performing at nightclubs. She knew he and the band had to get back to work and fulfill their contracts, but the evenings were still long and lonely. And yet, for some reason Cuppy could not understand, she found herself refusing the comfort Bill wanted to give her when he came home, and that she knew he needed as well. She felt as if she were frozen emotionally.

Bill turned to Dr. Grey for help. He wanted to know how he could get his wife back, the way she was before this happened. Dr. Grey advised him that Cuppy should have another child right away. "Having another child will keep her busy and help her forget," he said.

Bill wanted to be strong for Cuppy, and outwardly he didn't show much emotion over the death of his daughter. After renting a house in Cape May for the rest of the summer, he installed Cuppy there with family members including Sharyn and Jackie, thinking that having them around would take Cuppy's mind off what had happened to Doreen. It did not. Although she did her best to conceal her emotions,

Cuppy resented the burden of watching the children. She was consumed with grief and guilt and barely able to eat, although already thin as a toothpick, and would sob every time Bill tried to comfort her. She blamed herself for what had happened, thinking over and over Doreen wouldn't have died if she, Cuppy, hadn't slept so soundly.

There was also a hint of further tragedy to come for Bill and his family. Bill had rented a Jersey Shore cottage near his family's cottage for the other Comets, and one day that August, his father, Will, wandered over there, turned on all the gas burners on the stove, and wandered out. No one was there at the time except Joey Ambrose, a notoriously late sleeper who was roused when someone smelled the gas from outside and rushed in to wake him. The gas was quickly turned off and no one was hurt, but . . .

Meanwhile, the Comets' career was accelerating. "Shake, Rattle, and Roll" held steady on the pop charts and sold more than two and a half million copies in less than three months. The song stayed in the Top 40 for twenty-seven weeks and was a moderate success on the R&B charts as well, becoming one of Decca Records' best sellers of 1954.

The Comets' appearance fees rose to $2,500 per night, and soon they began a national tour. They also broke onto the UK charts, which "Shake" climbed for fourteen weeks, topping out at No. 4.

The group's next record, "Dim Dim the Lights (I Want Some Atmosphere)" was written by Beverly Ross, the white daughter of a New Jersey chicken rancher, and black songwriter Julius Dixson (sic). "Dim Dim" had what is now known as a doo-wop sound, and after being released in September 1954, it eventually rose to No. 11 on the pop charts and No. 10 on the R&B chart. Decca inspired sales by distributing auto bumper tags to major automobile dealers bearing the song's title, which had a double meaning for night-driving motorists.

As the Comets broke through racial barriers, they also starred in what has come to be known as the first rock video, *Round Up of Rhythm*. Filmed at Universal Studios, this short movie was the earliest-known rock 'n' roll film to play in theaters. In this, their motion picture debut, Haley and the Comets are introduced by a DJ and his female guest and perform "Crazy Man, Crazy," "Straight Jacket," and "Shake Rattle and Roll." It's easy to see why the movie's producers picked "Straight Jacket." While performing the song, bass player Marshall Lytle throws the fiddle up on his shoulder, puts it on his knee, plays it like a guitar, and finally lays it down on its side and rides it. Joey Ambrose straddles, and wails on, his sax. The whole band claps and sways in unison.

As the group's prospects improved, so did Bill and Cuppy's home life. Just before Christmas of 1954, the couple learned that Cuppy was pregnant, and their shared excitement over the prospect of having another child helped Cuppy continue to work through her grieving process for Doreen. Bill's mother Maude was elated. Bill and Cuppy even visited Bill's first wife, Dottie, and Bill's children from that marriage, Sharyn and Jackie, on Christmas Eve.

15

Bill Triumphs in Hollywood as His Mother Dies an Early Death

In early 1955, the Comets recorded "Birth of the Boogie" for Decca. Although it did fairly well, eventually hitting No. 17 on the pop chart, the song was the first fruit of the band's decision to record only songs they owned the publishing rights for, or could acquire a piece of. This decision, based on greed, eventually had disastrous effects.

As their latest releases continued to hit the charts, the band toured relentlessly, with engagements in Philadelphia, Baltimore, Washington, DC, Kansas City, St. Louis, and many other cities. Bill went home after each show when he could, even if it meant driving a few hundred miles. He wanted to be with Cuppy, now three months pregnant. One evening, Bill picked up his guitar and began singing "Candy Kisses" to Cuppy, and the phone rang. It was band partner James "Lord Jim" Ferguson, who told him that someone making a Hollywood film wanted to use "Rock Around the Clock" on its soundtrack. "I think Glenn Ford is starring in it and it's something about a jungle," Lord Jim said. Bill's reaction was that he didn't want to be "overexposed." But he was immediately overruled by Cuppy, Lord Jim, and the other band-member partners.

It turned out that a month earlier, screenwriter and director Richard Brooks had begun working on a film for the teenage market about a band of juvenile delinquents rebelling against authority in an inter-racial public school. The movie would be based on, and named after, Evan Hunter's 1954 novel *The Blackboard Jungle*, a blockbuster that eventually sold more than one million copies. (Under the pen name Ed

McBain, Hunter went on to write the "87th Precinct" detective novels, as well as the screenplay for Alfred Hitchcock's movie *The Birds*.)

At that particular moment, young rebels were the new darlings of Hollywood. In 1953, Marlon Brando had played the leader of a motorcycle club in *The Wild One*, and in 1955, the year the *Blackboard Jungle* movie was released, James Dean would portray a disaffected young man in the movies *East of Eden* and *Rebel Without a Cause*.

During production of the *Blackboard Jungle* movie, Brooks would occasionally meet with Glenn Ford at Ford's house to go over upcoming scenes. During one such get-together, Brooks told Ford he was looking for music to use on the film's sound track and needed something appropriate for what would be a controversial and perhaps shocking film. Ford suggested that the two of them listen to some of the records in his pre-teen son Peter's collection, since Peter loved music and was up on all the latest records.

Together they walked over to Peter's neat stack of records next to the family phonograph and flipped through the disks. They sampled quite a few, and Brooks asked to borrow three of them to share with the movie's producer, Pandro Berman, and assistant director, Joel Freeman. The records Brooks borrowed were black musician Big Joe Turner's "Shake, Rattle and Roll"; "All Night Long," played by the all-black Joe Houston Orchestra; and Bill Haley and His Comets' "(We're Gonna) Rock Around the Clock," one of Peter's favorites. After consulting with Berman and Freeman, Brooks decided to use "Rock Around the Clock" for *Blackboard Jungle*'s soundtrack.

In February 1955, Glenn Ford took Peter to see *Blackboard Jungle* as an early birthday present, telling him that "his song" was going to be used in the movie. Seated in the back row of the theater with his father, Brooks, and Berman, Peter nearly jumped out of his seat when he heard the opening rim shots of "Rock Around the Clock" begin to reverberate through the theater. Although Peter remained seated, many other teens who saw this movie jumped out of their seats and began dancing in the aisles when "Rock Around the Clock" hit the speakers. Fearing this reaction, some theater owners turned down the sound when the song started.

Blackboard Jungle opens with the roar of the MGM lion and a written onscreen message to the audience expressing deep concern about juvenile delinquency in the nation's schools. This message is immediately followed by Haley's recording of "Rock Around the Clock" on the movie's soundtrack, cementing the connection between the song and the alleged problem. Adding to the film's seriousness, a lengthy, ominous drum solo, which hadn't been in the original recording, precedes the first playing of "Rock." Later on during the film, an instrumental version of the song is played again, and the moment the onscreen action ends, its full version, with both voices and instruments, is heard once more. The fact that musical issues are a substantial part of the movie's plot tightens the connection it seems to make between juvenile delinquency and rock 'n' roll, particularly the song "Rock Around the Clock."

The plot somewhat eerily prefigures Bill's career as a pop music innovator, as well as an imitator and friend of black musicians. Glenn Ford plays a sensitive new teacher (Richard Dadier) who's starting his career at an all-boys manual-arts high school in a mixed-race, but still white-dominated, urban neighborhood. In the film's first scene, "Rock Around the Clock" is playing when Dadier enters the schoolyard, and some male students are dancing to it. Another new teacher tells Dadier he has a great collection of swing records that it took him fifteen years to assemble, and he's going to bring the records to school to play for the kids. In a scene in which he plays his class a recording of "Jazz Me Blues" by Bix Beiderbecke, however, the students revolt. Obviously on their way from part-time delinquency to full-time crime, they demand "bop" records or tunes by Frank Sinatra or Joni James, and they then destroy the teacher's precious record collection right in front of him while holding him down.

Later in the film, Dadier, whom the students mockingly call "Daddy-O," befriends the black student Gregory Miller, played by Sidney Poitier, when he sees Miller playing the piano for an all-black male singing group. Backed up by Miller, Dadier finally confronts the evildoers among his own students, and the two decide to work together from then on, just as Haley worked with many black musicians during his career.

The movie's real achievement was to latch onto the real-life discontent among many white and black teenagers trying assert themselves against their parents. The US economy was booming after World War II, and the kids saw their parents as self-satisfied sticks-in-the-mud who'd won the war and were now glorying in their own prosperity. *Blackboard Jungle* managed to merge this dissatisfaction with a rebellion against the dominant music of the era, which celebrated peace, complacency, and consumerism over all other values. (In 1953, the No. 1 song in America, on both the *Billboard* and the *Cash Box* pop charts, had been Patti Page's treacly and excessively sentimental "How Much is That Doggie in the Window?") The scene in *Blackboard Jungle* in which a sneering group of teenagers smash the records belonging to a white authority figure said it all. The fact that a teenage song like "Rock Around the Clock" in a teenage movie like this one was recorded by Bill Haley, a twice-married thirty-year-old with three children, adds to the drama of its success.

Made on the eve of a decades-long, eventually world-wide period of teenage rebellion that it may well have started, the film was later designated as "culturally significant" and selected for preservation in the US National Film Registry. *Blackboard Jungle* was also a boffo box-office success and was nominated for four Oscars, although it didn't win any.

Peter Ford wasn't the only youngster enthralled with the movie and its soundtrack. As the film opened around the country, tens of thousands of teens stormed record stores to buy "Rock Around the Clock" or asked that it be played on their favorite radio stations. They also bought thousands of paperback copies of Hunter's novel.

Everywhere the movie was shown, radio station music directors began to dig out their year-old promotional copies of "Rock Around the Clock" and play them on the air, inspiring Decca to promptly reissue the disk in the now industry-standard 45 rpm format. This time, however, "Rock" was on the A-side. By July 1955, the song would rise to No. 1 on the *Billboard* pop chart, where it stayed for eight weeks, and to No. 17 on the British charts, where it remained for two weeks.

The use of "Rock Around the Clock" in the movie *Blackboard Jungle* made Bill Haley and His Comets famous worldwide. In the minds of parents and conservative society in general, however, the song linked thirty-year-old Bill, the Comets, and rock 'n' roll in general to a growing adolescent rebellion against authority and, by extension, to juvenile delinquency. Soon a wide array of conservative voices and governmental agencies, including the FBI, would investigate, criticize, and condemn the Comets as the most prominent and visible representatives of this threatening new music. Bill and his bandmates—white, striving middle-class husbands and fathers, heading toward middle age and building houses for their families—would strive for years to change this perspective. They would not succeed.

Meanwhile, numerous musicians whom some middle-class parents would find much more disturbing because of their race, sexual preference, or personal peccadillos were also starting their careers. A month after the Comets performed in St. Louis, for instance, Chuck Berry, a twenty-four-year-old black St. Louis hair stylist and songwriter, made his first record, "Maybelline." Far from attempting to crush such competition, Bill and the Comets encouraged black soloists and groups. Soon after "Rock's" release, for instance, the Comets performed in Cleveland with the black group Billy Ward and the Dominoes, featuring lead singer Jackie Wilson.

Bill reacted badly to the negative light *Blackboard Jungle* had cast on the band. After returning home from a group tour in 1955, he asked office manager Sam Sgro to join him for a two-and-a-half-hour ride to see the movie in New York City. Sgro and Bill sat in the back row. The crowd clapped as the movie ended, but Bill was clearly disturbed by some of its scenes, and by the implied association of rock 'n' roll with juvenile delinquency. He started the car and took off, looking straight ahead, and didn't say a word to Sgro until they'd almost reached home. Finally, they pulled into a rest stop, went inside, and got coffee. When they came out, Bill got behind the wheel again, lit a cigarette, looked at Sgro, and said, "If this is what I do to those kids, I don't want to sing any more. No more!"

From then on, Sgro had to argue with Haley to get him to do public appearances or to take certain bookings. Bill was obviously of two minds on this subject, however, because when the movie opened in Philadelphia, he took his mother and Cuppy to see *Blackboard Jungle* and hear his song on its soundtrack.

Shortly after doing this excursion, Haley, following his usual custom, was spending Monday at home with his family. It was April 25, 1955, and earlier that day Maude and Cuppy had had a little tiff over some insignificant matter involving Bill. Feeling badly about it, Cuppy said to Bill, "I'm going to call mom and invite her to dinner," and Bill agreed. After dinner Maude returned to her house, after which she quickly called Bill and Cuppy to say she was having trouble breathing. She was frightened, and Bill ran over there while Cuppy phoned Dr. Grey. She then went to Maude's house to find her mother-in-law in the living room sitting on an overstuffed chair in the corner, mumbling "Oh my God! Oh my God!" and wincing in pain as she gasped for air.

Bill fretted while they waited for the doctor, and Cuppy, now six months pregnant, paced anxiously. Memories came back to her of having waited in that same room for medical personnel to arrive after Doreen died. Seeing that Cuppy was terribly upset and worried she might miscarry, Bill told her to go into the kitchen. From the kitchen Cuppy heard Maude say, "Oh my God, I'm doomed!" When the doctor arrived, he pounded on Maude's chest trying to revive her and then said, "She's gone."

Bill was devastated. The loss of his young daughter a year earlier had been tragic and frightening, but the suddenness of Maude's death, and the severing of their emotional bond, was almost unbearable. He felt a terrible sense of loss, as well as a sense of great gratitude, thinking about how hard she'd worked to help support their family by cleaning houses, taking in other people's wash, growing vegetables to sell, and keeping chickens.

Bill had always been the apple of Maude's eye. From the very beginning she'd told him he was talented, and as an adult, he'd wanted to protect and take care of her. During the early years, when Bill was making very little money and also had to support Dottie, Sharyn, and Jackie, Maude always had helped him care for his family. Right up until she died, she gave Sunday school lessons each week to Joanie, Sharyn, and Jackie, playing the piano, singing hymns, and reading to them from the Bible.

16

The Comets Enter the Stratosphere as Will is Committed to a Mental Hospital

On May 6, 1955, a few weeks after Maude's death, the Comets became the first rock 'n' roll band to perform at New York City's famous Carnegie Hall. They continued to release record after record, including "Razzle Dazzle," another composition by black writer Charles Calhoun. Soon "Razzle" would be heard playing on the jukebox as actors playing young people danced in the 1955 movie *Running Wild*, starring Mamie Van Doren.

Advertised on movie posters as "the stark brutal truth about today's lost generation" and "the first jolting story of organized teen-age gangs," *Running Wild* tightened the link in both teen and parental minds between rock 'n' roll and juvenile delinquency. It also tightened the connection between rock and sex because of the way the statuesque Van Doren behaved in the film. One image from a poster advertising the movie showed her "dancing" with a young man with both legs wrapped around his torso. In the movie, which is about a fictional young rookie cop who goes undercover to bust up an auto theft ring run by juvenile delinquents, Van Doren tells a male character, "When I want something, I want it now," presumably igniting parental rage throughout America.

Partly as a result of its use in the film, "Razzle Dazzle" quickly hit No. 15 on the pop chart and remained in the Top 40 for a month. It did even better in the UK, rising to No. 13 for two months. With "Rock Around the Clock" also still high on the charts because of the *Black-*

board Jungle movie, Decca decided it was time to release the Comets' first long-playing album, *Shake, Rattle and Roll*, containing eight tracks. Suddenly "Rock Around the Clock" was being played at teen and college parties and sock hops all across America. The scope of its success may be judged by the fact that it was cited as the cause of a mini-riot on the Princeton University campus, described by the *Philadelphia Inquirer* as "feverish though harmless." The representation of pop culture in music had reached a tipping point, and the flood gates were opened. "Rock Around the Clock" gave kids a music and a voice of their own,

On May 31, soon after *Running Wild*'s release, Bill and his Comets made their first national network television appearance on *Milton Berle's Texaco Star Theater*. During the show, Berle himself danced to their music. One of the earliest nationally televised performances by a rock 'n' roll band, the Comets' appearance on the Berle show gave rock a much wider audience.

By June 1955, "Rock Around the Clock" had also risen to No. 3 on the national R&B charts, and every radio and jukebox in America seemed to be playing the song continuously. On one drive from Buffalo to Boston, some of the Comets kept pushing the car radio button and heard "Rock" playing on five stations simultaneously.

Now afloat in cash, Bill was advised by his accountant to reduce his taxable income by spending some of it on items that could be deducted as business expenses. When the band's van broke down near Chicago and they were waiting for it to be repaired, they strolled over to a Cadillac dealer. Bill and his partners—Lord Jim, Billy Williamson and Johnny Grande—were casually dressed. The seasoned salesmen in the showroom dismissed them as tire-kickers and told the new kid on the staff to wait on them. That lucky young salesman ended up with juicy commissions on the sale of five new cars: a fully loaded blue two-door Cadillac Coupe de Ville for Cuppy, a pink Fleetwood for Bill, and a white convertible, a dark blue sedan, and a silver-grey El Dorado for Bill's companions.

While Bill, Lord Jim, Williamson, and Grande shared in the band's profits, the rest of the Comets, who worked on salary alone, reacted to the car purchases by demanding a raise. When no action was immediately forthcoming, they quit the band and formed a new group, the Jodimars, which went nowhere. Bill soon replaced them but resented their desertion for many years.

Meanwhile, two months after Bill's mother died, it became too difficult for Cuppy and Bill's sister Peggy to care for Bill's now-senile father. Will had to be placed in a nearby Veterans' Hospital. He'd been an intelligent, musical man, but had deteriorated to the point of becoming noncommunicative. Half the time, he had no idea whom he was speaking to.

Simultaneously with these personal challenges for Bill, in 1955 "Rock Around the Clock" became the first rock 'n' roll record ever to reach the No. 1 position on *Billboard*'s Hot 100 chart. Decca announced that in a little more than a year, the Comets had sold more than three million records for the label. "Shake, Rattle and Roll" and "Rock Around the Clock" had each sold over one million copies; a third Comets release, "Dim Dim the Lights," had sold seven hundred fifty thousand; and a fourth, "Mambo Rock," had sold more than three hundred thousand copies.

In July, another Comets tune, "Two Hound Dogs," joined "Razzle Dazzle" and "Rock Around the Clock" on the pop charts, and "Rock Around the Clock" simultaneously reached the top of the pop, R&B, and country charts. That same month, Bill and Cuppy's first son, William John Clifton Haley Jr., was born. Sadly for Bill and Cuppy, Bill Jr.'s birth was three months too late for Maude. His birth couldn't bring back Maude or Doreen, but it gave Cuppy a renewed sense of hope and optimism after a year filled with so much personal loss.

When Cuppy was in the late stages of pregnancy, Bill had stayed with her every step of the way. He never left her side when she was about to go into labor with Bill Jr. When the baby was born on July 28, 1955, Bill Sr. thanked Cuppy for giving him a namesake, noting that he'd always wanted one, because that's what his mother had wanted for him. The fact that Bill had consented to naming this son Bill Jr. while he had refused to give that name to his first son with Dottie indicated to Cuppy that he thought their marriage was permanent.

In August 1955, the band made its debut on Ed Sullivan's *Toast of the Town* show on the national CBS network, performing "Rock Around the Clock." The Sullivan show was an unprecedented maker or breaker of pop acts. A former reporter for the *New York Daily News*, Ed Sullivan had been an odd choice as the show's MC. He wasn't handsome; he bent too far forward, held his hands together either behind or in front of him, or stood onstage with his arms folded. Pronouncing *show* as "shew," he blew his lines regularly and often mumbled incoherently. Still, TV had been new and insecure when the show was about to start in 1948. To CBS executives at the time, a man such as Sullivan, credentialed by the obviously solid *Daily News* and a former MC of some war relief performances during World War II, had the best shot at winning audience acceptance for their planned national variety show.

Their gamble paid off: at 8 p.m. every Sunday night, millions of people gathered round their TV sets to watch and listen to the entertainers Sullivan had chosen for them. He became the star maker of the age, introducing more than ten thousand musical and performing acts to the American people from 1948 to 1971.

Bill and the Comets were the first rock 'n' roll act that ever appeared on the Sullivan show, and Sullivan let them know he wasn't impressed. He made no attempt to disguise his disdain for the Comets' sound and teased Bill about his trademark kiss curl, tugging at it off camera. "Is that thing real?" he asked Bill, out of earshot of the audience. "What are you, a fag or something?"

Sullivan's disdain didn't stop the band's progress, however. Their appearance on his show tremendously increased their popularity. They soon received and accepted offers to appear for the first time on *The Sammy Kaye Show* and a second time on *The Milton Berle Show*.

Meanwhile another song that the Comets had made very popular, "Shake, Rattle, and Roll," was heard on the soundtrack of yet another Hollywood movie, joining "Rock Around the Clock" and "Razzle Dazzle" in receiving that honor. "Shake" is played by a band at the commencement exercises of the fictional Bristol College in the Twentieth Century Fox production *How to Be Very Very Popular*, starring Betty Grable and Sheree North and released in 1955. In this film, strippers Stormy Tornado (played by Grable) and Curly Flagg (played by North) hide out in a fraternity at Bristol after it becomes known that they can identify the killer of a fellow stripper at their cabaret. Trouble ensues, and the fact that Curly has been hypnotized adds to her problems.

The release of *How to Be Very Very Popular* linked sex even more tightly with Haley and His Comets, and with rock 'n' roll in general. It didn't help that Grable's character was named Stormy Tornado and the leading stripper of the day was named Tempest Storm. (The Stormy Tornado character and the real stripper Tempest Storm may have inspired twenty-first century adult film star Stephanie Clifford to adopt the stage name Stormy Daniels.) The poster for the film showed the two women shimmying so vigorously in their caps and gowns that those gowns have fallen forward, revealing their spangled stripper costumes beneath.

Meanwhile, as the Comets stepped up their national touring schedule, a youngster named Elvis Presley joined them onstage in Omaha

Bill Haley (2nd from left) as a
member of the Range Drifters, 1946.
Photo Credit: Michael Ochs Archives.

Bill Haley, 1948.
Photo Credit: Michael Ochs Archives.

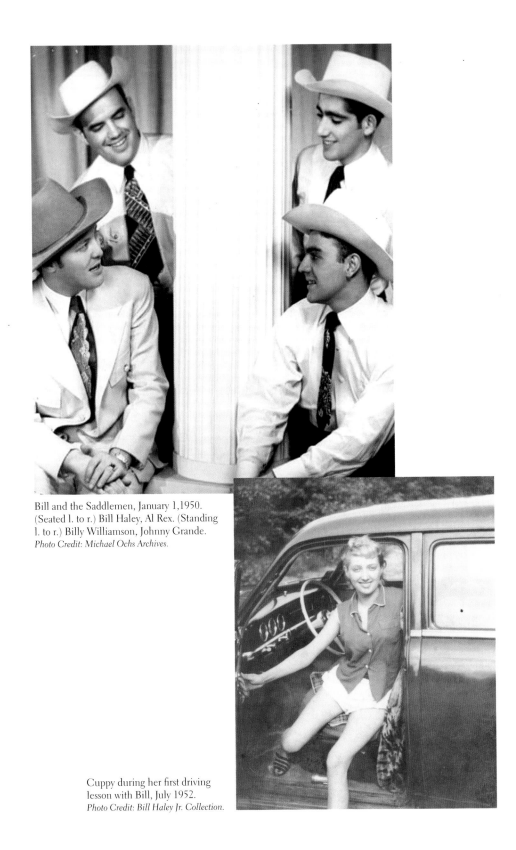

Bill and the Saddlemen, January 1,1950.
(Seated l. to r.) Bill Haley, Al Rex. (Standing
l. to r.) Billy Williamson, Johnny Grande.
Photo Credit: Michael Ochs Archives.

Cuppy during her first driving
lesson with Bill, July 1952.
Photo Credit: Bill Haley Jr. Collection.

(Standing l. to r.) Harry "Reds" Broomall, Cuppy holding Joanie. (Seated l. to r.) Bill's mother Maude, Bill's daughter Sharyn, Bill's father Will. Summer 1953.
Photo Credit: Bill Haley Jr. Collection

Bill performing in a night club, 1953.
Photo Credit: Bill Haley Jr. Collection.

Bill playing upright bass, performing in a night club, 1953.
Photo Credit: Bill Haley Jr. Collection.

Bill and Cuppy, September 1954. *Photo Credit: Bill Haley Jr. Collection.*

(l. to r.) Bill's father Will, Bill's sister Peggy, Bill's cousin Danny, Bill's mother Maude, Peggy's daughter Sylvia, Cuppy, Bill, and Harry "Reds" Broomall, September 1954. *Photo Credit: Bill Haley Jr. Collection.*

Bill Haley & His Comets pose with their new Decca van, 1954. (l. to r.) Bill Haley, Dick Richards, Marshall Lytle, Joey Ambrose, Johnny Grande, Billy Williamson.
Photo Credit: Bill Haley Jr. Collection.

Bill posing with the new Decca
van, 1954.
Photo Credit: Bill Haley Jr. Collection.

The Comets performing
at Hershey Park, PA, 1954.
Photo Credit: Bill Haley Jr. Collection.

Bill and Cuppy in England, February 1, 1957.
Photo Credit: Harry Kerr/BIPs/Getty Images.

Bill and Elvis Presley backstage at Brooklyn
High School, Brooklyn, Ohio, October 20, 1955.
Photo Credit: Tommy Edwards.

Bill at the Pythian Temple,
Decca Recording Studio, 1955.
Photo Credit: Bill Haley Jr. Collection.

Bill Jr. and Bill Sr. at home, 1956.
Photo Credit: Bill Haley Jr. Collection.

when they appeared there for a few shows. He did so at the request of Presley's new manager, Colonel Tom Parker, a friend of Lord Jim's who wanted Elvis to gain exposure and experience.

Bill didn't catch Elvis's act that first night in Omaha, and he also missed his next two shows at the forty-five-hundred-seat Nebraska University Auditorium in Lincoln and the six-thousand-seat Municipal Auditorium in Topeka. He finally met the Colonel's young prospect when the Comets' tour reached the Municipal Auditorium in Oklahoma City on October 16, 1955. Elvis mustered the courage to approach Bill backstage that evening and tell him that he'd been a long-time fan and was eager to learn from him. Bill, fondly recalling a similar meeting between himself and the great Hank Williams, liked the young man and offered a few words of encouragement.

The two became better acquainted, speaking together frequently over the next couple of days and playing cards backstage with some other musicians. They drove in Bill's Cadillac to Tulsa for Elvis's last appearance on the tour, with Bill graciously offering Elvis the opportunity to drive part of the way. Elvis was thrilled and told Bill that someday he was going to buy a Cadillac for himself and one for his mama too. The polite, respectful youngster repeatedly addressed Bill as sir. He said his favorite song was "Crazy Man, Crazy," and that it had made him want to be a singer. Both men also were huge Hank Williams fans, and as they discussed their shared love of Hank's music, they became friends.

A few days later, Bill and Elvis crossed paths again when radio personality Bill Randle brought them together during a show to stage an iconic photo. This classic color picture, taken by fellow DJ Tommy Edwards during entertainment night at Cleveland's Brooklyn High School Auditorium, showed a confident Bill Haley grinning at the camera and shaking hands with a weary-eyed Elvis Presley. That night, the Comets appeared on the same bill as Elvis, the Four Lads, and Pat Boone, and the nervous young Elvis asked Bill for permission before doing his own versions of "Shake, Rattle and Roll" and "Crazy Man, Crazy."

In November 1955, Elvis sang his version of "Rock Around the Clock" on the TV show *Louisiana Hayride*. Also, on November 26th—the same day the readers of *Cashbox*, voting in the magazine's Annual Readers' Poll, named the Comets the No. 1 Small Instrumental Group of 1955 and "Rock Around the Clock" the No. 1 Record of 1955—Presley signed a three-year record deal with RCA Victor. Not long afterward, in January 1956, Presley would record "Heartbreak Hotel," the first of a string of hits that propelled him to superstardom.

Continuing to perform virtually nonstop, the Comets began a one-week engagement at the Brooklyn Paramount, joining La Vern Baker and headliner Johnnie Ray, known as "Mr. Cry." According to a print advertisement for the event appearing in the November 19, 1955 issue of *New York Age*. Tension was built into this arrangement for three performances per day because Ray had an unrequited crush on Bill and therefore disliked Cuppy. Also, Ray had made certain to be the contractually designated headliner of, and the last act on, every show. Finally, he also insisted that no one use the freight elevator to reach his dressing room behind the stage until after his appearance, which included a dramatic "fainting" routine, because the elevator was noisy.

After a couple days spent watching from backstage following his own performance, Bill grew impatient with the delay. He ordered the elevator to take the band up while Ray was still lying on the stage. When Ray heard the elevator moving, he made a sudden and miraculous recovery, ran offstage, and pounded on the elevator door, indignant that his demands had been ignored.

A little while later, Bill and Cuppy went to see a new movie, *The Big Knife*, released in late 1955. It was based on a Clifford Odets play and starred Jack Palance, whom Bill had met backstage a few weeks earlier when they'd both appeared on the Ed Sullivan show. Bill was intrigued by, and strongly identified with, Palance's portrayal of Charlie Castle, a successful actor whose life is controlled by a studio. The film is a tale of blackmail and infidelity, and the character becomes a victim of his own success to such an extent that in the end he slits his own throat with a big knife, giving the movie its title. Bill and Cuppy talked about the movie for weeks, and it's hard to believe Bill didn't think about it later in his life.

On December 12, 1955, the Comets recorded "See You Later, Alligator," written by Robert "Bobby Charles" Guidry. Guidry's roots were in New Orleans R&B. He was white, a Cajun, and such a Haley fan that he sported his own kiss curl. His composition was inspired by "Later for You Baby," a song written by black composer Guitar Slim. For the Comets recording, Bill and producer Milt Gabler added a few "jive" phrases of their own and a gimmick: Comet Franny Beecher opened the record by speaking its title in a falsetto voice.

Gabler was in a particular hurry to record "See You" because not only was the tune already a regional hit for Guidry, but Gabler himself had recorded another version of it with vocalist Roy Hall. He knew the Comets could do the song better, however, and therefore had scheduled a rare weekend session to record it. Bill hadn't heard "See You" yet, but the recording session was a success. Later, Gabler announced at the Comets' annual Christmas party that the group had sold more than five and a half million records that year and already had booked 175 appearances for 1956. The sky was the limit, and Bill was certain he'd acquired the Midas touch. In January 1956, "See You Later, Alligator" would rise to the No. 6 position on the pop chart, where it would remain for 15 weeks. In February, it would rise to No. 7 on the R&B chart as well.

To top everything off, the readers of the December 28, 1955, issue of *Downbeat* had named Bill their No. 1 Rhythm and Blues Personality of 1955 in the magazine's annual poll. That may have raised eyebrows: R&B was considered black music, and Bill, a white man, had been favored over Joe Williams, Dinah Washington, Ruth Brown, and Big Joe Turner, all of whom were black. Even so, United Press named Bill and His Comets No. 1 R&B Artists of the Year in its annual poll.

On January 6, 1956, "Rock-A-Beatin' Boogie," another recent Comets recording, reached the No. 4 slot on the UK charts. It was one of several Comets songs that did very well in the UK around this time while never charting in the US. That same month, the readers of *Record World*, a US magazine, named Bill and His Comets their No. 1 Instrumental Group, and "Rock Around the Clock" their No. 1 Favorite Record and Artist. Bill and his band had risen from an up-and-coming novelty group to the most popular band in America.

With all this happening, neither Bill nor any of his Comets had taken much notice of a full-page ad in the December 3, 1955, issue of *Billboard*. Elvis Presley, the ad said, was now "the most talked about new personality in the last 10 years of recorded music."

17

The Comets Shine in Hollywood While Elvis Shines in the Heartland

Singing "Rock Around the Clock" on the soundtrack of *Blackboard Jungle* had vastly increased the Comets' fame. Although they hadn't appeared in a Hollywood movie yet, in 1956 the group was hired to appear onscreen as the musical heroes of Hollywood's first rock 'n' roll musical. Named *Rock Around the Clock* after the song, the film was a fictional version of how rock 'n' roll was discovered. Besides the Comets, it also featured onscreen performances by the Platters, the Ernie Freeman Combo, Tony Martinez and His Band, and Freddie Bell and His Bellboys.

"Rock Around the Clock" introduces the soundtrack of this movie, just as it did for *Blackboard Jungle*. In the film, the ex-manager of a big band orchestra—Steve Hollis, played by actor and singer Johnny Johnston—is driving to New York City with the band's ex-bass player, Corny LaSalle, played by Henry Slate. Johnston plays his role well but somewhat oddly doesn't sing in the movie, although he'd had three Top 10 hit records in 1945 on the Capitol label.

At the beginning of the film, Hollis has just resigned as the band's manager because he can't find gigs for the group, and he is driving to New York to find a job with a musical booking agency. LaSalle accompanies him, apparently to get a free ride to the city. When the two men stop in the fictional town of Strawberry Springs for the night, they can't help but notice that everyone in town is heading for the local auditorium to dance to the music of the town's own band, a group of farm kids called . . . you guessed it, Bill Haley and His Comets. After watching the band's boffo performance, Hollis signs on as the group's manager. In the movie, the band includes a teenage brother-and-sister dance duo: Lisa Johns, played by Lisa Gaye, and her brother Jimmy, played by Earl Barton. Hollis decides to use them all to popularize rock 'n' roll in America.

Unfortunately, Hollis soon falls in love with Lisa and wants to marry her. This angers his booking agent, Corrine Talbot (played by Alix Talton), who herself wants to marry Hollis. She takes revenge by trying to halt the Comets' rise. Toward the end of the picture, when all seems lost for the band and its supporters, DJ Alan Freed, playing himself, comes to the rescue, providing a way for the Comets and other acts to get the major exposure they'll need to hit the big time.

Bill delivers his few spoken lines in the film somewhat stiffly. He comes alive, however, when he leads the Comets in six of their songs, including "See You Later, Alligator," "Rock-A-Beatin' Boogie," and "Razzle Dazzle."

Teenagers loved the movie and showed it by rocking, stomping, and singing along loudly during screenings. Adults, by contrast, criticized the film's "wild" music and "offensive" dance movements. (Some critics also pointed out that while Bill's actual music appealed to teenagers, most of the "kids" dancing to Comets tunes in this and subsequent Comets movies appeared to be expert professional dancers well into their twenties.)

Freed, who'd become the nation's most popular DJ while broadcasting from station WINS in New York, at first demanded a straight fee up front for participating in the film. He was convinced to take a generous percentage of the profits instead, and he ended up making a small fortune rather than the $15,000 he would have settled for. Bill and his partners were paid $20,000, a respectable amount at the time but a bargain for Columbia Pictures, which produced *Rock Around the Clock*. The film became a huge commercial success.

On the group's first night out in Hollywood, where the film was made, Cuppy found herself in a dimly lit, smoky nightclub full of movie stars, DJs, and musicians drinking champagne, dancing, and laughing. During the evening she became trapped in a one-sided conversation with actor Johnny Johnston, who wanted to tell her all about his successful singing and acting career and his ex-wife, Kathryn Grayson, an opera singer who'd starred in several movie musicals. Grayson had successfully sued Johnston for divorce five years earlier, and he couldn't conceal his lingering resentment as he poured his heart out to Cuppy, denigrating his ex-wife and claiming he was the one who'd divorced her. He did confess that one of Grayson's claims was true, however: he really had read her letters aloud to some young girls in his fan club, including some all-too-graphic details about what Grayson liked most about his lovemaking.

With a silent shudder, Cuppy excused herself and joined Bill and a group of other people who were watching surreptitiously as band associate Jim Myers approached actress Gloria DeHaven. Band member Billy Williamson, always looking for a laugh, had told the chubby Myers that DeHaven had recently divorced real estate developer Martin Kimmel and might be looking for a companion. Having set the bait, Williamson stepped back with the others to see what would happen. Sure enough, as he'd anticipated, the boisterous, overconfident, starstruck Myers approached the legendary actress and requested her company for dinner. DeHaven, with a mixture of outrage and pity in her eyes, declined his offer and dismissed him. Stifling snickers, the band members later joked mercilessly about the rejection, eventually even mocking Myers, good naturedly, to his face.

Soon after Bill and His Comets completed *Rock Around the Clock*, Bill bought a new 1956 pink Fleetwood Cadillac and left with the band on a ten-day tour. He was on the road almost continuously now, mostly without Cuppy, and the constant travel was beginning to create tension in their relationship.

Unable to watch TV while flying to a Birmingham, Alabama, appearance one Saturday night in April, neither Bill nor the Comets could see their young friend Elvis Presley make his national debut on CBS-TV's *Stage Show*. On that show, he performed a medley of the Comets hits "Shake, Rattle and Roll," "Flip, Flop and Fly," and "I Got a Woman." During the next eight weeks, Presley would make five more appearances on *Stage Show*. While the Comets were on the road selling out stadiums and reaping the rewards of their string of hits over the previous year and a half, he was busy capturing the imagination of the nation.

Bill and His Comets were the only white act on the ten-day tour that began in Birmingham in April 1956. They were joined on that tour by the Platters, LaVern Baker, Shirley and Lee, the Drifters, Big Joe Turner, the Five Keys, the Turbans, Bo Diddley, Roy Hamilton, and the Red Prysock Band. In Birmingham, the Comets performed only in the afternoon, while the black acts performed only in the evening, because in this pre-integration era, "colored" artists in the South were not allowed to appear onstage at the same time as any white person.

"I hope soon the South will do away with its ideas on segregation," Bill wrote in his diary after appearing in Birmingham. Nevertheless, attendance at the Birmingham shows was phenomenal: 6,000 people in the afternoon and 7,000 at night, a total of 13,000 for one day. It was a new record for a Birmingham audience. Shortly thereafter, the band played to a full house at the Charlotte Coliseum, establishing a new world record for a single rock 'n' roll show: 11,534 paid admissions. As scheduled, the band ended their tour shortly thereafter.

Meanwhile, Elvis's fame kept growing. On February 1, 1956, Decca rereleased "See You Later, Alligator" in both 45 and 78 rpm formats, just two days before Elvis recorded his own version of "Shake, Rattle and Roll." Three days later, on February 4, Presley appeared on *Stage Show* again to sing "Baby Let's Play House" and "Tutti Frutti." He returned there a week afterward to sing "Blue Suede Shoes" and "Heartbreak Hotel." Resenting the time spent away from his family, Bill turned down a $5,000 offer to go to Las Vegas to appear again on Milton Berle's TV show during the third week of February and instead went away with Cuppy. On that vacation, when they heard "See You Later, Alligator" being played on almost every station on the car radio, Bill sang with it and laughed a lot. He told Cuppy that Elvis was a good kid with a lot of talent and a respectful, polite country boy.

On a later tour, Bill and the band visited Omaha, Nebraska. *Variety* magazine noted that while the Comets were performing there, "kids took over the aisles to jitterbug to 'Rock Around the Clock,' 'Shake, Rattle and Roll,' and 'See You Later, Alligator' despite attempts of gendarmes to keep 'em seated." In Milwaukee, the owner of the Million Dollar Ballroom hugged Bill onstage after the show and told him the Comets were the answer to the fading dance business.

On tours like these, when Cuppy wasn't with him, Bill would call her three or four times a day, including when he arrived in each new city and before and after each show. He'd send roses to her at home and call to tell her she was his inspiration and that without her he never would have made it. Every time he left for a tour, he'd make sure Cuppy had money for anything that came up and leave blank signed checks for her to use.

In March 1956, "See You Later, Alligator" entered the UK charts, where it stayed for thirteen weeks, reaching No. 7. That month, the Comets flew through a blizzard to Washington, DC, for the world premiere of their *Rock Around the Clock* movie. Shortly after Cuppy joined them by train, Bill wrote in his diary, "Everything's all right now that my baby's with me." The movie certainly did well, ringing up revenues of $1.1 million against a production cost of $350,000. Although Bill thought his speaking appearances in it were terrible, he certainly was interested in aiding its climb, spending eight hours meeting and greeting fans in the lobby of the Philadelphia theater that was showing it.

18

The War on Rock 'n' Roll Becomes the War of Whites Against Blacks

American culture has one great theme, race,
and one great art form, pop music, and the two are and
always will be inseparable,
will always be the twin helices of our national DNA
–David Kirby, from his 2015 book
Crossroad: Artist, Audience,
and the Making of American Music

Soon other recording artists began following Bill's lead, or at least pretended to. Kay Starr's "Rock 'n' Roll Waltz" became the nation's No. 1 record. "See You Later, Alligator" held strong at No. 6, and Elvis's "Heartbreak Hotel" shot up the charts to No. 2. Meanwhile, on March 26, 1956, Bill and Cuppy's first child and only remaining daughter, Joanie, reached her third birthday. It was a relief to her parents, who'd been permanently scarred by the sudden death of their second child, Doreen.

While continuing to cut new disks they hoped would be hits, Bill and the Comets performed "See You Later, Alligator" and their all-instrumental song "Rudy's Rock" on CBS-TV's coast-to-coast *Arthur Godfrey Show* in March. "Rudy's Rock" was great for television because it featured some spectacular onstage antics by band members. While playing his bass fiddle, Comet Al Rex stood the fiddle on its side with its

93

strings facing the audience, lay down on its top edge with his right hand dangling over the strings, and played the instrument while pretending to swim on top of it. Rudy Pompilli, the saxophonist after whom the song was named, then climbed on top of Rex, "riding" him while Rex "rode" the bass fiddle, and both men continued to play while a widely grinning Bill strummed his guitar.

Although the Comets performed "Rudy's Rock" spectacularly on-stage, the tune lacked both romance and lyrics, and it was no match for Elvis at his peak. While "Rudy's Rock" entered the *Billboard* Hot 100 Chart on November 3, it never climbed higher than No. 34. Pompilli became a great friend of Bill's, however, and his death years later would affect Bill greatly.

The night after their *Godfrey Show* performance, Decca presented Bill and his band with their third gold record, this one for "See You Later, Alligator." Ominously, however, resistance was rising to the spread of rock 'n' roll. The Eisenhower Administration had blocked *Blackboard Jungle*, which featured "Rock Around the Clock" on its soundtrack, from being shown at the Venice Film Festival, and the august *New York Times* published an editorial declaring rock 'n' roll "a communicable disease." Soon afterward, the Alabama White Citizens Council organized an anti-rock 'n' roll rally in Birmingham, charging that the National Association for the Advancement of Colored People (NAACP) was corrupting and seducing white teenage girls by condoning this new form of music.

Ignoring such criticism, Bill and his group kept touring and recording, and so did Elvis. On April 3, the Comets drew capacity crowds during a four-day engagement in Pittsburgh and were called back for multiple encores. Meanwhile, Elvis appeared on *The Milton Berle Show* to sing "Heartbreak Hotel," "Blue Suede Shoes," and "Money Honey" live from the flight deck of the USS Hancock, which was anchored in New York Harbor. Presley had just officially ended his association with the *Louisiana Hayride* TV show after eighty-four appearances, and now Colonel Parker was orchestrating an avalanche of Elvis appearances on national television. "Heartbreak Hotel" would soon become the first of an unprecedented string of eighteen No. 1 national hits for the emerging superstar. When Elvis made his first appearance at the Frontier Hotel in Las Vegas, however, poor attendance forced the cancellation of his two-week engagement after the first week.

Meanwhile, Bill and the Comets began a forty-five-day Galaxy of Stars show, billed as the biggest rock 'n' roll show of 1956. It immediately ran into a problem caused by its own success: too many fans. "Got hit in the eye as I came off stage and we were mobbed by fans," Bill wrote in his diary in Scranton, Pennsylvania. "It's hard to control mobs of people like this." In White Plains, New York, Bill noted that he "had to turn away 5,000 people and they were unruly and hard to control. Kids danced in the aisles and wouldn't behave. . . . They mobbed me after the show and I got hit again." In Newark, where all went well, Bill penned a reminder to himself that "we have to . . . prove this music can be played right and it's not barbaric as *Variety* says."

When thirteen thousand fans showed up in Toronto, Bill noted that "Newspaper, magazine, radio and TV interviewers all ask me the same thing: is this music hurting teenagers? My nerves are getting bad." He complained of feeling tremendous pressure from critics accusing him of inciting juvenile delinquency. In Buffalo, New York, by contrast, Bill wrote that "Everything went fine, proving so far that rock 'n' roll does not cause riots."

As the leader of a country and western band, Bill had allowed his band members to drink alcohol, but when they switched to rock 'n' roll and their music came under attack, he forbade the Comets from drinking while touring. As band member Al Rex told author John Swenson, "When we were riding high, Bill wouldn't put up with alcohol on our breath, because we were playing for kids. He wouldn't let us drink when we had a [rock 'n' roll] performance, because he always contended the kids would go home and tell their parents, 'He was drunk.'"

Although the tour had begun in Hershey, Pennsylvania, on April 20, 1956, it was headed for the South, and once again the Comets were the only whites on the show. Included on the bill were the Charms, the Teen Queens, the Flamingos, the Colts, and Frankie Lymon and the Teenagers, plus the acts that had accompanied Bill on his previous Southern tour: LaVerne Baker, Big Joe Turner, the Platters, Clyde McPhatter, Bo Diddley, the Drifters, and Red Prysock.

Bill was worried. "This tour is like sitting on a keg of dynamite," he wrote in his diary. "The show is all colored but our act. With the racial situation in the South broiling . . . I hope my nerves hold up." His worry was well founded. A few weeks earlier, on April 10, Nat King Cole had been beaten up onstage at the Municipal Auditorium in Birmingham by five members of the Northern Alabama Citizens' Council. Even though arrests had followed the incident, some resentful and vocal blacks in the area had vowed revenge. Things were starting to heat up on both sides.

While the Comets traveled in style, driving their Cadillacs with a Decca van carrying their instruments, they followed the same route as the bus carrying the other acts on the tour. It bothered them that the black entertainers on the same tour would not be served in white establishments. They'd have to settle for sandwiches served from the back door, and eat, and often sleep, on their bus.

Such treatment was not confined to the South. On May 4, 1956, after a performance in Columbus, Ohio, the tour drove off toward Canton, Ohio, for a show at Memorial Auditorium. Bill and the band stopped and ate at a restaurant on the Ohio Turnpike. When some of the black acts on the tour tried to buy meals at the same place while the Comets were still there, however, they were refused service. "They got in a fight, and we left in a hurry," Bill wrote. Bill and the band sympathized with their colleagues and were angered by the injustice, but other than getting food for them, they felt powerless to change firmly entrenched prejudices held by others.

The Comets themselves were still riding high. While on tour, Bill had to turn down an offer to perform in an RKO picture with Eddie Fisher and Debbie Reynolds. He and the band had already been booked for appearances on the proposed filming dates.

The band moved on to New Orleans, where Bill was met by Cuppy, now three months pregnant with her fourth child. They had a wonderful dinner with New Orleans native Fats Domino. Cuppy had a great time learning the latest dance steps from the Platters, while Bill and the band members passed much of their idle time backstage playing poker or throwing dice.

At their next stop, Birmingham, where Nat King Cole had been attacked a month earlier, members of the Alabama White Citizens' Council picketed the appearance by the Comets and the black groups, and attendance was low. The council's vitriolic tirades made front-page news all over the country. After its anti-rock 'n' roll rally the previous month, it had started campaigning to force radio stations and jukebox owners to "boycott this immoral music." The council's spokesman called Bill a "Judas goat" who'd "betrayed for thirty pieces of gold the youth of America with white-washed nigger music." The whole town was in an uproar.

"These people are fanatics," Bill wrote. He suggested in his diary that all touring bands should stop visiting the South "until the race situation is straightened out."

Chuck Berry, a late addition to the tour, was chased by an angry mob after one show where he was seen with a white woman. The mob tracked him to the bus the Comets had rented and tried to board it, but Bill got them to back off by assuring them that whoever they were looking for wasn't there. "Do I look like a nigger lover to you?" he asked the mob. More than once on this tour, Cuppy had to feign kinship with Berry's white girlfriend to avoid potentially violent confrontations.

When Bill and Cuppy stayed in a small motel in Birmingham, they talked to the owner, a woman, about the uproar over the shows. "Well, it's not us down here," the woman said to Bill and Cuppy matter-of-factly. "It's the people up North that are doing this. Our niggers know their place down here." Bill and Cuppy looked at each other with disbelief as it dawned on them exactly what was happening. She wasn't deliberately being nasty, they realized. She was simply expressing an opinion she assumed was universal. After they'd received death threats, calls to their hotel, and anonymous notes left for them at various venues on their Southern tour, Bill asked Cuppy to wait at their hotel in Greenville, South Carolina when he and the band performed there rather than accompany him to the concert.

As at the other southern shows, the racial tension at the Greenville performance was very real, and very acute. Audience seats were segregated, with blacks in one section and whites in another. The MC for the show was Hal Kromber, a black man, and when the tour reached the South he had to announce the Comets from the wings because he wasn't allowed to appear onstage at the same time as a white act. The first show that evening was a full house, but the second show was canceled.

During the first show in Greenville, as the band was finishing its first set, Lord Jim came up behind Bill and whispered in his ear, "There's a bomb under the stage. Don't run. Just stop playing and put the instruments down."

The band quickly exited out the back door and took off running for about a block. A Greenville newspaper recounted the incident the next day: "An anonymous tipster phoned police that a time bomb had been placed [in the hall]," it reported, and said that the Greenville police gave Haley just enough time to play "See You Later, Alligator" before clearing the hall. Several thousand fans still seeking admission to the show were denied entrance without being told why. Police roped off the area, and at about 3:30 a.m., they found a crude dynamite bomb that had failed to explode only because it was badly constructed.

"What next?" Bill wrote in his diary afterward. From that point on, for the rest of the tour, he carried a gun, even onstage. It turned out to be unnecessary, although in Atlanta five teenage boys were arrested after fights broke out at one of the Comets concerts, and another teenage boy was hit in the head by a flying beer bottle. According to an Atlanta newspaper, "Spectators said it was hard to figure out who was doing the fighting and who was dancing in the aisles."

In Savannah, Georgia, black audiences began resisting enforced segregation at Comets performances. "The Negroes refused to come to the second show," Bill wrote in his diary. "Results: 2,500 people first show, second show canceled. This race problem is not mine. I'll be glad to finish this tour and let the South alone for now."

Washington, DC, was only arguably part of the South, but there was trouble there as well. At a night show at the National Guard Armory, *Newsweek* reported, that "Even before the joint began to jump there was trouble . . . 5,000 people, mostly teenagers, poured in for some rock 'n' roll. Knives flashed and one young man was cut in the arm. Inside, 25 special officers waited for Bill Haley and His Comets to swing into the big beat."

When Bill and the band started singing one of their new songs, "Hot Dog Buddy Buddy," the fists really starting flying. Seventeen-year-old William Warfield was rushed to a nearby hospital with a severe cut over one eye and was diagnosed with a brain concussion. "Before I knew it, everybody was pounding everybody," he said. The press had a field day with this mini "riot."

Bill held himself blameless for the violence at his concerts. He himself, however, had written "Hot Dog Buddy Buddy," which included the verse "Fourteen days, fourteen fights, fourteen lefts, and fourteen rights," referring to the blows a fighter might inflict on his opponents. The song doesn't refer to the hot dogs people eat. Instead, it lovingly describes what's often called "hot dogging," which means doing something reckless and flamboyant to attract attention, such as ripping up seats in an auditorium or starting fights with other attendees.

In fact, Bill had been singing about violence ever since the very beginning of his rock 'n' roll career, when he sang "Rock the Joint." And although he'd expressed shock at what had happened on this tour, he soon began performing a new song called "Rip It Up" that included such lyrics as, "I'm gonna rip it up, I'm gonna shake it up," that could easily be construed as a call to rip up the seats in a theater. "Rip It Up" became an instant hit.

People began denouncing not only Bill himself for inspiring misbehavior by his fans, but also one of Bill's competitors. On June 5, 1956, Elvis Presley, with "Heartbreak Hotel" still holding strong on the national charts, made a final appearance on *The Milton Berle Show*. This time, however, he pushed his gyrating too far. It angered and offended many members of the press, who began derisively dubbing him "Elvis the Pelvis."

19

The Comets Keep Rising as Bill's Father Dies and Elvis Closes the Distance

Bill and the band continued to tour nationally and in Canada, but Bill got word in Manitoba that his father had died of tuberculosis. Although only Cuppy was with Will in his final agonizing, wheezing moments, Bill went home for the funeral and placed Will's prized mandolin beside him in his casket.

Meanwhile, FBI agents based in Philadelphia were questioning Bill's friends, neighbors, and associates to find out if he drank a lot, fooled around with young girls, or was a member of any communist or Negro-rights organizations. In those days, the FBI and its boss, J. Edgar Hoover, thought rock 'n' roll performers, along with members of civil rights groups, were subversives deserving investigation.

Trying to assuage parents and detractors who feared rock 'n' roll music was corrupting children, the Comets soon recorded a new tune, "Teenager's Mother (Are You Right?)." In this oddly tuneless song, Bill attempted to reassure mothers of teenagers by telling them that dancing to rock 'n' roll was no more damaging to youth than dancing the Charleston had been a generation earlier. "The same thing that's worrying you is the same thing you used to do yourself" he sang, urging them to be kind. With no tune and lyrics like these, it was no surprise when "Teenager's Mother" didn't chart.

As the Comets continued to tour, "See You Later, Alligator" passed the one-million mark in sales in July 1956, and the band began pulling in a million dollars a year. Soon "Rock Around the Clock" hit the top of the Australian charts as well. Elvis scored another huge US hit in July with "I Want You, I Need You, I Love You." That same month, his new singles "Don't be Cruel" and "Hound Dog" made the Top 40, and another young rocker named Gene Vincent burst into the spotlight with "Be-Bop-A-Lula."

The Comets continued to defend rock 'n' roll with another new record called "Don't Knock the Rock." They also began working on a new movie of the same name in fall 1956 for Columbia/Screen Gems. In that film, a DJ and a rock star try to convince parents and a female newspaper columnist that rock 'n' roll won't turn their children into juvenile delinquents.

Although Bill and His Comets performed five songs in the film, they weren't its stars. Probably because Alan Freed was still the nation's major disc jockey, the producers cast Freed as a crusading DJ once again. Freed's friend, singer Alan Dale, became the star of the movie. A better actor and singer than Bill, Dale did a good job playing Arnie Haynes, the rocker at whom the movie's stodgy parents directed most of their scorn. Dale's two Top 10 songs, "Heart of My Heart" and "Sweet and Gentle," were hardly rockers, however, and when he appears onstage in the film, his backup group looks like a combination of some former big band musicians and a barbershop quartet. Dale did close the movie by doing a decent job of singing Bill's song "Don't Knock the Rock."

This film also features Little Richard in his first onscreen appearance, singing his hits "Tutti Frutti" and "Long Tall Sally," as well as the Treniers and Dave Appell and His Applejacks. Nevertheless, Bill's music is dominant. He and his band sing their own songs "Hot Dog Buddy Buddy," "Goofin' Around," "Calling All Comets," and "Rip It Up" onscreen. "Hook, Line and Sinker," another of his creations, is heard on a record player while a young couple is dancing.

As a defense of rock's wholesomeness, *Don't Knock the Rock* is much less convincing than its predecessor, *Rock Around the Clock*. In *Rock Around the Clock*, the people dancing to the music are mostly young women wearing petticoats and wholesome-looking young men. In *Don't Knock the Rock*, Dale, presumably influenced by Elvis's continuing rise, does what appear to be pelvic gyrations onstage, and the girls in the audience blush and scream. As the movie continues, shapely women gyrate in tight leotards, or equally tight short shorts and tight blouses. Four of those dancers, all well-endowed males and females, are inexplicably wearing tight bathing suits in a suburban living room as they writhe to the music. In a fourth scene, a voluptuous girl wearing tight clothes, who announces herself as underage, tries to seduce Dale in a parked car.

For 1956, this movie bordered on porn. Such scenes destroy in advance the argument the characters make at the end of the film comparing rock 'n' roll dancing to the much less sexy Charleston, which the parents of the kids in the film presumably danced in their own youth. The pro-rock spokesmen in the film also fail to mention that while most Charleston tunes had no lyrics, most rock 'n' roll tunes do, and some of them are nasty.

Possibly for these reasons, *Don't Knock the Rock* was much less successful at the box office than *Rock Around the Clock*. Although the producer of both films, Sam Katzman, told an interviewer he was planning a third film on the theme featuring Bill Haley and Alan Freed, none was ever produced. Nevertheless, the fact that the Comets' music had been featured in three Hollywood movies in a row, and that they themselves had appeared as singers and actors in several scenes in both movies, added greatly to their popularity.

Apparently unconvinced by the films' pro-rock propaganda, anti-rock 'n' roll forces gathered considerable strength. Music industry personalities started to take sides: Frank Sinatra, Rosemary Clooney, Teresa Brewer, and Mitch Miller spoke out against rock 'n' roll while Kate Smith, Benny Goodman, and Duke Ellington publicly expressed their support for the upstart musical form.

Sinatra was especially harsh, calling rock 'n' roll "phony," "false," and the product of "cretinous goons." He also insisted the music was characterized by "almost imbecilic reiteration," and was "sly, lewd . . . and dirty."

Despite all the furor, the Comets soon had five titles in the British Top 20 simultaneously: "Rockin' Through the Rye," "Saints' Rock 'n' Roll," "Rock Around the Clock," "See You Later, Alligator" and "Razzle Dazzle." The film *Rock Around the Clock* caused riots in theaters in South London and was banned in several British cities, paradoxically making the movie, and rock itself, even more popular. London's first rock club, Studio 51, opened in the summer of 1956, preceding the opening of the celebrated rock club Studio 54 in Manhattan by twenty-one years.

On Oct. 8, 1956, four days after the band recorded "Don't Knock the Rock," Bill and Cuppy's second son, James Stephen Haley, was born. Three days later, Bill and His Comets left on a twenty-five-day tour of the US and Canada, playing to sold-out shows in ten-thousand-seat auditoriums. By October 28, however, after another appearance by Elvis on Ed Sullivan's *Toast of the Town* show, there was no doubt about it: Elvis was the nation's king of rock 'n' roll, with both the No. 1 and No. 2 records, "Don't be Cruel" and "Love Me Tender." The Comets still topped charts in the UK and Australia though, and Bill and the band decided to tour both countries.

On November 16, with "Love Me Tender" No. 1 in the US, Twentieth Century Fox released Elvis's first feature film, which bore the same name. A preview of the movie at the Paramount Theater in Brooklyn nearly turned into a riot when fifteen hundred "bobbysoxers" discovered their idol wouldn't appear there in person. (Promoters had led them to believe Elvis would hand out gifts to the first thousand people in line.) "It'll be a miracle if this theater is in one piece when we get out," fifteen-year-old Carol Olsen told the *New York Journal American*. It was becoming obvious that teenage girls, as well as teenage boys, could be incited to violence by their rock 'n' roll idols.

That same day in Louisville, Kentucky, a "no wiggle restriction" was placed on Elvis's upcoming appearance at the Kentucky State Fairground Exposition Center and Jefferson County Armory. Police Chief Colonel Carl E. Heustis said he wouldn't permit any "lewd, lascivious contortions that would excite a crowd." Heustis told agents from the FBI's Louisville office he was alarmed that Presley and Bill Haley and His Comets were booked for simultaneous appearances at the Exposition Center and Armory. He was wrong about the simultaneous booking, but he accurately described the Comets and Elvis as "rivals for the attention of quote rock 'n' roll unquote fans." Heustis said that he'd received reports of riots at Presley's and their appearances in other cities, and that he was trying "to prevent such recurrences here." In Syracuse, New York, a group of housewives denounced Elvis's "physical contortions" as "vulgar, suggestive, and disgusting."

The British opening of the movie *Rock Around the Clock* later in 1956 further hurt rock's reputation. Spontaneous destructive behavior by "Teddy Boys" at showings of the film created public alarm. Although the Teds liked to dress in Edwardian suits, they also carried straight razors, which they occasionally used to slash seats in theaters. The music of the Comets, especially the song "Rip It Up," provided just the rallying cry they needed.

In spite of Elvis's rise, in 1956 the Comets had completed what might have been the most successful year for any act in the history of show business. Having played more than three hundred live performances before half a million Americans that year, starred in two feature films, and scored twenty-four straight hits in both the US and Britain, they were poised to take their act abroad to lands where rock 'n' roll was still relatively new.

With the Comets' income dramatically increasing, Bill turned down several other big moneymaking opportunities. By 1956, the group's gross income had escalated from an average of a few hundred dollars a week in 1952 to more than ten thousand dollars a week, the equivalent of more than one hundred thousand per week in 2018 dollars. It was such a grand figure at the time that as the holidays approached, Bill once again turned down a lucrative offer to appear on the top-rated *Dinah Shore Show*. He said he needed to go home to be with his family.

The band's pre-Christmas party in December and its annual Christmas party at Bill's new house, Melody Manor, were celebrations of momentous proportions. Filled with toasts and boasts, they echoed with the sound of champagne glasses being thrown into the fireplace.

Bill gave $1,000 bonus checks to all band members and generous checks to everyone else in the organization. He told the band members they were all going to be millionaires, and at one point draped his arm around drummer Ralph Jones's shoulder. Gazing out of the large picture window in the living room, Bill told the crowd, "I'm going to have busts made of each guy in the band and put them out on the lawn." One band staffer read aloud a newspaper headline from 1954, "Haley and His Rock 'n' Roll Given Six Months," and everyone roared with laughter.

Downstairs in the den, which was decorated for the holiday, guests enjoyed drinks from the bar and gorged themselves on a sumptuous buffet of foods and desserts. Games of pool and darts, music and dancing, and raucous merriment prevailed. The band's booking agent boasted once again that this was just the beginning. He said he was going to make Bill Haley and the Comets the "biggest act in the history of show business."

20

The Second Battle
of Waterloo

It was the nearest-run thing you ever saw in your life.
—THE DUKE OF WELLINGTON
DESCRIBING HIS VICTORY
AT THE FIRST BATTLE OF WATERLOO

On New Year's Day 1957, Bill and the Comets left on the first leg
of an eleven-thousand-mile journey to Australia. After landing
at Nadi International Airport in the Fiji Islands for a refueling stop,
they went to a local restaurant for a bite to eat. Unaware that the *Rock
Around the Clock* movie had just opened nearby and that the word
was out that the Comets would be passing through, they were quickly
confronted by a huge celebrity-struck mob that carried Bill off on its
shoulders. During his two-and-a-half-hour abduction, Bill was stripped
of his jacket, his wallet, and the rings on his fingers while the rest of the
band members and the plane crew anxiously waited for him to return.

At their final destination, Sydney, Australia, the Comets performed
for eight thousand fans, while another ten thousand were turned away.
Unlike the band's concert audiences in America, which were predominantly composed of teenagers, three-quarters of the attendees at the
Australian concerts were adults. Many of those grown-ups may just
have been eager to find out what the fuss was all about, because rock
'n' roll had been banned from radio stations in Sydney and Adelaide.
The restrictions were lifted after the band's first performances. As the
tour continued, Bill developed throat problems and could barely sing,
but no one noticed because of the deafening noise in the enormous
venues where he and the band performed. Haleymania was sweeping
the nation. The Comets entertained more than three hundred thousand Australian fans during this tour, breaking every known attendance
record in that country.

They were so astoundingly successful that Frank Sinatra, who'd been scheduled to tour Australia and had already reached Hawaii, backed out. As a result, the tour promoter offered Haley and the Comets $100,000 in cash in 1950s dollars to stay one more week. He also promised that if they said yes, he'd pay for flying the band's wives and families to England for their next tour of that country.

Exhausted and homesick, Bill turned down the offer. A year and a half of constant traveling, performing for huge audiences, promotional appearances, and giving constant interviews to answer the critics of rock 'n' roll had worn him down physically and emotionally. Unable to go anywhere now without being approached by fans, he said he needed to go home to Cuppy and the kids, which he did as soon as he'd completed his final appearance Down Under.

On returning to the States, Bill was informed that while he and the Comets had been gone, their young rival for the rock 'n' roll crown had continued his relentless ascent and had scored another No. 1 hit while the Comets had been touring Australia. Feeling more and more pressure to produce hit records, overwhelmed, and isolated from a normal existence, Bill was comforted to know that at least Cuppy would be with him for the upcoming British tour.

At this point, all Great Britain had been abuzz for weeks in anticipation of the Comets' upcoming tour. The press fanned the flames with accounts of "disturbances" in movie theaters by Teddy Boys while *Rock Around the Clock* was being shown. After two Teds were arrested and fined for their refusal to stop dancing and jiving during a showing of the film in London, they explained to one reporter that Bill Haley's music had compelled them to keep going. "This music is just different from anything I ever heard before," one of them said. "There's nobody sends me like Bill Haley— except for Elvis Presley." His partner in crime agreed. "I think Bill Haley is a great musician," he said, adding that he'd keep on jiving in the cinema anyway, regardless of the circumstances. "It's worth it for the rhythm," he said.

With tabloids such as the *Daily Mirror* feeding interest in Bill with endless stories, Haley fever swept across the United Kingdom. On January 25, 1956, "Rock Around the Clock" had become the first record to sell one million copies in the UK, and a British tour by Bill and the Comets was scheduled to begin in February 1957.

The promoters of the fourteen-city UK tour were Londoners Lew and Leslie Grade. (Lew Grade later became known as "Low Grade" for some of the films he produced.) It was set up as an exchange: Lonnie

Donegan and his skiffle group from Scotland were scheduled to tour the States simultaneously. (Skiffle was a mix of folk, blues, and jazz music often played partly on washboards and other improvised instruments.) Donegan already had had a million-seller of his own in the US in 1956: "Rock Island Line" on the London label.

On the last day of January 1957, after only a short break at home from their Australian tour, the Comets drove 130 miles in the snow to New York City's Pier 90 to board the Cunard ocean liner *RMS Queen Elizabeth*. Bill and Cuppy got to New York later than the others and were permitted to board right away when Bill told the officials that his passport was in his baggage. Down in his cabin, however, he rooted through his luggage, couldn't find his passport, and realized he must have left it at home. Officials told Bill he'd have to deboard the ship and stay behind.

At 9:55 a.m., five minutes before the scheduled departure time, two stewards entered the cabin and removed Bill's luggage from the ship. Bill offered to have the passport sent by mail but was informed that that was illegal. In desperation, he called the State Department in Washington and requested special permission to travel without the passport. He fidgeted nervously at the gangway until 10:10 a.m., when a State Department official finally told him he could leave on the condition that his passport be flown to Washington, and then by special courier to Southampton before his arrival. The luggage was loaded back on board, the ship embarked—and shortly afterward, Bill went to change his shirt and found the passport. It was in the suitcase where it should have been all along, but it had been hidden by some clothing when he searched for it the first time.

During the trip, Bill and Cuppy enjoyed a large cabin that included a sitting room, bedroom, and bathroom. For the duration of the voyage, their bathtub was filled with bottles of champagne on ice, so they bathed next door in a cabin occupied by the band's booking agent and his wife.

On the first night of the trip, a large celebrity-filled reception was held in the captain's stateroom. Actor Victor Mature imitated Elvis onstage, gyrating his hips and clutching an imaginary microphone, while Bill and Cuppy talked with British actors Brenda de Banzie, Jennifer Jones, and Jack Buchanan. Cuppy danced with actor Zachary Scott and sipped cocktails in a corner of the room with Mature, who confided to her what a "bitch" Rita Hayworth was. (Hayworth had been one of Mature's movie costars and was briefly engaged to him.) Cuppy looked at Mature and thought, "If he told me to leave with him right now, and Bill was over there in the corner, I'd walk right past Bill."

Pearl Bailey provided entertainment for the party, singing and trying to pull Bill onto the dance floor at one point. Bill was mortified because although he had good rhythm, he couldn't dance, and he was afraid of making a fool of himself. Sensing the awkwardness of the moment, Zachary Scott sprang from his chair, glided across the floor, took Pearl's hand, and said, "I'm afraid Mr. Haley is too slow to accept your offer, so I will take you up on it." Scott twirled and swirled Bailey around the dance floor and brought her back to the table. Looking first at Cuppy and then Bill, he said, "And now, with your permission, sir, I'm going to ask the lovely Mrs. Bill Haley to dance." Cuppy obliged.

On the third day of the voyage, the Atlantic got rough. The *Queen Elizabeth* caught the tail end of a hurricane, got tossed and slammed by sixty-five-foot waves, and lost a stabilizer bar. "Trip gets rougher," Bill wrote in his diary. "Can't wait till we get off this blooming boat." The crew put up extra safety ropes, but there were a few injuries, including broken legs, among some of the passengers. Nearly everyone on board got seasick.

On February 5, the liner finally reached Cherbourg, a small port city in the lower Normandy region of France. When Bill and Cuppy emerged from their cabin, they were met with a barrage of flashbulbs by the hundred or so British photographers who'd crossed the English Channel to cover their arrival. After a brief stop to pick up even more reporters, photographers, and publicity people, the *Queen Elizabeth* made port in Southampton, England, where the party disembarked shortly after 2 p.m. It was a cold, drizzly, misty day, and Cuppy pulled her mink stole tightly around her neck to keep warm. She had no idea of the frenzy she was about to encounter.

After shuffling through the customs shed, where Bill signed auto-graphs for dock workers, members of the entourage were mauled as they inched their way to the shiny, black line of waiting Rolls Royce auto-mobiles. Frenzied teens pursued them as they and their families slowly began the mile-long auto journey to Southampton's Terminus Station. Screaming youngsters jumped on the cars, rocking them from side to side, rapping on the windows, and pulling at the doors. Cuppy, remem-bering how she'd hidden in her closet as a child when her father would come home drunk, was shocked and frightened and burst into tears.

Finally, they arrived at Platform 11 at Terminus Station. After Cuppy pushed Bill out of the car in her panic, it took a group of policemen, who formed a protective corridor with their own bodies, fifteen minutes to get Bill to the platform and onto the train. A mob of five thousand shrieking fans, many of them girls in bright jeans, sweaters, and socks, had paid for, or won, tickets to ride with the band from Southampton to London's Waterloo Station on the *Daily Mirror* "Rock 'n' Roll Express" train. The fans screamed Bill's name, took his hat, pulled his hair, tore at his cream-colored camel-hair coat and trousers, ripped off his buttons, and grabbed his suitcase and gray suede gloves. One girl shrieked, "I nearly got his wedding ring! I nearly pulled it off!" When he was finally on board, Bill cowered behind closed curtains in his Pullman coach as frenzied, ecstatic teenagers banged on the windows and shouted, "We want Bill!"

"No ribs broken," Bill said, smiling but white as a ghost. "I thought for a moment that my arm had gone." Someone said the violence came from sheer admiration. Bill replied, deadpan, "Then they must be glad to see me."

Suddenly, realizing that his wife was missing, he ran into the corridor, shouting, "Where's Cuppy?" She and Bill had been separated when the policemen took him aboard the train, and because she was overwhelmed and frightened, she'd stayed in the car. Finally, the police got her on the train too. It took thirty officers to close the gates to the platform, and the group finally departed Southampton Station on the *Daily Mirror* Rock 'n' Roll Special at 2:35 p.m.

Because The *Daily Mirror* had run competitions for tickets to board the train, the eight-car Rock 'n' Roll Special was packed with frenzied fans. When they reached Waterloo Station at 5:15 p.m., the mob scene repeated itself. More than two thousand fans, contained by about one hundred regular police and officers from the Criminal Investigation Division, had been waiting there, chanting "We want Bill," for hours. They were now at a fever pitch, bathed in a barrage of floodlights for the benefit of photographers. Hordes of them broke through a police cordon and engulfed the Haleys' entourage. A police sergeant leading a dozen policemen charged into the frenzied mass of bodies to get the celebrated guests to their waiting cars. Once everyone in the band was safely in the limousines, however, they were unable to drive away. The fans mobbed Bill's black, square-topped Rolls and held it stationary for fifteen minutes, snapping off its wing mirrors and wipers.

Bill saw a girl who'd been thrust under the front of his Rolls by the mob and then dragged by the car after she caught her ankle on the fender. She suffered a broken leg, but her claim for injury compensation was turned down later because no driver reported the accident. A policeman climbed on the roof of Bill's car and fought off a chanting youth who had "Bill Haley" tattooed on his arm, and who was trying to get into the Rolls.

In the car behind Bill's, Cuppy was covering her face with her hands and sobbing. Sick with claustrophobia, she gamely hung on as the mob rocked her Rolls from side to side. The other band member and their families experienced similar feelings of awe and panic.

Soon, a screaming woman with a baby in her arms was pushed under the wheels of Cuppy's Rolls, but a policeman rescued her. Another girl's face was smashed into the windscreen pillar and she fainted, with her glasses broken and blood running down her temple. Finally, someone in the car behind Cuppy's leaned on their horn, and sure enough, the crowds parted and they were off, shortly after 5:30 p.m. As the autos drove away, the mob chanted, "See You Later, Alligator." A dozen or so shoes, as many gloves, several scarves, handbags, police helmets, and a "ball of wool" were left strewn about the station, inspiring a railway official to set up a lost property office on the platform.

Following the battle at Waterloo Station, three women were treated for fainting and shock at a station first-aid post. One mother with a baby was hurt and treated there. A woman station attendant was knocked unconscious and taken to a hospital, and so was a uniformed policewoman who'd been crushed against railings. Dubbed by the press "The Second Battle of Waterloo," this event was the first serious rock 'n' roll riot. Seven years later, the Beatles would start similar riots in America.

21
Rockin' in the British Aisles

After their ordeal at Waterloo Station, Bill and Cuppy made it to the Savoy Hotel in London and were escorted in through the back entrance. Cuppy was still shaken, and she breathed a huge sigh of relief as they finally entered their hotel room and closed the door. They embraced, and Cuppy told Bill how terrified she'd been. Bill said, "Somebody pushed me out of the car!"

Embarrassed, Cuppy replied, "I don't know who," and it wasn't until a few years later that she told him she'd been the culprit.

As they explored the amenities of their enormous suite, Bill and Cuppy heard screaming and hollering outside, and when they looked out one of the windows, they saw people in the office buildings across the street straining to get a look at them. (The British press corps had strategically rented rooms directly across the street from Bill and Cuppy's suite at the Savoy and set up a camera watch.)

Cuppy reminded Bill that this was the dream he'd worked very hard for and never expected to achieve. They closed the drapes, hugged, and took stock of their situation. There wasn't time for a nap, just time enough to take a bath and dress for the reception and press gathering downstairs.

When they'd first arrived at the terminal, Bill had rebuffed questions from reporters about possible riots at his shows with the nonreply "I just got here." Now, as cameras rolled and clicked, Bill conspicuously sipped from a glass of milk and took every opportunity to reassure parents that rather than harming their children, his music gave them a healthy and harmless way to enjoy themselves. Nevertheless, Bill asked young people planning to attend his concerts to "take it easy, please," and behave.

He was determined to present himself to his critics as an upright, respectable family man. Bill spoke of Cuppy and his children frequently at the press event, and he pointed out that he'd turned down a lucrative offer to extend his Australian tour so he could spend time at home before leaving for Britain. He added that the Comets' entourage included several of the band members' wives and children, and his manager had even brought along his seventy-seven-year-old mother. He also emphasized his British roots at the affair by repeatedly talking about his mother's Lancastrian origins, noting that she'd been born in Ulverston, birthplace of comedian Stan Laurel. "I owe England a deep affection," he said.

Cuppy, wearing a slinky black dress, was described by the press as "blonde, glamorous and slim." She sat quietly in the background, but she did talk to one reporter. Asked how she felt about Bill's music, she honestly replied, "As a matter of fact, I'm not all that keen on rock 'n' roll. We don't play it at home at all, and we don't dance to it much at parties." Cuppy also said that as soon as her children were old enough, she'd be taking them on tours too. "It's important for family life that we should all be together," she said.

The next day, not knowing about the reporters in the room across the street, Cuppy read the papers and wondered, "How did they know that Bill hugged me and kissed me when we entered our room?" The morning was bright and sunny, and Bill and Cuppy had breakfast in their suite with the reporters, who couldn't get enough of the Haley story.

The warm-up acts for the tour included a well-known British ensemble, the Vic Lewis fourteen-piece swing band, which regularly kicked off its set with a rock 'n' roll version of "In the Mood." Also featured were vocalist Irma Logan, the comedy-singing team Earle and Vaughan, and "penny whistler" Desmond Lane. Luxury cinemas, which averaged about twenty-seven hundred seats, were chosen over large halls for the tour because of their supposedly more intimate atmosphere; and a nationwide chain of cinemas, Rank, agreed to pull its films on weekdays for concerts of popular music events. Before each Comets appearance, Rank made an announcement that if anyone attempted to leave their seat and dance in the aisles, the show would be stopped.

The Comets officially hit the stage for the first performance of their UK tour at 7:27 p.m. on Wednesday, February 6, 1957. It was at the spacious three-thousand-seat Dominion Theater, jam-packed with rows of Teddy Boys and Teddy Girls. The *London Observer* described the boys as "nearly all short with hairbrush hair" and said the girls "wore tight black skirts or tartan trousers, with their thick thatches of hair overhanging their foreheads like lettuces, making their intent, small faces look oddly the same." It said the audience also included "a few square business types . . .drawn by curiosity and the hype."

Tickets for the two sold-out Comets shows at the Dominion ranged from the US equivalent of thirty cents to three dollars apiece. Wearing tartan tuxedo jackets with blue trousers for opening night, the Comets opened with "Razzle Dazzle" and proceeded to run through thirteen numbers in thirty minutes. At this, and at most of the stops on the tour, the band performed two shows per night.

Cuppy was a part of the promotional package as far as the tour organizers were concerned, and they orchestrated her brief "public appearances" and photo ops. She'd go with Bill to the shows, wait backstage until the band went on, and then be escorted to a private balcony section where other entourage members and VIPs were seated. She also was taken backstage before the finale, "Rock Around the Clock," so she could exit smoothly with the band.

The Comets promoted two new singles beginning on this tour: "Don't Knock the Rock" and "Forty Cups of Coffee." For the opening show on the Dominion stage, they used only three microphones and three amplifiers. Yet they still managed to create an unprecedented wall of sound, thanks in large part to the powerful drumming of Ralph Jones and searing saxophone playing of Rudy Pompilli.

By now, their stage act had reached the height of polish and professionalism. Rudy performed writhing snake-like movements, twisting and turning, playing on his knees, and playing while lying on his back and then on top of bass player Al Rex. Rex became world famous for his pants-splitting routine, for riding the bass fiddle and throwing it around like a toy, for looking and acting like a circus clown, and for wearing one red and one yellow sock. Bill beat his fingers raw on his trusty, black hollow-body Gibson guitar, furiously bobbing back and forth. He wore a perpetual grin and shouted out the lyrics of hit after hit, straining to be heard over the deafening din of the band and the shrieking youngsters in the audience.

After its opening rock numbers, the band would cool things down. Guitarist Franny Beecher would sing a falsetto, comedic version of "You Made Me Love You" while Billy Williamson crept up behind him and outlined a large "square" symbol with his hands. Haley then introduced each band member, and each individual answered back with a one-liner or some other comedic gimmick. After Bill implored the audience to buy a copy of "Rudy's Rock" because Pompilli needed the dough, for instance, Pompilli would turn out his pockets. Bill would then introduce Billy Williamson or Al Rex to sing a song in his own style, such as Rex's rendition of "Tutti Frutti." The Comets would conclude their performance by playing their already familiar hits, culminating in the already classic "Rock Around the Clock."

The first night the Comets played at the Dominion ended abruptly, however, after teens began jiving in the aisles during "Rock Around the Clock" and ushers forced them to return to their seats. Possibly spooked by the crowd scenes of the day before, Haley quickly finished the number. He hurriedly backed off and the curtain came down, followed by a second safety curtain, while "God Save the Queen" blared over the loudspeakers. Afterward, nearly one hundred policemen tried for half an hour to disperse a crowd of thousands outside, and there was a rush at Bill when he darted out the stage door and toward his waiting car. Several girls fainted with excitement and had to be lifted to safety over the heads of the crowd.

Later that night, the band members and their wives gathered in Bill and Cuppy's suite at the Savoy. They ate, drank, and chatted until 4 a.m. when they could read the reviews of their performances in six different publications. Smiling and laughing, they read the ecstatic quotes aloud to each other.

"Supersplendiferous and just plain colossal," somebody read out loud from one of the reviews. "The supercharged voodoo rhythm of the emperor of rock 'n' roll crashed into Britain last night with jet-age impact." The *Daily Mirror* reported that "the joint jumped!" and "the floor vibrated!"

Following their opening-night success with double shows the next three nights at the Dominion, the band played to a total of more than twenty-four thousand fans before continuing their musical assault on the industrial cities of the Midlands and North. Late on Thursday, February 7, after the second show on the second night at the Dominion, Bill and Cuppy went to Hammersmith Palais, where two thousand people were attending a rock 'n' roll ball. The celebrated couple materialized on the dance hall balcony, bathed in white light, and Bill cried out to the crowd, "Enjoying yourselves rockin' and rollin'?" After introducing Cuppy to the youngsters, he sang "See You Later, Alligator" from the balcony, with the stage band down below playing the music. When the spotlights went off, Bill and Cuppy slipped out, but they were besieged by hundreds of fans on their way to the waiting car.

While Bill was accustomed by now to being mobbed by fans, Cuppy still couldn't quite believe it was happening. Early on in London, she and a female member of the entourage had gone to a bookstore without telling anyone. After doing so, they'd continued on to do more shopping, and Cuppy noticed that a crowd was starting to form. She thought, "Gee, they must be going shopping too." The crowd grew larger and larger, and soon the two women were surrounded by a sea of people who began pulling at Cuppy's hair and clawing at her. Just as suddenly, she was encircled by the British security men who'd been assigned to follow her everywhere and who quickly escorted the two women back to the hotel.

Once it became obvious that Cuppy couldn't shop anonymously at the local stores, some local clothiers brought dresses and accessories directly to her hotel room. The idea came from an aide who'd been assigned by the *Daily Mirror* to accompany them during their visit.

During the course of this tour, Bill's "kiss curl" haircut became more and more popular in Great Britain. London hairdresser Barry Ross raked in more than a few pounds and shillings by designing and providing a "Haley haircut." Glasgow barber Cyril Breene also cashed in on the craze by providing a curl that was "permanent and shockproof" after a thirty-minute treatment. He soon established a waiting list.

Shortly after their arrival in England, the Comets had announced that they'd add as many as twelve dates to their English tour, and they were soon on their way to Coventry by bus. Bill, disguised in a wool trilby hat, upturned collar, and dark glasses, entered that city's Hotel Leofric through the back door with Cuppy. After the evening show in Coventry, an enthused crowd of one thousand gathered outside their hotel and chanted "We want Bill" for fifteen minutes. Eventually, Bill emerged on the balcony dressed in an overcoat and fur slippers, and they asked him to sing. When he declined, they sang to him instead.

On Monday, February 11, 1957, Bill, Cuppy, and Lord Jim were given a tour of the Warwickshire countryside in a demonstration model Jaguar Mark VII Saloon. Bill visited the Jag factory and ordered three cars, but as fate would have it, the factory burned down that very night, and the deal was never consummated.

That evening, the band appeared at the J. Arthur Rank Odeon Theater in Nottingham, playing to five thousand people in two shows. Their attire: crimson jackets with black velvet collars and black trousers. During this tour, scalpers, or "spivs" as they were known locally, sold excess tickets for Comets shows, and other enterprising youths hawked homemade "programs" outside theaters. The programs consisted of a folded piece of paper with a picture of Bill and the Comets pasted inside, and a written list of the band's song titles.

The following night, the show was disturbed in Birmingham. Held at the Odeon Cinema on New Street and Worcester, the show had been extended by ten minutes due to pressure from promoters after some fans who felt it was too short had booed at the final curtain. There were minor disturbances outside the theater between shows, including intentional traffic tie-ups, as two thousand young toughs gathered, smashed bus windows, and trampled a few people without seriously injuring them. Because of its potential to cause such "disorders," the *Rock Around the Clock* film had been banned in Birmingham by the city's Public Entertainments Committee the previous September.

That Wednesday, looking snappy in their pillar-box red jackets, the band played the first of two sold-out shows at the 2,916-seat Odeon Theater in Manchester. "Riots" had occurred there during the showing of *Rock Around the Clock*, so management set the highest prices for seats in the stalls, where it was easiest to disrupt a performance. Graham Nash, eleven days past his fifteenth birthday, was in the Odeon's balcony that evening attending his first-ever concert, having ditched school the previous day to stand in line for tickets. After the show, he joined the throngs of Comets fans waiting for a glimpse of the band at the stage door, and he managed to touch Rudy Pompilli's elbow as Pompilli and the other Comets made a mad dash for the limousine. The Haley concert was a life-changing event for Nash, a founding member of the Hollies and of Crosby, Stills, and Nash. He'd keep his ticket stub in his wallet from that point forward. "Over the years I've lost houses . . . I've lost wives . . . but I've not lost that ticket stub," Nash would say.

Young Pete Townshend, who'd soon form a band called the Who, also attended one of the Comets shows on this tour. Later, he said that seeing Bill Haley and the Comets was "the birth of rock 'n' roll for me."

When Bill arrived for his second show at the Odeon in Manchester with Cuppy, a small group of fans who'd waited ninety minutes in the rain for his arrival broke through a cordon of police. They mobbed him, snatched his hat, and pulled his coat half off before he was able to pull away and get into the theater.

Some people at the show that evening were disappointed when the band limited itself to a short set that night. They jeered, catcalled, and whistled. Later, a large crowd formed outside the band's hotel chanting the familiar "We want Bill." In a novel display of grass-roots commercialism, Manchester University students hawked "Bill Haley bathwater" on campus at lunchtime after the band left town.

On Valentine's day, Bill held a pre-show press conference before the Comets played two evening concerts at the Leeds Odeon Cinema. Dressed in a gray, small-checked suit and a bright red Royal Stuart tartan shirt with no tie, he sipped tea and twirled a matchstick in his fingers. After telling reporters that his mother had raised him on tea, Bill announced that due to complaints about how short the bands' sets were, the show would be extended to forty to forty-five minutes at every remaining stop on the tour. Chain smoking and holding a stuffed koala bear, he boasted that the Comets were booked up for the next five years and had offers that would carry them through five more.

As one would expect, hotel managers wherever the band stayed wished to avoid crowd incidents at all cost. Sometimes they asked Bill and Cuppy to exit via the service elevator and through a tunnel to a waiting limousine to avoid the mob out front. Other times Bill left the hotel in the backs of service trucks or ambulances. Occasionally he disguised himself as a British police officer.

When the band pulled into St. Enoch Station in Glasgow, thousands of fans shouting "We want Haley!" were awaiting their arrival. With considerably less difficulty than the London bobbies, the Scottish police cleared a path. With a deerstalker's hat pulled down over his eyes and his topcoat collar pulled up, Bill was able to duck into a waiting cab with Cuppy. A few youngsters managed to jump onto the bumpers and running boards of the cab, but police got them off as it pulled away.

Trying to avoid more Scottish crowds, Bill and Cuppy rented a car and unobtrusively visited tombs and monuments of famous Scotsmen. Fascinated by the history of the British monarchy and anything related to it, Cuppy was a voracious reader of books about the wives of Henry VIII and other royal lore of the British Isles. She'd read and dreamed about the Scottish Moors as a child, and the historic aspects of their visit thrilled her. But the constant grind of the tour had strained her relationship with Bill, leading to frequent petty arguments. Ironically, after long periods of being apart for much of the previous year, the closeness of everything was starting to rub both of them the wrong way.

During their first two nights in Scotland, the band donned their tartan jackets and gave four performances in Glasgow. On the first night, three thousand frenzied fans clashed with police outside after the second show. The band snuck out the back entrance, and the frustrated mob turned down Nile Street, banging on the tops of cars and climbing lamp posts until dispersed by police.

The second night, one hundred policemen showed up to control a crowd of one thousand people after the final show ended at 10:30 p.m. During the last number, the "stay in your seat" rule was violated *en masse* when youths "jumped into the aisles, jived, threw hats and

scarves in the air, clambered over seats and chanted 'We want more!'"
according to people who were there.

On Wednesday the band traveled to Liverpool, another city that
had banned the showing of *Rock Around the Clock*. A young Paul Mc-
Cartney, who was in the audience that night, was the only one of his
mates who could scrounge up twenty-four shillings for a ticket. "I was
single-minded about it," he said later. "I knew there was something
going on here." Eight months later, McCartney joined a skiffle group
called the Quarrymen, which had been formed by John Lennon the
previous year. In August 1960, that group, after a change in personnel, would change its name to the Beatles. Ironically, the Beatles
auditioned in London for the Comets' recording company, Decca
Records, on January 1, 1962, but were rejected in favor of a group
called Brian Poole and the Tremeloes. Decca added insult to injury
by declaring that "the Beatles have no future in show business."

The next day, Bill bought a painting in Liverpool titled *Festival of
Youth*. Obviously painted very recently, it depicted the frenetic scene
outside the Birmingham Odeon between the two Comets performances
there on February 12. The painting showed lines of police officers con-
trolling the "jiving and shouting crowds," and Bill told reporters it was an
"ideal souvenir of one of the most tremendous welcomes I have yet had
on the tour." Shortly after the Comets arrived at the Angel Hotel in Cardiff, two girls burst out of the hotel doors holding one of the band's prized
tartan jackets, shouting, "We've got it!" After ten minutes, however, a
policeman reclaimed the jacket and returned it to its rightful owner.

The next morning, the band took a train from Cardiff Central Station to Temple Meads Station in Bristol, where Bill, wearing a plain,
dark suit with white socks and sunglasses, put Cuppy on a train back to
London. Afterward Bill wrote in his diary, "Cuppy went back to London
today to wait for me . . . I miss her."

The same day, the *Manchester Evening News* carried a poem by a
reader, J. A. Pitt, about Bill Haley. "He's cool," the poem began. "He
rocks a body to death. He creeps in through your toes, starts 'em tap-
pin'. Up through your legs, starts 'em knockin'. Up to your hips, and
starts 'em swingin'. Captures your brain, and then you're rockin'."

By the end of February 1957, after two straight months of touring
Australia and Great Britain, the Comets' Decca record sales totaled
twenty-two million, including six million copies of "Rock Around the
Clock." The band was pulling in royalties and performance fees total-
ing $30,000 a week.

In Dublin, Bill had to be rescued from a group of frenzied fans by a dozen policemen. Bottles and other missiles were thrown at the police, who then drew their batons and charged into the demonstrators. Store windows were broken, and some gasoline pumps were damaged. "Crowds outside theater of about 4,000 people," Bill wrote in his diary. "They scare me."

On March 1 and 2, the band performed at the Belfast Hippodrome in Northern Ireland, where the Catholic Church had banned the film *Rock Around the Clock*. The first Comets show was only half full, and the second show two-thirds full. "Damn it," Bill wrote in his diary.

On Monday, March 4, 1957, Bill received a gold record for "Rock Around the Clock" on the Brunswick/Decca label. The presentation was made by Sir Edward R. Lewis, managing director of Decca, at a gala reception held at the Savoy Hotel in London. Sir Edward also gave Bill a solid gold watch, and each of the Comets received a silver cigarette box. The award celebrated the sale of one million copies of "Rock Around the Clock" in the British Isles, the first time any record had sold that many copies there. The next day, Bill was the guest of honor at another reception held on behalf of Germany's Deutsche Grammophon record company. There he received a gold record for selling one million records in Germany, Austria, Switzerland, Norway, and Holland.

During their second stay at the Savoy, after dinner and a show, Bill and Cuppy tried drinking Irish whiskey with ginger ale. When they returned to their hotel room they began arguing furiously, shouting so loudly they were sure everyone on their floor heard them. Afterward they got sick and began throwing up, Bill in one bathroom and Cuppy in the other.

Cuppy had never really been falling-down drunk before, and the next day they laughed about it. They stayed away from Irish whiskey after that, but during this English trip, Bill was introduced to Johnny Walker Scotch. He developed a passion for it and would ultimately become an alcoholic. Ironically, photos of the "battle" of Waterloo Station show a large, lighted billboard advertisement in the background reading, "Johnny Walker. Born in 1870. Still going strong."

On the way back to London after his last show in Ireland, Bill broke his own "no alcohol" rule with the band and drank out of a bottle of Scotch on the bus. Drummer Ralph Jones joined him, and the two men began a heated argument. Bill criticized Ralph's drumming abilities, and Ralph responded that he'd forgotten more about drumming than Bill would ever know. Bill fired Ralph, and Ralph said Bill couldn't fire him because he quit. Ralph called Bill a dumb hillbilly and Bill called Ralph a half-assed milkman who couldn't keep time. The next morning, Bill went to Ralph's room and apologized.

After playing to 350,000 fans on the whirlwind-paced tour, everyone in the band was understandably frazzled and drained. Bill and Cuppy had become short with each other, and both were in foul moods. When a female reporter at their London hotel came in for one last interview, Cuppy, her patience worn thin, was rude to her. "That's it, we're leaving," she screamed. "We're leaving today!" and she slammed the door.

When they arrived in New York, Bill and Cuppy stopped at a Howard Johnson's restaurant for lunch and feasted on sandwiches made of orange cheese and processed ham. They loved them. They were home again.

22
Success Takes Its Toll

The very word *star* summons up images
or remoteness, of loneliness.
–MICHAEL NEWTON

A year and a half of nonstop touring had taken a physical and emotional toll on everyone. Band member Rudy Pompilli was hospitalized for exhaustion, and Bill was mentally and physically exhausted as well. The constant travel and pressure to perform were hard enough, but the relentless questions from the press about allegations that his music was causing juvenile delinquency was putting Bill through an emotional wringer.

The long UK tour and some nasty arguments had also put stress on Bill's relationship with Cuppy. After their return, Bill seemed preoccupied and was increasingly less affectionate toward her. At the same time, they started having cocktails before dinner. When first married, they'd drunk only coffee at home and when they went out. Even when Bill worked in bars at night, he usually drank coffee on his breaks. After a time, he and Cuppy had drunk alcohol socially, but only in moderation. Now they drank every night.

Adopting the European custom, they also started having dinner later in the evening, after the children were fed and put to bed. Sunday traditionally featured a family dinner, often with guests, and the kids were served Rob Roys and Shirley Temples while Bill and Cuppy had cocktails with the other grown-ups. Aside from her concern over what she perceived to be a change in her husband's mood, Cuppy felt empowered as a result of her British experience. Visiting museums and attending the theater for the first time had opened a new world of culture to her, making her feel worldlier and more self-confident.

On the business side, even with Elvis's rise, money was still rolling in and likely would continue to do so for the foreseeable future. Bill told the *Delaware County Daily Times* that as a result of the tour, bookings were "pouring in from all parts of the globe."

Outwardly the dynamic among the band members seemed the same after the UK tour. They were all still boastful and confident. But there was a hint of change. To one degree or another, everyone in the band had felt a little bit of air come out of the balloon during the last week of their tour—and it seemed a bit like that at home now too. They'd learned that the entire time they were away, Elvis Presley had dominated the charts with his latest No. 1 record, "Too Much." Now he had another smash hit climbing the charts, "All Shook Up."

No one said it out loud, but every band member knew they were no longer the No. 1 act in America, or even still hitting high on the charts there. The chart positions of the newer Comets releases fell far short of previous highs. During the last half of '56, Presley had been knocking them for a loop. Coming back to the US with a fresh perspective, they couldn't help noticing that the uniquely identifiable Comet sound, which had dominated the US charts for nearly two full years, had lost some of its appeal. They were better musicians than before, but the style and feel of the records was more of the same, and the kids just weren't buying them as much as they used to.

The new competition wasn't limited to Elvis and his erotic gyrations. There was also a huge crop of raucous newcomers competing for the Comets' audience, including Gene Vincent, Buddy Knox, Chuck Berry, Eddie Cochran, Ricky Nelson, Little Richard, and the latest rock 'n' roll sensation, Jerry Lee Lewis. Not to mention a local kid out of Philadelphia, Charlie Gracie, who'd scored a big hit in March with "Butterfly." Competition was coming out of the woodwork.

Nevertheless, there was cause for optimism. On March 24, 1957, the Comets appeared again on Ed Sullivan's *Toast of the Town* show, commanding a fee higher than Elvis Presley had received for all four of his appearances on that show combined. Moreover, the band's overseas tours had been successful and profitable. Record sales abroad were still strong. Riding on the success of their British tour, the Comets' "Don't Knock the Rock" entered the UK charts just before they departed, hitting the No. 7 spot in seven weeks. At home, even though the band had been out of the public eye for more than two months, their latest release, "Forty Cups of Coffee/Hook Line and Sinker," had just entered the Hot 100 Chart, although it would only reach No. 70. Bill Haley and His Comets were still a huge name in the entertainment industry, and rock 'n' roll was more popular than ever.

Right now, what Bill and the band wanted most was another big US hit. Determined to give it their best effort, they went back to the recording studio, producing "(You Hit the Wrong Note) Billy Goat," "Rockin' Rollin' Rover," and "Miss You" in one day. Over the next several days, they recorded a dozen more: "Please Don't Talk About Me When I'm Gone," "You Can't Stop Me from Dancing," and "Rock Lomand." Four days later, they recorded "Is It True What They Say About Dixie?" "Carolina in the Morning," "Ain't Misbehavin'," "The Dipsy Doodle," and "The Beak Speaks," and a week later, they recorded, "Moon Over Miami," "One Sweet Letter from You," "Apple Blossom Time," and "Somebody Else Is Taking My Place," for a total of fifteen new songs. It remained to be seen whether any of them would chart.

After the recording sessions, trying to keep his promise to Cuppy and himself to tour less and stay closer to home, Bill resolved that he and the band would spend more time composing, recording, and promoting other musicians they'd hire to work for them and pursuing new business opportunities. These plans would have made sense if any of these ventures had been successful, but they weren't.

Nevertheless, Bill and the Comets struggled hard to hold onto their place near the top. In May, the band drove to New York for a repeat appearance on Ed Sullivan's *Toast of the Town* series, where they performed "Forty Cups of Coffee" and "Rudy's Rock." They followed that up by appearing on *The Ray Bolger Show* on May 9, performing "Rock Around the Clock" and "Huckleberry." For the rest of that month and into early June, the band also performed a series of twenty one-night concerts in cities in the Midwest and on the East Coast.

23

The Struggle Continues

Where there is no struggle, there is no strength.
—OPRAH WINFREY

In June of 1957, the Everly Brothers were the hottest new act in America with their smash hit "Bye, Bye Love." Meanwhile, the Comets' "(You Hit the Wrong Note) Billy Goat" crept up the *Cashbox* charts to No. 54 on June 8, hitting the *Billboard* Hot 100 two days later. At the same time, Elvis kept churning out hits. His latest one was "(Let Me Be Your) Teddy Bear."

Even without chart success, Bill Haley and His Comets were still popular in the US, and they continued to command top fees for performances. Royalties from sales of their records outside the US also were strong, boosting the band's total receipts to $86,632 for the first half of 1957.

After taking a month off for fun and fishing at the Jersey shore, the Comets embarked in August 1957 on a seven-week tour of forty-nine American cities. Their venues, and receipts, were smaller than they'd been in 1956, but they still went first class, spending freely and gambling often. As a result, most of the money they made touring never made it back to the office.

They also found themselves at another crossroad of sorts. Bill and producer Milt Gabler had different opinions about the musical direction they should take. Gabler often drove down to Bill's house to work with Bill on new material, and Cuppy would cook them a nice dinner. Later in the evening, she'd hear them arguing about song selections. Bill wanted to go back to the western sound that worked for them in the past, and Gabler wanted to stick with the rock 'n' roll formula that had brought them so much recent success. He told Bill he didn't have the right type of voice to be a top-selling country singer.

There were other ways for the Comets to make money as musicians, however. The band still had plenty of offers for concerts and personal appearances, including television shows. But other such opportunities went begging. Bill and manager Lord Jim Ferguson glibly turned down several potentially lucrative deals, some because of scheduling conflicts but others out of arrogance and overconfidence.

On one occasion Bill refused to do ten short commercial spots for Coca-Cola for $250,000, telling Cuppy that he didn't want to be "overexposed." It was the same excuse he'd tried to use when he and the band were offered the chance to participate in the blockbuster movie *Blackboard Jungle*. On that occasion, at the urging of his advisers and Cuppy, Bill and the Comets had accepted Hollywood's offer and had gone on to greatly increased popularity. This time, although Bill relented and agreed to participate in the Coca-Cola ad campaign, he changed his mind and backed out after three days of shooting, saying he didn't like the way it was going. He and the band were paid only union scale for their time, thus losing most of the $250,000 and the massive publicity a Coca-Cola ad campaign would have given them.

In a revengeful mood, Bill shortly thereafter turned down a chance to host a weekly half-hour variety show on NBC-TV. The show would have been produced by Desilu Productions, which had created the fabulously successful *I Love Lucy* sitcom and later produced the also-successful *Star Trek* and *Untouchables* series. Bill insisted in advance on banning the Jodimars as guests, because they consisted of former Comets who had quit his band. He also demanded a ban on using any songs by Frank Pingatore, partly because Pingatore was managing the Jodimars, but also because Pingatore had taken Cuppy to dinner once when Bill was working, told her she could do much better than Bill, and made advances she rebuffed. Desilu withdrew its offer.

As the Comets' popularity and earnings declined, and the money going out of the organization began to catch up to and exceed the amount coming in, Bill continued to spend as if money were no object. In June 1957, he told Sgro to purchase a brand-new thirty-two-foot Pacemaker twin-engine boat to replace Bill's single-engine, unreliable "Comet," even though the organization didn't have the cash to pay for it. The Pacemaker was priced at $25,000, a price that was increased to $32,000 when Haley insisted on adding extras such as outriggers, a ship-to-shore phone, depth finders, and a three-hundred-thirty-gallon fuel tank.

Sgro managed to raise the required $15,000 down payment by trading in the band's old boat. The rest of the purchase price was financed through the dealer. The new vessel was dubbed the *Comet IV*, and Bill took a month off from performing and recording to go deep-sea fishing every day. His guests on these excursions included Chuck Berry, Frankie Lymon, and Big Joe Turner, among many other musicians.

Bill may have exceeded his sailing ability with the purchase of the Comet IV. One day he and some other Comets were twenty-four miles out to sea when a bad storm came up. Bill, who thought the boat was unsinkable, was steering the vessel when it began to list to one side. Luckily Lord Jim, a former Navy man who had some idea of what to do to keep the boat from being capsized, forcefully took the wheel and said, "Bill, I'm taking this boat in."

Comet Ralph Jones, who was aboard that day, was petrified because he couldn't swim. He had a life jacket on, and he hung on for dear life, saying the Rosary. When they finally got back to the pier, Jones jumped off and said, "Bill, that's the last goddamned time you're ever going to see me on this boat!" Looking at the first stranger he saw, he asked, "Do you fish?" He then sold him his rod, reel, tackle box, and other fishing equipment for a total of five dollars. That was the last time Jones ever set foot on a fishing vessel.

During the first two weeks of September 1957, the band went back to work, doing a brief tour of the Midwest before a combined audience of 137,000 fans. They played at clubs and halls in Minnesota, Iowa, Indiana, Kansas, Missouri, Wisconsin, and Illinois, before heading back East. Bill took another week off after that and drove down Skyline Drive in the Appalachians with Cuppy.

Cuppy was happy to get away and be alone with Bill, but the trip turned out to be a bit disappointing. They visited many of the same places they'd seen on a previous trip in the fall of '54 when Bill's career was starting to take off. They'd been so much in love then, and giddy with hope and optimism. This time, although everything looked the same, it felt different. They had some nice dinners together, but Bill was distant and moody most of the time. He was silent for long stretches while they drove, deep in thought. Cuppy tried to engage him, but he was often annoyed, and she didn't feel she could get close to him. He never opened up to her as he had in the past, and it was frustrating. When they returned home, Bill left immediately to do a show in St. Louis.

On October 14, 1957, Bill and the band appeared in a star-studded show at the Hilton Hotel in Los Angeles with some of their major competitors: Jerry Lee Lewis, Chuck Berry, LaVern Baker, Eddie Cochran, Fats Domino, Bo Diddley, and the Everly Brothers. Somewhat ominously, many of these individuals and groups were doing better than the Comets. Jerry Lee Lewis had a pair of hits: "Whole Lotta Shakin' Goin' On" and "Great Balls of Fire." The Everlys were riding high with "Bye Bye Love" and their current chart topper "Wake Up Little Susie." Fats Domino had scored with "I'm Walkin'," and Chuck Berry was ringing up sales with "Rock 'n' Roll Music" and "School Day (Ring! Ring! Goes the Bell)." Finally, Elvis Presley was climbing the charts again, with "Jailhouse Rock" on its way to becoming his sixth No. 1 smash hit in two years. The Comets had nothing comparable.

After the Los Angeles show, the band did a brief, well-received return engagement in Jamaica. On this trip, Billy Williamson cooked up another one of his classic practical jokes, with Lord Jim as the victim. After noticing that Jim was making overtures toward a young lady at the bar, in a resort where they were all staying in little huts, Williamson grabbed his bandmates and sprang into action. While Lord Jim was distracted, the Comets pulled the mattress off the bed in his hut, dipped it in the pool, put it back in place, and covered it with a dry bedspread. They then hid in an adjacent hut and awaited Jim's return with his conquest. Sure enough, about ten minutes after Lord Jim and his lady friend entered the hut, Jim burst out its front door bellowing, "You dirty rotten sons of bitches! I'm gonna kill you bastards!"

The Jamaica appearance, combined with the fact that they were now selling more records internationally than they were in the US, inspired the Comets to return to the studio in November to record fourteen songs with themes from around the world. Although the album included familiar international folk songs as well as rock numbers, it was titled "Rockin' Around the World." The Comets' final diversified singles for the company in 1957 were the country and western tune "It's a Sin" and the rocker "Mary, Mary Lou."

Neither the album nor the singles were hits, but Decca was still happy with the Comets at the end of 1957. That year, "Rock Around the Clock" had sold another two million copies worldwide, reaching No. 1 in France. In all, twenty-three Comet singles were released in 1957 on the Decca, London, and Brunswick labels, along with nine extended-play recordings and five albums. Total Comet record sales for Decca worldwide now topped eighteen million. For the second half of 1957, Haley and his partners received a total of $111,771 in Decca royalties, including advances.

Before taking off early to enjoy the holiday season with their families, the Comets appeared on *American Bandstand*, an extremely popular music TV performance show, to lip-synch "(You Hit the Wrong Note) Billy Goat." Another Christmas bash was held at Melody Manor at the end of 1957, and a sense of reckless optimism prevailed once again. Bill handed out the customary $1,000 holiday bonus checks to the band members as they toasted each other to continued success in 1958.

24

Bill Dallies with a South American Dolly

The Comets, although still popular, were heading downhill when Uncle Sam gave them a break. Elvis was drafted into the Army in December 1957, severely restricting his recording and performance opportunities, although Colonel Parker had shrewdly stockpiled a dozen recordings for periodic release during Elvis's absence from the public eye. The Comets also aided their career prospects by deciding to tour South America.

The reception at their first stop, Rio de Janeiro, was tremendous, reminiscent of the greetings they'd received in Australia and England. They played a series of standing-room-only shows in other big cities, as well as in remote jungle towns. In both cities and towns, many fans knew Bill and each of the Comets by name. Meanwhile, in April 1958, one of their newly pressed disks, "Skinny Minnie," climbed to No. 22 on the *Billboard* pop chart back home.

While band members' optimism about their future was rising, they met Alex Valdez, an Argentinian promoter who offered them a deal to tour Europe in the fall. The deal had a bad side, however. Valdez had worked his way into Bill's good graces through a beautiful woman named Dani, whom he called his wife. Dani proceeded to cling to Bill at every opportunity, making sure she sat with him on the plane, bringing him coffee, and showing him around the various cities they visited. Bill, who'd never been unfaithful to Cuppy, resisted Dani's advances for weeks. By the end of the tour, however, he was clearly smitten by her, and the band's previously strict ethical code began to decay. The rules against cavorting with women and drinking eroded even more than they already had, and Bill ended his practice of making nightly informal bed checks of the other band members.

Meanwhile, the IRS found out that some of the payroll taxes on revenue from Comets road trip had never been paid, and they slapped the band with a bill for $59,000 dollars. To keep the group going, Bill had to take out a mortgage on the house he shared with Cuppy, and another one on the band's office building in Chester, Pennsylvania.

The Comets' insistence on recording only their own compositions also continued to hurt them. One particularly bad idea was an album they made called *Bill Haley's Chicks* that contained nine songs, each based on a different woman's name. It's hard to believe that when Bill thought up the idea for this album, he hadn't been thinking of Dani, or of straying in general.

It's also possible Bill was thinking of Dani when he established a record label of his own in 1958 and called it Clymax Records. That Bill would choose to name his new label Clymax while defending rock 'n' roll as innocent music showed the divided and somewhat contradictory nature of his business and his personality. His bifurcated personal nature would become even more obvious on his next foreign trip.

Meanwhile the band stayed busy in the Chester studio, backing the organization's signed artists on a fresh, new series of records released by Clymax. They consisted of five singles, three extended play disks, and one album. First the Comets cut a record featuring The Matys Brothers, "Sweet Sixteen," backed with "I'm Alone Because I Love You," and next, they backed WFIL-TV personality Sally Starr on "Rockin' in the Nursery" and "Little Pedro." Finally, the band backed Charlie Gray on "Completely Satisfied/Wastin' Time" and Lou Graham on "Wee Willie Brown/You Were Mean Baby." The partners also wrote songs for and backed Sally Starr on an album produced by Johnny Grande, which they recorded at Frank Virtue's studio in Philadelphia, entitled *Our Gal Sal*.

25

Bill and Cuppy Continue to Fight While Bill's Sister Dies Young

When Bill left for South America with the band, he and Cuppy had been going through a rough stretch in their marriage. Their relationship had gradually deteriorated since they'd returned from Great Britain. From Cuppy's perspective, Bill had turned into a different person. He'd always had a short fuse and a quick temper, but after the UK trip he gradually became moodier and more silent, and easily irritated by the children and almost everything Cuppy said to him. He was often emotionally cold and argumentative. Others also noticed a change in Bill's personality. He was more reluctant to make personal appearances, interact with fans, and socialize, even within his circle of friends. The band members often had to make excuses for his absence at private promotional parties, press gatherings, and other events.

Soon Cuppy had a hard time getting her husband to come home in the evening. She'd call him for dinner, he'd say he'd be home in half an hour, and two hours later he'd still be at the office. Once Bill did get home, however, he seemed to enjoy it. The couple would have dinner, go for a walk around the grounds, and put the children to bed. Then Bill and Cuppy would retreat to the den in the basement to play a game of billiards, throw darts, or watch television. Bill loved Westerns, but variety and quiz shows were his favorites. He'd been an avid reader as a boy, and he was very good at answering questions correctly, despite not having finished high school. He frequently said in jest that one day he was going to go on a quiz show and win a lot of money for Cuppy and his mother.

Quite often on these evenings with Cuppy, Bill would pick up an acoustic guitar and entertain his audience of one. The couple would have a few drinks, and afterward Bill was as happy as a big sunflower, singing his wife his favorite country and western songs. As the drinks kept flowing, however, his mood would change, and soon they'd begin to argue. Eventually Bill started drinking at night to the point where he no longer made sense. He started blaming band staffers and others for his mounting financial difficulties, and he would exclaim repeatedly, "I'm Bill Haley!"

The financial pinch Bill endured in 1958 further exacerbated tensions with Cuppy. Their frequent squabbles became constant bickering. "You weren't meant to be a father," Cuppy said during one of their many fights about the situation at home. "You show no interest in the kids. You're not there for them. And I'm not just talking about being on the road. Even when you are home." Bill offered no defense other than to say his work came first.

The discord eventually reached the point where Cuppy, as a bluff to force Bill to talk about their deteriorating relationship, had suggested a trial separation before he left for South America. When he returned, she was happy to see him but not sure he felt the same way. She and Bill fell back into their usual routines, but she couldn't help feeling that he was pulling away from her.

At the band's offices, Bill started spending hours with his office door closed, making long phone calls to Dani in South America. When office manager Sam Sgro saw the large phone bill, he wondered what was going on. He was angered at this outrageous expense when money was so short. With diminished cash flow, Sgro was borrowing to meet payroll and pay expenses. He marched into Bill's office and hollered, "You just ran up a $2,000 phone bill! Two calls to South America, $2,000!" Bill, visibly intoxicated in the middle of the afternoon, opened his desk drawer, pulled out a .38-caliber handgun, and held it to his head as if he were going to shoot himself. Stunned, Sgro turned around and walked out.

Not long after that, partner Billy Williamson walked into Sgro's office and said, "Bill is up there playing around with that gun." Sgro climbed the stairs to the third floor, entered Bill's office, and saw the handgun sitting out on Bill's desk.

"Bill, do you want something?" Sgro asked. Bill just looked at him, expressionless, and didn't answer, and after a moment, Sgro turned around and left. A couple of hours later, Bill walked down the stairs, got in his car, and went home.

The drama was far from over. Missing the new object of his affection, Bill came up with the idea of inviting Alex Valdez and Dani to a party at his home celebrating a new deal for the Comets to tour Europe again in the fall. The whole band gathered at Bill's house waiting for Alex and Dani to arrive. The members knew about Bill's dalliance with Dani, but no one had said a word about it to their wives or Cuppy. Bill seemed impatient and nervous while waiting for his guests to arrive, pacing around the house and the driveway. Cuppy suspected something had happened on the South American trip, but she had no clue what it had been until Alex and Dani arrived at Melody Manor.

Valdez, well-dressed, slightly balding, and of medium height, struck Cuppy as a shifty con-man type, charming in a European sort of way. "You just look absolutely gorgeous," he told her with his South American accent when they met. "Bill never told me you were so beautiful," he continued, introducing his "wife," Dani, a raven-haired, dark-eyed South American beauty with a very nice figure. Cuppy instinctively suspected that something had happened between Dani and Bill, and her suspicions were confirmed later that evening when the two of them snuck off to spend time alone. When she saw Bill and Dani standing together under the apple tree in the front yard, her heart sank and her blood boiled. That was where she and Bill had spent many romantic evenings. It was *their* tree.

Bill invited Alex and Dani to stick around for a few days before continuing on to Manhattan, their next destination. He and Cuppy took them to the Diamond Beach Lodge resort in Wildwood Crest, on the Jersey Shore. They stayed in adjacent motels at the Motel Beach Club, *the* place to go that year. Cuppy could see that Bill was trying to show Dani what a big star he was. He treated her and Alex to extravagant restaurant dinners and took them to see the Andrews Sisters and Teresa Brewer, one of Bill's favorite entertainers despite her past criticism of rock 'n' roll.

After their stay in Wildwood Crest, Alex and Dani went on to New York. Bill and Cuppy returned home, but before long, Bill found an excuse go to New York alone. Looking lovestruck, he was photographed there having dinner with Dani and a couple of Comets staffers at the Starlight Roof restaurant in the Waldorf Astoria.

After Bill returned home from that trip, his heavy drinking and moodiness continued. While he was still struggling to produce another hit record, his rival Elvis managed to score another megahit with "Hard Headed Woman," even though he was still stuck in the Army. Chuck Berry, the man Bill had once saved from a lynch mob, was also rocking the charts with hits like "Sweet Little Sixteen" and "Johnny B. Goode."

Unable to contain herself, Cuppy challenged Bill about his relationship with Dani when he returned from New York. He denied it, but the frequent arguments at home resumed. Cuppy traveled with Bill and the band to a series of engagements in Florida, hoping to rebuild their relationship, but when they returned, they received some devastating news. Bill's beloved sister Peggy, a hospital nurse, was dying from liver cancer at age thirty-five.

Peggy was well liked by her coworkers at the hospital, who gave her a thirty-fifth birthday party in her room. But at 2 a.m. on the morning of June 21, 1958, one of the nurses called Bill and Cuppy and said, "I'm not supposed to do this, but I think you should get over here now." When they arrived, Peggy was drifting in and out of consciousness. Cuppy sat down and held her hand, Bill at her side. Bill told his sister that he loved her. She said she loved him and died. Bill was devastated.

Shortly after Peggy's death, the band played an engagement in Atlantic City, and for the first time in their relationship, although Cuppy went with him, Bill shut her out completely. Between sets he went outside and sat in a rocking chair overlooking the ocean, talking to no one. He and Cuppy had always been close even when they were fighting, and this was the first time he'd acted this way.

As the organization's cash flow worsened and creditors harassed band staffers daily, summer turned to fall. Bill and Cuppy's relationship continued to deteriorate, and his drinking continued. They argued all the time. At one point, they discussed selling the house and moving to New Jersey. The house—on the land where his parents had raised him, with the rock where Bill and Cuppy had pledged their future together—had always been sacred to him. That Bill was willing to give that up troubled Cuppy. One argument followed another until it reached the point where Bill provoked a huge blow-up and they barely spoke for several weeks, each waiting for the other to apologize. Then Bill left for Europe. Cuppy figured she'd better start thinking about the possibility of being forced to make it on her own with the children.

That fall, a few days after Bill left on his European tour, Cuppy began attending a nearby branch of Patricia Stevens Career College and Finishing School, a school for "models and career girls," two nights a week. Cuppy's classes included Visual Poise, Drama, Makeup, Personality, Styling, Figure Coordination, Hair Care, and Typing and Secretarial Skills.

26

The Second Battle of Berlin

Bill's 1958 European tour marked the first time the band had accepted a booking of this magnitude without receiving any money in advance. Sgro was wary and mistrustful of promoter Alex Valdez, and the Comets were short on funds. Still, Sgro remained hopeful that the five-week, twenty-three-city tour—which included fifty-six scheduled performances in Italy, France, Belgium, Germany, and Spain—would turn out as planned, and that the money collected would be wired to the home office as promised.

The Comets' first few appearances went well, but soon after they arrived in Rome, Pope Pius XII died, and Italy went into shock. Every nonessential business shut down for a period of official mourning, and the remaining Comets shows in Rome were cancelled. Another four shows in Naples and Venice were poorly attended. Valdez tried to reschedule the lost Rome dates for the end of the tour in November, but he couldn't because halls weren't available.

The band's bad luck continued. In Barcelona, Spain, after the band completed a sold-out performance with no trouble from the audience, the local authorities decided they didn't have enough police to patrol the auditorium and cancelled the rest of their shows. People who'd lined up for blocks to buy tickets had to line up again the next day to get their money back. Generalissimo Francisco Franco, citing a Catholic Church ban on rock 'n' roll, ordered that the Comets' remaining scheduled concerts in Seville and Madrid be cancelled as well.

On October 14, 1958, the Comets were wearing suits and ties when they arrived at the Bourget Airport for a performance at the Paris Olympia Music Hall, just as though they were in town for a business meeting. A contingent of restless, frenzied young men led by the Black Leather Jackets, the French version of Britain's Teddy Boys, seized upon this opportunity to release their anger and frustration. Fifty youths were arrested after the first show, and ten more were hurt in riots outside the theater when one hundred policemen couldn't control the crowd. Despite the scuffle, the band was a huge hit, and the show was broadcast live throughout Europe on the American Forces Network.

With a few free days left before the band's next scheduled appearance in Marseilles, Valdez managed to get them a couple of shows in North Africa in the same month, even though most people there weren't familiar with the Comets' music. Valdez refused to go with them, and the musicians found out why after they arrived in Tunisia: there was an outstanding warrant there for his arrest. The chartered single-engine DC3 cargo plane that flew them there had barely enough room for the band and their equipment, and its seats were made from pipes and leather straps. To muster the courage to board the plane in Marseilles for a two-and-a-half-hour flight across the Mediterranean to Tunis, where they were to appear that night, some band members drank heavily.

Because most of the Tunis audience had never heard of Bill Haley, let alone "Rock Around the Clock," the Comets altered their set list and played numbers they didn't normally do, such as "Night Train" and a lot of other semi-rock songs. The men in the audience wore fezzes with red and black tassels, and most of the women wore veils, but despite the cultural differences, the performance was a smash hit. When the Comets played "Rock Around the Clock" at the end of the show, more than one hundred men swarmed the band, hoisted Haley to their shoulders, and paraded him around the stage. Many of the men kissed him.

Although the theater where the band played in Tunis was in a very modern shopping center, camels walked down the streets outside. The hotel the Comets stayed in had a beautiful foyer, but the rooms were filthy and the food was so bad the Comets lived on peanuts for three days. Band assistant Vincent "Catfish" Broomall, Harry Broomall's nephew, was so frightened someone would come in and slit his throat in the middle of the night that he propped a chair under the doorknob of his room and lay wide awake as long as possible.

After another show the following day, the band flew back to Marseilles on the same plane that had brought them there. The return flight hit a headwind and took six hours, with the band members feeling as though they were standing still over the Mediterranean. After landing in Marseilles, they swiftly changed planes and flew to Brussels for a hastily arranged appearance on the final night of the World Fair that was broadcast live on Belgian TV.

In the Comets' next stop, Le Havre, France, a small group of excited fans captured two of the Comets and held them hostage. Carrying the musicians on their shoulders to a central square, they deposited them on a pedestal that held a statue of a military hero on a horse. Unfazed, the two musicians sat there and signed autographs for several hours.

By the time the Comets reached Frankfurt, Germany, Bill was despondent. His fling with Dani had fizzled out, and back home, his relationship with Cuppy was in tatters. The band had performed well and often on the tour despite the difficulties in Italy and Spain, but because they often were staying in the best hotels and eating in the best restaurants, they were spending every penny they received. Meanwhile, back in the States, the public seemed to miss Presley, who was still in the Army, more than they missed Bill and the Comets.

The band's next scheduled appearance was on Sunday, October 26, 1958, at the West Berlin Sportspalast, an arena that was set up with seven thousand folding wooden chairs. The Berlin Wall hadn't been built yet, and the CIA had warned the Sportspalast director that members of East German communist youth groups were going to arrive by subway and try to disrupt the show. As a security precaution, eighty extra police officers were waiting in the Sportspalast's basement in full riot gear.

All went well until the band performed "Rock Around the Clock," their usual finale. Numerous youths wearing leather jackets and white motorcycle hats and armed with clubs began pounding those weapons on the stage. Some hopped up on it and began dancing as security personnel struggled to push them back. Then a riot started, captured on film by the American Forces Network. The film showed crowds destroying amplifiers and microphones, along with stage lights and decorations. The grand piano was overturned, chairs were smashed, and equipment belonging to the American Forces Network was vandalized.

As soon as they saw what was happening, the Comets left the arena through a rear door, intending to board a waiting bus. But their path through the alley was blocked by pockets of brawling teens. Then the German bus driver, a big, burly man, opened the door, hopped off the bus, and proceeded to grab each hapless teen within his reach. He picked up each youth he caught, held him over his head, and threw him over a nearby six-foot wall. After the first three teens had been disposed of this way, the rest of the revelers fled.

By the time calm was restored, one police officer was permanently blinded and twenty more were hurt. Thirty-four young people had been severely injured, and eighteen were arrested. All in all, about thirty thousand marks (approximately seven thousand dollars) worth of damage was inflicted on the Sportspalast, mostly due to the cost of replacing shattered chairs. Footage of the riot appeared on the evening news in the US, and the official East German Communist Party newspaper, *Neues Deutschland*, ran a front-page editorial accusing the Comets of "turning the youth of the land of Bach and Beethoven into raging beasts."

None of this stopped a German film company from recruiting the Comets to appear in a movie. Titled *Hier Bin Ich: Hier Bleib Ich* (Here I Am; Here I Stay), it was being filmed in Berlin at CCC Studios. Before leaving Europe, the Comets visited the set to perform their song "Vive la Rock and Roll" for the cameras. Bill and the movie's costar, Caterina Valente, sang the lyrics, and Valente danced in front of the band. An Italian singer and actress, Valente was popular in both Germany and the US.

The scene in *Hier Bin Ich* in which the Comets appeared had been written to depict a riot in a nightclub during the band's performance. After the real riot at the Comets' real performance, however, director Werner Jacobs rewrote it so that the only violent person on screen during the band's performance was actor Wolfgang Mueller. Playing the club's head waiter, he smashed a chair in a comedic musical frenzy.

The riot inspired a second comedic reference the next morning, when the band went to CCC Studios to record their songs "Hot Dog Buddy Buddy" and "Whoa Mabel" for the movie soundtrack. The petite, multilingual Valente, Europe's biggest musical comedy star at the time, entered the studio wearing riot gear, carrying a club, and asking for directions to the Haley concert.

After another real riot occurred during a Comets concert in Hamburg, the authorities were prepared when the band arrived in Essen on October 28, 1958. Some 570 police were on hand, including 50 hidden behind a huge curtain, some holding trained police dogs on leashes. The Comets began playing, and this time, the troublemakers did not wait until the end of the show. Someone threw a potted plant at the stage, scoring a glancing hit on musician Billy Williamson. The band kept playing for a few seconds, but when audience members began jumping onto the stage, Bill decided things were getting out of hand. He stopped singing mid-song, and he and the other band members left the stage with their instruments as quickly as possible.

As soon as the Comets went backstage, the police sprang into action. Security personnel led the band up a flight of steps, through a set of fire doors, and onto the roof. When band members asked a German policeman on the roof how they were going to get out of the theater, he lifted a bullhorn and said, "Watch this! Bring on the hoses!" Suddenly, large vehicles arrived and sprayed the crowd with water cannons, dispersing them only momentarily. "Aaagh! Watch this! Bring on the horses!" the officer said. Mounted police appeared and attempted unsuccessfully to disperse the crowd with their horses. Finally he said, "Aaagh! Watch this! Bring on the *dogs!*" and a number of fierce dogs appeared, all on thirty-foot leashes. The crowd retreated and the band was able to escape the theater area.

The following night, the Comets played to six thousand people at two nonviolent shows in Stuttgart, and Elvis Presley, accompanied by his father, stopped by to see them again. (Elvis was still stationed in Germany with the US Army.) In the dressing room between shows, he and Bill chatted and sang country and western songs together. Elvis told Bill that "if it weren't for you, I'd still be working on a truck back in Tennessee."

Because Elvis's mother had recently died, he was subdued and slightly depressed. He offered to join the band onstage for a cameo appearance, but was discouraged by local authorities, who didn't want to press their luck because of the rioting at some of the previous shows.

By now, Cuppy hadn't heard from Bill for nearly two months. That never had happened before; he'd always called constantly when he was on the road and sent her roses. Even during Bill's South American travels, when he'd been distracted by Dani, he'd still called to see how the kids were.

During their last argument before Bill left for Europe, Cuppy had once again suggested a trial separation. She was trying to force Bill's hand, naïvely believing that he could never stand to be away from her. They'd been fighting more and more lately, however, and she remembered that the last time, Bill had said, placing the blame squarely on her, "With each fight we have, you place another brick in the wall. Pretty soon the wall will be so high neither one of us will be able to climb over it."

Although heartbroken, twenty-six-year-old Cuppy wasn't one to sit home waiting by the phone. While Bill was gone she was off in the car, visiting friend after friend, but lonely, unhappy, and fearful. As the days rolled by, she felt progressively more worried. Even if Bill was still angry with her, it was unlike him not to call to at least see how the children were. Each day Cuppy would walk down the driveway to the mailbox, hoping that Bill had sent her a letter saying what she wanted to hear: that he was sorry and couldn't live without her.

Finally, in early November 1958, Cuppy opened the mailbox, and there it was, a letter from Bill with an airmail stamp, postmarked in

West Germany. She looked at his familiar handwriting on the envelope and her heart raced. She briskly walked back to the house, pressing the letter against her heart and stopping to look out the large dining room window at Joanie on the swing and Billy and Jimmy digging in the sandbox. "I did it," she thought to herself. "He couldn't stand being away from me. How could he have been so blind not to see our love was meant to last forever?"

Cuppy went back to their bedroom and closed the door, savoring every moment in anticipation of reading Bill's letter of surrender. She propped herself up on the fluffy, pink pillow on her side of the bed and slowly opened the envelope. What she read was not what she expected:

> I am sorry that it has taken me this long to answer your letter about having a trial separation. I know that we have been fighting a lot and we have both been unhappy. A lot of things have happened to bring us to this point.
>
> I want to do the right thing for you & my little Junebug & Bill Jr. & Jimmy— but I feel that you were right to suggest a trial separation. In this way you can feel free to seek companionship that you have been so lacking in. I must concentrate on getting my life's dream back together & to make money for you & the kids.
>
> You were right to say we must try this. I will see my little Junebug & the boys whenever I can & I will send you money when I have it. Remember— we stopped saying 'I love you' and got to 'I like you.' Hopefully we still "like" each other.

Cuppy was stunned. Bill, confused over the muddled state of his personal and professional affairs, flew to Spain and stayed there. Finally, as Thanksgiving 1958 approached, his money ran out and he flew home. When he called Cuppy from the airport, he was drunk. Before Cuppy could answer, he hung up, called Sam Sgro, and asked him to pick him up at the train station in Wilmington, Delaware. When Sgro got there, Bill said, "I want to get home. I want to see Cuppy and I want to see the kids."

Sgro drove him home and asked Cuppy if she'd let Bill stay. "He has nowhere to go," Sgro said.

Cuppy looked at Bill, his head bowed. He couldn't look her in the eye. "All right. Bring him in," she said.

Sgro helped Bill inside, gave Cuppy a wink, and said, "He's too drunk to know anything." Bill stayed the night, although he and Cuppy didn't sleep together.

The next morning, Bill walked into the kitchen while Cuppy was making breakfast. "Cuppy, I'm sorry," he said. "I made a mistake. I did a bad thing. I'm really sorry. I love you. We can make it together."

Because there was no place else for Bill to go, they gradually began to mend their relationship. Cuppy still loved him and felt sorry for him. They never again directly discussed Bill's illicit affair with Dani and their trial separation, but it left a nasty stain on their relationship.

27

The Financial Noose Tightens and Bill Flirts with Suicide

By 1959, the Comets had no money. They had nothing to show from their tumultuous European tour. Cancellations and expenses had eaten up all the money that tour and previous tours and recordings had produced.

Valdez was trying to set up another tour in South America and one in India as well. This time, however, the partners were determined to insist on receiving half their money up front before even setting foot on an airplane. In the meantime, they began finding gigs again in states where they'd always been successful: Wisconsin, Pennsylvania, New Jersey, Delaware, and Maryland. They looked for dates in Canada as well.

At Melody Manor, meanwhile, Bill noticed that Cuppy was trying to make herself more employable, possibly as a hedge against his permanent departure. He saw her typing homework for a course at Patricia Stevens Finishing and Career School and felt surprised, impressed, and even a little bit threatened. "Wow," he said. "You must really like that. I couldn't do that."

"I do," she said confidently. For the first time in their relationship, she felt she'd turned the tables on her husband and had the upper hand. He asked her what was going on, and she told him she'd decided to go back to school after he'd left for Europe without saying goodbye. She said she was doing it to help him, herself, and their children.

Bill smiled and said he was proud of her. When he went on the road with the band, he instructed Lord Jim to attend Cuppy's graduation ceremony in his place, and she greatly appreciated that. Slowly, husband and wife began to put the troubles of the previous year behind them.

Meanwhile, a few of the Comets, particularly Franny Beecher and Ralph Jones, were becoming increasingly frustrated by the poor quality of the material they were bringing into the studio to record. After a disappointing session, Franny would say to Ralph and the others, "Jesus Christ. We've got to get professional writers! We've got to get somebody who knows how to write this music for us!"

Band producer Milt Gabler had implored the partners to use professional songwriters, but Bill, on the advice of Lord Jim, kept insisting on only recording original songs they could own a piece of, many cowritten with Bill's old friend Rusty Keefer. Gabler was furious with the way Lord Jim, a.k.a. James Ferguson, was behaving. Ferguson would get on the phone and try to extort outside songwriters and publishers. He'd threaten not to use their song if he hadn't secured a writing credit or a piece of the publishing rights, or throw it out if they'd already recorded it. Bill backed Lord Jim's approach in the hope that the publishing royalties from the songs he'd composed himself, or had gained the rights to, would ease his own financial plight. But it wasn't working out that way.

It was pointless to gripe to Bill about the studio mess, however, because by now, he had his own way of doing things. Meanwhile, unknowns like J. P. Richardson, a.k.a. "The Big Bopper," and Eddie Cochran had been beating the Comets on the charts. Even Alvin and the Chipmunks—a group consisting of animated cartoon characters—had come up with a current No. 1 hit, while the Comets, who were very much alive, had *nada*.

As Bill and Cuppy worked on improving their relationship, Cuppy's increasing sense of independence and desire to learn and acquire new work skills began to concern and threaten her husband. His daily drinking hadn't stopped, but he'd been civil and somewhat restrained at home since returning from Europe. The couple's level of intimacy had improved, and sometimes they felt that everything was going to work out. As time passed, however, the same old petty arguments began to re-emerge, and new ones arose. When Bill drank, he'd reach a point where he'd be convinced that Cuppy was the spouse who'd been unfaithful, instead of the other way around. He'd blast Hank Williams's "Your Cheatin' Heart" on the record player and belligerently accuse his wife of having had an affair while he was in Europe.

Cuppy was deeply troubled by Bill's baseless accusations and his growing disinterest in his family life and the home he'd once cherished. Hurt that he no longer looked at or touched her the way he once had, she was reluctant to question him, afraid it might give him an opening he might be looking for to end their marriage. Meanwhile, although Bill hid his mounting financial troubles from Cuppy, he clearly was feeling the strain of trying to sustain a crumbling business.

In early June 1959, Cuppy unexpectedly learned she was pregnant again, with what would be her and Bill's fifth child together, even though their lovemaking had become infrequent by now. Despite this news, and adding to the band's pressing need for cash, Bill let another money-making opportunity slip through his fingers late that summer when he and the Comets once again played for low rates on the New Jersey shore. Toward the end of the season, just before Labor Day, Sam Sgro received a call from Colonel Tom Parker, Elvis's manager, who was apparently keeping busy booking concerts while his young protégé was on duty with Uncle Sam in Germany.

Bellowing into the phone, Parker said, "They want Haley down in Australia! Haley's bigger than Elvis there! You get him down there. I'll guarantee him $50,000 and the plane fare."

Sgro relayed the offer to Bill, and Bill told him to refuse. Hearing the response, Colonel Parker said, "Let me talk to Haley!" but Sgro said Bill was on the phone with another caller. When Parker called back less than an hour later, Bill still wouldn't talk to him. "Haley said he'll tour Australia after Labor Day," Sgro told the Colonel. "Book him two or three other dates on the way back plus California and Las Vegas."

Colonel Parker replied, "Tell him to go down there now. $50,000 and plane fare. Five days work."

Bill's response was, "No. Tell him $75,000 plus two bookings on the way home."

After the third call, Parker gave up. Sgro figured Bill didn't like Colonel Parker because Elvis, under Parker's management, had deposed Bill as the King of Rock 'n' Roll. Nevertheless, Sgro shook his head in disbelief. Instead of going to Australia for $50,000 for a week's work, Bill and the Comets closed out the summer playing at Diamond Beach in Wildwood Crest, New Jersey, and lost money.

Decisions like that added to Sgro's problems as he struggled to make payroll during the band's long downward slide. Although he often had to issue the band members' checks late, Sgro did everything he could to make ends meet. He sold the band's bus and the company truck, and laid off a couple of the young women who worked in the office.

By late 1959, most singers who managed to become popular in America were clean-cut, modern-day crooners such as Bobby Darin, Paul Anka, Frankie Avalon, Bobby Rydell, and Guy Mitchell. A backlash against rock 'n' roll vocalists had taken hold, and an "instrumental rock" craze was in full swing. All record-buying teenagers wanted from music at the moment was a happening beat and a catchy riff to dance to such as the one in the Champs' "Tequila," an enormous 1958 hit. Duane Eddy, Johnny and the Hurricanes, the Ventures, and countless other bands also captured the imagination of America's youth with simple but catchy instrumental releases.

The Comets, masters of the instrumental genre, were desperate for another hit, so it was natural for them to go into the studio and finish out the obligations of their Decca contract by making an instrumental album of their own. Decca released the Comets album *Strictly Instrumental*, but Bill and Decca disagreed about the material to be recorded on it, and the album failed. With the band's Decca royalties shrinking dramatically, thirty-four-year-old Bill began negotiations for a contract with Warner Brothers Records.

He got it, but there were signs he was in no shape to record anything. While waiting in a fifteenth-floor Manhattan hotel room with Sgro one morning as the negotiations dragged on, Bill became despondent. He sat by the phone, picking up magazines and putting them down, unable to concentrate, then ordered a bottle of wine from room service around noon and started drinking. As the day wore on and nothing happened, Bill paced up and down, drinking straight from the bottle. When it was empty, he walked over and opened a window. Sgro, who was leafing through a magazine, looked out of the corner of his eye just in time to see Bill with one foot on the windowsill, leaning out at a terrifying angle. Bill stayed in that position for what seemed like half an hour, apparently waiting for Sgro to say or do something. Finally the phone rang, the caller told Sgro the contract had been granted, and Bill climbed down.

The next year, the Comets would record two singles and two LPs for Warner Brothers, and that company said it expected Haley's popularity "to spread even wider than it has to date." And indeed, one of the records the band recorded for Warner—"Skokiaan," their version of a song about drinking illegal liquor in Africa—became a hit in Europe and Australia, although not in the US.

Three

BILL MARRIES HIS THIRD WIFE AND BECOMES A MEXICAN POP STAR

28

Viva Haley!
Bill Plummets
in the US but
Rises in Mexico

A preacher was talking, a sermon he gave,
said every man's conscience is vile and depraved.
—FROM "MAN IN THE LONG BLACK COAT"
BY BOB DYLAN (1989)

Recording sessions for the Comets' first Warner Brothers album, *Bill Haley and His Comets*, got underway at Bell Sound Studios in New York City in early 1960. For this first album, Bill was asked to cover the top twelve rock 'n' roll songs of the fabulous '50s. They included "Blue Suede Shoes," "Whole Lotta Shakin' Goin' On," "Kansas City," "Stagger Lee," "Blueberry Hill," and remakes of three classic Comets hits: "Crazy Man, Crazy," "Shake, Rattle and Roll," and "Rock Around the Clock."

The band was busy throughout January and early February, returning to Bell Studios to record additional numbers for a second Warner album, *Haley's Juke Box*, that was scheduled for release that August. And on January 22, 1961, Warner Brothers released its first Comets single, "Tamiami," backed with "Candy Kisses" and supported by an advertisement in *Billboard*.

While Bill was struggling for a comeback, rock 'n' roll received a black eye on January 25, 1960, when Chuck Berry was indicted for violating the 1910 Mann Act in connection with an alleged incident in Kansas in 1958. Under that law, it was a felony to transport "any woman or girl for the purpose of prostitution or debauchery, or for any other

officially
it's Warner
Bros.
-JF
(I worked
there for 6
years)

153

immoral purpose" across state lines, and Berry was already under a 1959 indictment for another alleged violation of that law.

On January 26th, 1960, Bill and Cuppy's fifth and last child together, Scott Robert Haley, was born. Bill rushed Cuppy to Sacred Heart Hospital in her pink Cadillac, driving 70 m.p.h. on the narrow, winding back roads. He clutched the steering wheel so tightly he actually pulled it off. Sgro, riding in the back seat, screamed, "Put it back on!" which Bill did, but his reverence for Cadillacs was never quite the same after that.

By now, with the new baby about to arrive, the financial situation at home was close to desperate. Adding to the problem, reporters had heard a rumor that Bill and the Comets were broke. The 1959 $50,000 Warner Brothers advance hadn't gone far, but it did temporarily get the press off Bill's back. He'd requested the advance payment in four checks—three for $10,000 and one for $20,000—and instructed Sgro to hold onto them. Over the next two weeks, every time a reporter approached Bill about the rumor, Bill would turn to Sgro and say, "Tell him if we're broke. In fact, show him. Don't you have something in your pocket?" Sgro would produce the checks, fan them out, and say, "This is nothing. We get checks like this all the time!" Finally, Bill instructed Sam to deposit the checks.

The advance money was soon gone, however: the records the Comets had made for Warner Brothers weren't selling, and there were no royalty payments on the horizon to speak of yet. Meanwhile, in Washington, Congressional investigations of payola—the illegal practice of paying radio DJs to broadcast records—were picking up steam. And with Chuck Berry's highly publicized trial receiving mass publicity, another anti-rock 'n' roll backlash was building in the US.

In March, salvation arrived from the south, when the Comets were offered a series of performance dates in Mexico. With the exception of Louis Armstrong, very few American acts had appeared there before. Mexican promoters, however, having noticed Bill's popularity in South and Central America, thought he would be a tremendous draw in their country.

The band soon responded with their first Mexican performance tour. As well as performing live, they shot scenes for two films in Mexico during their stay. The first, *Jovenes y rebeldes* (Young and Rebellious), a Mexican version of *Blackboard Jungle*, tells the story of a young man who committed a crime and was sentenced to prison. After completing his term, he tries to guide a group of college students toward leading good lives. The Comets participated in the movie by lip-synching "Shake, Rattle and Roll" and "See You Later, Alligator" onscreen.

The second film, *Besito a Papa* (Kisses for Daddy), starring Mexican actress and singer Lola Beltran, was about a man trying to get approval for his wedding from his intended's parents. Inadvertently, he becomes involved in a scheme hatched by the greedy suitor of another woman. In this production, the Comets mimed their recordings of "Crazy Man, Crazy," and "Blue Suede Shoes."

The tour would have been a success if the Comets had stopped their excessive spending on the road. But they did not. Although money was needed at home, the band not only failed to send any back to the US but also stayed an extra ten days in Mexico after their initial one-week engagement ended, spending all they'd earned. Bill stayed even longer than the others and spent even more. It was the first time his attraction to Mexico and Mexicans became apparent.

For Bill's first night back at Melody Manor, Cuppy prepared one of his favorite meals, home-made spaghetti and meatballs. She lit candles on the dining room table, poured wine, turned the lights down low, and put on a Ray Charles LP as they sat down. The children were allowed to stay up late and eat with their parents, a rare treat. Normally they had dinner earlier, in the kitchen.

Bill drank his wine quickly and ate slowly, in silence, seemingly lost in thought. Joanie noticed, looked at Cuppy and asked, "Is Daddy okay? I think he's going to cry."

"Daddy's only tired, honey," Cuppy replied. "Remember he just got back from a long tour. He's fine. There's nothing to worry about." Bill managed a forced smile and told Joanie, whom he called Junebug, that Mommy was right.

After serving dessert, Cuppy ushered the children off to bed before rejoining Bill. As she sat down he said, "I want you to learn Spanish."

"Why?" she asked, surprised by the request.

"I've been thinking maybe I should move to Mexico," Bill said. "There's work for the band down there. Once I get established, I'll send for you and the kids. We can sell the house and buy a new house in Mexico."

Cuppy was stunned. "What are you saying?" she asked. "This is the first time you've mentioned any of this to me."

"I've been thinking about it for a while," Bill explained. "You know how rough it is out there." He acknowledged that his popularity in the US was fading and that it was taking a financial toll on him. Once it had been so easy: American fans couldn't get enough of the band. Nevertheless, he continued, they were still selling records in Europe and Australia, where "Skokiaan" was a big hit, and the fans in Mexico loved the band.

Refilling his wine glass, Bill explained that he was making good connections in Mexico and meeting influential people who could help him. With all the money troubles at home, however, it was getting hard to pay the band, and maybe it was time he went off on his own. Not that the band wouldn't still be together, but when they didn't have any gigs, he could live in Mexico and make some good deals that would benefit everyone.

Bill said he felt he was torn in two living in Pennsylvania, with the IRS still breathing down his neck about unpaid taxes and enormous bills continuing to arrive. Blaming managers and agents for the situation, he said, "You have to understand that a man has to do what he has to do to take care of his family." He lit a cigarette and blew a cloud of smoke toward the chandelier.

Cuppy sipped her wine, but now it tasted bitter. "What's going on?" she thought, wondering why he would want to leave his family behind and live alone in a strange country, even if it was going to be temporary.

Crumpling his cigarette pack, Bill said they'd talk about the subject later; he had to go get more cigarettes. He rose from the table and reached for his jacket. Taking the car keys out of his pocket, he gave Cuppy a slight hug with a disingenuous smile, the one he used with strangers. She walked him to the door and threw her arms around him.

"Be careful," Cuppy said, but Bill gently pushed her away.

"Oh, I always am. You know that," he said, deflecting her attempt at intimacy. Cuppy stood in the doorway and watched Bill drive away, praying that he'd turn and look back at her. He didn't.

Cuppy told herself that Bill was tired and had a lot on his mind, but she also admitted to herself that things hadn't been great with them during the past year. He was showing almost no interest in his children or his home. And he didn't seem interested in her either.

A few days later, the subject of Mexico came up again. This time, when Bill said, "We can sell the house and buy a new house in Mexico," he added, "I know you would like it there once you got used to it."

Cuppy said it was something to think about. Hoping for the best while fearing the worst—that he really did not intend to take his family with him—she didn't confront Bill or question him, afraid of what the answer might be.

Meanwhile, Bill's friend, disk jockey Alan Freed, was having his own troubles. On May 20, 1960, during the congressional payola investigation, Freed was arrested in Los Angeles on charges of commercial bribery. Prosecutors alleged he'd received $30,650 "under the table" from six record companies for promoting their products. The charges were plea bargained down to a six-months suspended sentence and a $300 fine, but later Freed was indicted again for evading $47,920 in income taxes. He died from the effects of alcoholism in a Florida hospital in 1965 at age 43.

There were other ominous portents. Kids used to go crazy when the Comets appeared on *American Bandstand,* but the last time the Comets performed on the show, on April 16, 1960, one of the Comets noticed the bored, gum-chewing youngsters in the audience. They were forcing smiles for the camera while rolling their eyes and mechanically clapping to the beat, obviously waiting for the song to end. That same month, Elvis Presley, who'd returned stateside in March, scored another No. 1 hit with "Stuck on You."

Moreover, after another Comets show in Toronto, which had always been a great town for Bill and the band, he was escorted as usual by four police officers as he left the venue to protect him from being mobbed. Not a single fan approached Bill for his autograph, however, or even tried to get near him. It was over. A few of the band members began quitting. The partners replaced them with Chester, PA-area musicians, brought them up to speed on the Comets' repertoire, and resolved to press on.

There were other troubling signs that the Comets' heyday in America was nearing an end. In July and August, Warner Brothers released its third Bill Haley single, "Let the Good Times Roll/So Right Tonight," and the album *Haley's Juke Box: Songs of the Bill Haley Generation.* Sales of both were dismal. The band left Warner Brothers and announced they would soon be recording for Gone Records, originally Real Gone Records, a much smaller company that was owned by alleged mob associate George Goldner.

Not long afterward, Elvis scored another No. 1 hit with "It's Now or Never," and Fats Domino charted at No. 4 four with "Walkin' to New Orleans." Finally, a new dance craze swept the US in September when Chubby Checker knocked Elvis out of the No. 1 spot with his rendition of the Hank Ballard tune "The Twist."

The Comets remained popular abroad, however, and soon they embarked on another Central and South American tour, visiting nine cities in Chile and continuing on to Ecuador, Peru, and the Dominican Republic. In marked contrast to the receptions they'd been receiving in North America, they drew enthusiastic crowds at shows, and throngs of fans greeted them at every airport. When the band arrived at Corpac Airport in Lima on November 20, Bill was caught in a mob of frenzied fans and lost his hat, his wallet containing $300 and other personal items. Back in the US, Elvis reached the No. 1 spot yet again in 1960 with his latest song, "Are You Lonesome Tonight?"

The Christmas and New Year's holidays at home didn't provide much cause for celebration. Bill went through the motions with Cuppy and the kids, but the joy of the season was absent.

29

Bill Finds the Third Love of His Life South of the Border

After the holidays, Bill and the band were off again, this time back to Mexico in 1961 for what was to be a two-week tour. Once again, their reception and popularity were so strong that they stretched the tour to three months, remaining in Mexico until April.

In early February the band worked with the Caravan Corona Extra, a vaudevillian troupe that travelled throughout Mexico on two double-decker buses. That's when Bill first saw Martha Velasco, a Mexican chorus girl working as a singer and dancer with the show who would soon shatter his life as a family man.

Their meeting took place on February 9, 1961, when Bill boarded the bus in Monterrey, Mexico, on the way to the Comets' first show with Martha's troupe in Reynosa. He was three hours late, and the bus had been waiting for him. When he sat down next to Rudy Pompilli, Bill was hung over and hiding behind a pair of dark sunglasses with a fedora hat pulled down low on his head. Martha was on the bus, chatting, laughing, and irritating the hell out of Bill, who turned to Rudy and asked, "How do you say 'Shut up, broad' in Spanish?"

As it turned out, Martha had been hired to sing with Bill on the tour and to prepare dance routines to accompany "ABC Boogie" and "Rock Around the Clock." Bill found this out after Martha walked by wearing a sparkling leotard at a rehearsal the next day. He asked Rudy, "Who's that?" That evening Bill and Martha had dinner together, and before long, they fell in love. Years later, Martha told *Texas Monthly* magazine that when she first met Bill, even though she and her fellow chorus girls had been waiting three hours in the heat for him to show up, "It was love at first sight."

According to her son Pedro, Martha had started to sing and dance in Mexican night clubs and supper clubs when she was seventeen. Born in the town of Villaflores in the southern Mexican state of Chiapas, she'd moved to Mexico City with her parents and siblings in the 1940s. Two of her brothers played the guitar, and her sisters sang and harmonized.

When Bill took up with Martha, the band members were surprised. They'd always been besieged by female followers, but before Bill's dalliance with Dani, they'd perceived him as a devoted family man who didn't tolerate fooling around. The ban he'd imposed on drinking and cavorting by the group was long gone, but it still seemed out of character for Bill to openly start a relationship with a woman he'd met on the road.

By now, Bill's excessive drinking was also on display for everyone to see, and the mean and nasty side of his personality became more and more evident. Martha became aware of Bill's drinking problem, but by then, "It was either sink or swim," she said later. "I chose to swim."

In Vera Cruz, it was fiesta time when the band arrived, and all the streets were jam-packed. The band played two shows nightly there as at least fifty thousand people crowded the city square.

In early April 1961, while Bill stayed behind in Mexico with Martha, the other band members returned home to find that Elvis Presley had yet another No. 1 hit, "Surrender." They also were appalled to learn that the band owed $17,000 to the IRS plus thousands of dollars in back commissions to agents, and that claims for payment from numerous other creditors were flooding in daily. Still impressed by their own international popularity, they'd continued to spend lavishly on the road and didn't have enough money left over to pay these debts.

This time around, the IRS had gone so far as to open a Chester, Pennsylvania, office near the Comets' location and station a federal tax agent there who'd been trying to meet with Bill and the partners. Sam Sgro would go there once or twice a day, trying to keep the agency appeased until the partners came back with some money. Sgro had set up a meeting with the tax agent three times so far, and all three times Bill had failed to appear.

Again and again, without success, Sgro tried to convince Bill to come back to the office to deal with the band's financial problems. But one of the reasons Bill stayed in Mexico was all the people hounding him for money in the US. When the band came back without Bill, and without any cash, Sgro was at his wits' end.

Bill called Sgro every day or every other day during this period. "How's Cuppy?" he would ask. "How are the children?"

Sgro would answer, "What's the use of telling you anything? If you want to know, come on back." About the fifth time Bill called, Sam said, "Bill, this is it. If you're not back here at nine o'clock tomorrow morning when I open the office, I'm closing up and going home."

Bill didn't show up at 9 a.m. or anytime that day, so Sgro closed the office for the final time at 5 p.m. and resigned his position with the band. He needed a visit to the doctor and a long rest.

30

The Night of
the Knife

With the IRS breathing down their necks, the Comets took whatever work they could get in the United States. Bill finally returned from Mexico in May 1961 and spent his days at his office in Chester. He spent much of his time there on the phone talking to Martha. At home, he went through the motions of being a husband and father, but he argued frequently with Cuppy and would slip into the library next to the dining room to call Martha in the evenings. Cuppy could hear him through the closed door, speaking softly in broken Spanish, and although she didn't understand Bill's words, she could hear the affection in his voice. More and more often, he would drink heavily in the evenings. Cuppy realized to her dismay that the progress they'd made in their relationship over the past year was all for naught.

Bill became angry and tense at home. He was quick to take off his belt and use it as a strap to discipline the boys, who were often unruly. Joanie would cringe in her bedroom as she heard her brothers' cries, feeling helpless and unable to intervene. While his father had been absent in Mexico, little Billy had found a box of Christmas light bulbs stored in the garage, brought them up to the house and thrown them, one by one, against the stucco wall, excited by the popping sound they made. He'd smashed the windows on a door to the garage with a croquet mallet too, making Bill even more furious.

Reflecting the tense, confrontational mood of their parents, Billy and Jimmy often would fight when Bill Sr. was away. At one point, Jimmy hit Billy in the head with a garden rake, drawing blood and prompting a visit to the doctor's office. Billy retaliated by pushing a playground teeter-totter set onto Jimmy, hitting him in the head, which resulted in an emergency visit to the hospital and stitches. Often unsupervised, Billy would wander the grounds alone, spending countless hours playing in the woods or the creek, running through the property and engaging in his favorite pastime, catching and releasing frogs.

Despite the Comets' financial struggle, there were still occasional gatherings and parties with band members and their families at Bill's house. Bill would try to play the role of loving husband and father, but the signs of his growing disinterest in his family were apparent. Cuppy was troubled that Bill, who'd always been so proud of his sons, didn't pay any attention at all to his newest son, Scott, who looked just like his father. One weekend evening, when there were people downstairs in the den and baby Scottie was upstairs crying his eyes out, Cuppy went to calm him. She brought him downstairs to say goodnight to his father, and when she placed him in Bill's arms, Bill recoiled. He finally took the baby, but that was the only time Cuppy ever saw Bill hold Scott.

That summer, while the family stayed in Stone Harbor and the band worked mostly at the small clubs on the Jersey Shore, little Billy often tried to get his dad to tie his shoes. Bill would snarl at him to get away; only Joanie, it seemed, could gain her father's affection. Cuppy often felt like she was walking on eggshells around Bill, but there was little she could do except try to be a loving mother and a good wife, and put on a good face when they were around other people. When Cuppy had first learned that she was pregnant with Scottie, it had been a surprise, but both she and Bill had resolved to recommit to their relationship and focus on creating a good life for their children. Bill's enthusiasm had quickly faded, however, and now he was distant and noncommunicative again.

In September 1961, Bill went back to Mexico to make records, perform, and be with Martha. There, the band began recording for the Mexican record labels Orfeon and Dimsa as "Bill Haley y Sus Cometas."

Almost immediately, Bill Haley y Sus Cometas produced a regional hit, "Twist Español." By that time, the Twist had become the most popular dance in North America, and "Twist Español," a Spanish-language recording, helped spread that craze into Mexico. The record was so popular that the band followed up with what would become the biggest-selling single in Mexican history to that date, "Florida Twist." Oddly, the song wasn't written by a Mexican but by Anthony Caruso, who owned the Caruso Music Store in Chester, Pennsylvania.

Because Chubby Checker and Hank Ballard, who'd started the Twist craze in the US, were little known south of the border, Bill Haley y Sus Cometas soon were proclaimed "Kings of the Twist" in Latin America. They appeared often on the Mexican TV series *Orfeon a Go-Go*. Bill revived vocalist Joe Turner's career by bringing him to Orfeon, and the two became even closer friends. (Turner had recorded Charles Calhoun's "Shake, Rattle and Roll" before Bill and the Comets had recorded their more popular version of the song, but he had quit popular music and was singing with small jazz combos before Bill brought him to Mexico.) The Comets eventually recorded a total of about one hundred songs in Mexico, most of them instrumentals, but others straight vocal and rock 'n' roll versions of traditional Mexican tunes. In April 1962, four of their songs were simultaneously at the top of the Mexican pop chart: "Caravan Twist" at No. 2, "Florida Twist" at No. 3, "Twist Español" at No. 9, and "La Paloma" at No. 12. Bill sang in Spanish, with Martha translating. She sometimes stood with him in the recording studio.

In spite of their success in Mexico, Bill and the Comets received very little financial return from the Orfeon label recordings. Eventually they had a falling out with the company. Nevertheless, the recordings got them bookings, and helped them earn performance fees that enabled them to live comfortably on the road. Back in Chester, Jim Ferguson and Jack Howard continued to manage the office and hold off creditors.

For nine years, Bill and Cuppy had spent every Christmas together. It was their favorite time of year, and no matter what, Bill had always made sure he was home to spend the holiday with his family. In 1961, however, he stayed behind when the Comets returned to Pennsylvania to be with their families. Cuppy learned that the other Comets were home from talking with their wives. When she asked them where Bill was, she got vague responses, such as that he was doing interviews or attending business-related meetings. This hurt, because the guys in the band were her friends, like big brothers, and their wives and children were like family. Every year, they all spent the winter holidays at Bill's house, trimming a Christmas tree, and on the Fourth of July, they had group barbecues out by the patio. Although she'd traveled all over the country and to parts of Europe with them, now they were mostly avoiding her.

Finally, on December 23, 1961, Bill called Cuppy and said he couldn't get out of Mexico. It had snowed in Pennsylvania, and he said too many flights there were canceled. Cuppy told Bill to keep trying. She recalled that he'd never accepted holiday bookings before, especially on Christmas and Thanksgiving.

On Christmas Eve, Cuppy and her mother, Sadie, made a fire in the living room fireplace at Melody Manor and sat there in silence. "In the past Bill would have done whatever he could to get home," Cuppy thought to herself. "The snow is just an excuse. He's with someone else."

After the holidays, Bill came back from Mexico to find Chubby Checker's "The Twist" at the top of the charts again and Elvis there also, with "Can't Help Falling in Love." Bill's business and personal lives both were now in shambles. In love with Martha, he fretted about how he was going to tell Cuppy goodbye, but they never talked about it. Meanwhile, he drank constantly, often becoming verbally abusive and blaming everybody else for his troubles. Cuppy started feeling more and more trapped in their failing relationship and nosediving business.

The other band members told Cuppy that while they'd been on the road, Bill had started to become violent. He smashed things and blamed everybody but himself for problems that arose. Soon he started behaving that way at home. The couple's usual routine was to have dinner with the kids, when everything would be all right. After putting the children to bed, they'd go downstairs to the den to watch television. Predictably, Bill would get drunk at this point and pick a fight. He'd say awful things, blame others for his loss of popularity, and drink even more, reaching a point where he would hallucinate. Sometimes Bill didn't even know that he was speaking to his wife; she became whomever he was angry at at that moment. He was out of his mind, Cuppy thought. He threw ashtrays and other objects at the walls, and was nasty and completely out of control.

One dreadfully bad night, Bill was in an especially vicious frame of mind, and it was as though a switch flipped in his brain. He and Cuppy argued, he went to their bedroom, and Cuppy, relieved, thought he'd gone to bed for the night. She was in the kitchen getting coffee when she heard him bellowing at her from the other room. She was shocked because she thought he'd passed out.

Suddenly Bill staggered into the kitchen and grabbed a carving knife from a drawer, still arguing and apparently not even recognizing her. Looking right at her, he said, "And you, you son of a bitch! This is what you did to me!" (It's possible Bill was remembering the Jack Palance movie *The Big Knife*, a tale of blackmail and infidelity he and Cuppy had seen a few years previously.) For the first time in their relationship, Cuppy feared for her life. In her terror, she realized that no matter what she did, Bill wasn't listening to her. She thought, "If I don't run, he's going to kill me."

It was too late. Bill approached her, grabbed her by the shoulder, and held the point of the blade up to her throat. Looking right at her, he said, seething, "I'll get even with you, you son of a bitch, for what you did to me." Instinctively, she said, "Who's going to take care of your kids? Are you going to take care of them?"

Puzzled, Bill said, "What?" He backed off, and as he did, Cuppy kicked him in the groin. Bill staggered back, drunk and disoriented. He dropped the knife, and Cuppy ran past him into Joanie's bedroom. There was a telephone there she knew she could use to call for help if necessary. Bill didn't try to come in, and Cuppy stayed in the locked bedroom until dawn. When she finally crept out, Bill was lying across the bed in their own room, face down. He had passed out.

When Bill woke up the next morning he came into the kitchen, where Cuppy was making breakfast. She told him what had happened, and he said he'd blacked out and didn't remember any of it. When he learned what he'd done, he was ashamed and remorseful. Embracing his wife, he looked in her eyes and said, sobbing, "My God, Cuppy. No wonder you're afraid of me. I have never been so ashamed in my life!"

"I was scared to death you would have killed me," Cuppy replied, and Bill knew she was telling the truth. Although he'd never previously been physically abusive toward Cuppy, he was now drinking to the point of temporary insanity.

Bill's business empire was crumbling, and the pressure was getting to him. Creditors lurked around every corner, and his cars, his biggest indulgence, had been repossessed. When he'd hit it big with Decca, he'd owned three or four automobiles at a time, trading them in for new models every year. The cars were always top of the line and loaded with every accessory, except air conditioning, which Bill always refused because it gave him a sore throat. He'd bought Cuppy a maroon and white T-bird, and several Cadillacs and a Lincoln Mark III for himself, along with a state-of-the-art Ford convertible that he loved, even though its automatic roof never opened right. Now, except for Cuppy's T-bird, the cars were all gone.

Bill and Cuppy were even losing their phone service at home because they couldn't pay their bills. A sympathetic agent at Bell Telephone had allowed Cuppy to keep one working phone line, however, in the one bedroom she'd locked herself into the night Bill scared her so badly.

After previous tours, Bill had retreated for sanctuary to the band's office building in Chester. Now creditors hounded him there, and he lost that sanctuary as well. He'd make excuses and go anywhere but home. When the Comets had a job that required them to travel, he'd go with them, but he often stayed behind when the band returned home.

Cuppy spent Valentine's Day 1962 alone while Bill and the Comets appeared in Milwaukee for a "Valentine Celebration" at William Block's

Cosmopolitan Club. A while later, she drove to New York to be with Bill for one of his appearances there, and she used the opportunity to try one more time to see if he had any feelings left for her. Even now, with everything that had happened, Cuppy thought that, somehow, Bill still cared.

At the Roundtable Nightclub in Manhattan, where Bill and the Comets were performing, Cuppy wore an attractive, sexy new dress. The band was playing, and a handsome man, a professional dancer who was appearing there, asked her to dance. She obliged, to see if Bill would be jealous, and when it didn't seem to bother her husband at all, it became clear to her that it was all over between them. In the past, he had always been extremely jealous of any attention she received from other men, the cause of many of their arguments.

A few months after the knife-wielding incident, the marriage effectively ended. Bill was under immense pressure from all sides. In June, he told Cuppy he was going on a promotional tour to Rome, New York, but once again, everybody in the band came home except him. Band members couldn't even look at her when they said, "He's staying for additional promotion."

Finally Bill called, and predictably, they had a terrible argument over the phone. He was saying he couldn't come home because he had to see disk jockeys, but Cuppy knew he was making excuses. Frustrated and angry, she slammed down her one remaining telephone and thought to herself, "That's the end. He's not going to call anymore." And he didn't.

In fact, Bill never came home again. Leaving behind most of his clothes, all his gold records and trophies, and everything else he owned, he went to Mexico and showed up at Martha's door. "Here I am, with my guitar, my suitcase, and my ass," he said. Martha let him in.

Cuppy was devastated. As the reality of what had happened sank in over the next couple of days she was on the verge of a nervous breakdown. Totally despondent, she couldn't even try to explain what was going on to the children. In the dining room, there was a hi-fi phonograph player where she and Bill had played Ray Charles records all the time. One of their favorites was, "I Can't Stop Loving You." Cuppy sat in the dining room playing those records, and that song, over and over. Joanie climbed into the cabinet where all the albums were, closed the door, and hid, crying because she didn't understand what was happening and nobody would tell her. Her father was gone, and her mother was walking around in a daze.

Barely nine years old when Bill left, Joanie loved her father. He used to tell her she was the most important person in the whole wide world to him. He'd sing her the song "You Are My Special Angel," and she believed him. He'd taken her to toy stores, riding on his shoulders, and let her pick out anything she wanted.

When Joanie was in first grade at the Francis Harvey Green Elementary School, across Bethel Road from Melody Manor, older girls had liked to walk her home. She'd thought at the time, "Oh boy, they like me." But at the edge of the Haley's property line, the girls had lifted her up over the fence, listened to the band practicing in the garage, and said, "Go get your dad."

Eager to please, Joanie had run into the garage, and right in the middle of practice, Bill had put his guitar down, taken Joanie by the hand, walked out to the fence with her, and met the girls. Joanie'd thought he'd done it for her, and that he was the most wonderful father in the world. Now she was left to wonder, "How could you be everything to somebody and then be nothing?"

Cuppy, on the other hand, wasn't surprised that Bill would flee to Mexico. He was trying to recreate the life he'd once had in the US, while the good times had lasted. "They make a big deal out of me," she remembered him saying after the first trip to Mexico, when he first talked to her about moving, "I'm a big star in Mexico. Everybody rushes after me and wants my autograph. . . . They really make me feel good. Like I'm really somebody."

31
Bill Haley: Business Failure

By the time Bill left Cuppy and moved to Mexico, misdirected investments and overspending had doomed him financially, depriving him of the ability to support his first and second wives and the six surviving children he'd had with them.

Bill's decline in popularity was the main cause of his financial problems. In addition, his pal and business partner James "Lord Jim" Ferguson had advised Bill in the making of many serious financial mistakes. Unfortunately, Bill didn't begin rejecting his advice until all the projects Ferguson had recommended had gone south. Bill's major competitor, Elvis, was much luckier in his choice of Colonel Tom Parker as his own manager and business advisor.

Many of the bad investments that Lord Jim advised Bill to make were in businesses unrelated to music. In 1956, for instance, on Lord Jim's advice, Bill and the Comets spent $40,000 to buy a 25 percent share of a struggling company called Industrial Mechanics, a metal fabrication firm specializing in ductwork and urinals. It was owned by two friends of Lord Jim.

Against the advice of their accountant, Haley and the band, who knew nothing about manufacturing, bought out the two owners and hired them to run the business as salaried employees. When the accountant pointed out that the former owners had thus become valuable assets, the band also bought $50,000 life insurance policies on each of them. This arrangement might have resulted in a substantial payoff when, as it happened, one of the former owners of Industrial Mechanics passed away unexpectedly. When the Comets applied for the $50,000 insurance payout, however, the deceased former owner's wife sued the band in an unsuccessful attempt to get the money for herself. Then the government took $28,000 of the payout for itself to cover the Industrial Mechanics' unpaid payroll taxes. The company never made a profit and eventually plunged into bankruptcy. When the Comets tried to sell it, there were no takers, and the partners' entire investment was lost.

Making matters worse, Lord Jim also fancied himself a shrewd art investor and convinced the Comets to back him in that business. He'd been collecting paintings since 1943, when he was on duty with the Navy in Naples, Italy, and at one point his paintings, priced at thirty-five to sixty dollars apiece, hung in nearly fifty restaurants in Philadelphia, Baltimore, and towns on the Jersey Shore.

Before joining up with the Comets, Lord Jim had earned $400 to $600 per week from the revenue those paintings generated. That was partly because he'd frequently eat at one of the restaurants where they were hung, and if he saw that any had been sold, he'd deduct that amount from his bill.

Eventually Lord Jim hit a real jackpot. In 1955, three floors in the Town House restaurant at the Jersey Shore burned down, taking seventy of his paintings with them. After claiming that their value was eighty to ninety dollars each, he received a sixty-five hundred-dollar insurance payout, double what he would have made if he'd sold them.

Bill and the Comets weren't aware of these facts when Lord Jim, now their adviser, urged them to invest in his art business. They were also unaware that he had previously deceived artists and collectors who had given him paintings to sell on consignment. Eventually Lord Jim's deceptive practices led to a private warrant being issued against him on charges of larceny and fraudulent conversion: Edna Gabriel, an artist who'd given him eighteen of her oil paintings to sell on consignment, charged him with failing to return the painting, which she valued at $2,000. At first Lord Jim told her he would make full payment, before sending her a letter saying that he'd been ill and would pay her when he was able.

The Haley-Ferguson art partnership had started out fairly well. In July 1958 an exhibition of their collection was held at the Cape May Theater in Cape May, New Jersey. It was moderately successful. Next, Lord Jim convinced Bill and the partners to buy a run-down building for $7,000 dollars, pay another $7,000 to renovate it, and open it as the Bill Haley and Lord Jim Art Gallery in Booths Corner, Pennsylvania. Using the band's money, he then acquired more than one thousand canvases by unknown artists from ten countries, plus some by the better-known Austrian painters Lily Spandorf and Walter Hessler. Lord Jim told Bill that the art would increase in value over time and provide them both with retirement income. Comets staffers and others spent many evenings in Booths Corner stretching and framing canvases and otherwise preparing for the opening, but the paintings were slow to sell.

When the band toured Europe in 1958, Lord Jim showed that he still hadn't learned much. He spent $50,000 buying even more European art with money he'd borrowed from their Paris hotel in Bill's name. When Haley found out, he sent Jim home with instructions to sell all the paintings immediately and then wire the $50,000 to the hotel before the tour concluded.

Things got worse. Unable to unload the paintings, Lord Jim took out a "short-term" loan that had long-term consequences from some questionable characters. For instance, as a condition of the loan, the band had to perform periodically for union scale in certain clubs in Las Vegas and elsewhere well into the 1960s.

At the end of March 1962, as part of their obligation to work off the debt, the Comets played their own array of "twist" tunes during an eleven-day stint at the Roundtable Nightclub in New York City. It was owned by Morris Levy, a member of the Genovese crime family. The tunes were honed from their Mexican set list, and included "Florida Twist," "Caravan Twist," and even "Lullaby of Birdland Twist." As the co-owner of the Roulette Records label with George Goldner, Levy recorded and released a live LP of the Comets Roundtable show.

Levy was convicted of conspiring to extort in December 1988 by a federal jury in Camden, New Jersey, but died in 1990 before he could begin his prison sentence. Known as "Moishe" by his crime family associates, Levy was the inspiration for the character Herman "Hesh" Rabkin on the hit HBO series *The Sopranos*.

Lord Jim didn't restrict his investments to art. When the band toured Australia, he spent a considerable portion of its proceeds on Australian opals that he hoped to resell for a profit. That investment that never yielded any return. Worse still, he was known as a gambler. Band members had reason to be suspicious when he claimed that he'd lost his entire bankroll to a pickpocket in Buenos Aires while the band was touring there. Jim said the thief had escaped with the proceeds from two weeks of appearances that he'd planned to wire home.

Lord Jim Ferguson, who died in 1969, wasn't the only sketchy spender Bill hired. At the height of his popularity, Bill Haley employed accountant to help with the Comets' business affairs while the band was on the road. Following their lengthy nationwide tour in 1956, however, the band members returned to Chester and discovered that at least $50,000 was missing.

The Comets also made some bad business decisions by themselves with little or no input from either Ferguson or the accountant. One such decision was spending too much buying and extensively renovating a permanent business headquarters. In 1956, they purchased a three-story stone house in Chester, Pennsylvania, and paid large sums to renovate it into offices and a music publishing house with a recording studio in the basement.

The buildings' optics were as ill-considered as its cost. Its top floor housed Bill's large office in the front, with his desk perched on a raised platform. The platform had been there when the house was purchased, but having Bill's desk there looked pompous. Two other band members also had private offices in the building. Later, as their musical fortunes declined, the Comets were forced to rent out the first and second floors of this building and move their own operations to the third floor. Eventually they sold the entire building, losing most of what they'd invested in it.

By mid-1958, the Comets had finally maxed out their credit line with the bank. Reluctantly, Bill agreed to take out mortgages on his own home, Melody Manor, to support the band. He believed that proceeds from their upcoming European tour, as well as royalties, would put the organization back on a firm financial footing soon, but that didn't happen.

In addition to all their other attempts to raise money in the late 1950s, the Comets tried to produce revenue by booking other artists into clubs and theaters. Starting in 1957, they signed and promoted over thirty talented but relatively unknown artists, but they never made any money on them.

Various Comets also tried to make money by writing and recording songs for other labels, in violation of the contracts they had signed with the labels producing their records. Under various pseudonyms—the Highlighters, the Kingsmen, the Lifeguards, the Scottsmen, the Merrimen, and the Greenlights—they wrote and recorded for the Arcade label, the Atlantic subsidiary East/West, and Casablanca/ABC. But these ventures didn't make any money either.

The Comets not only failed to profit while their popularity declined, but also continued to spend lavishly on tour. During 1957, after taking the now-customary month off for fun and fishing at the Jersey shore, they embarked on a seven-week tour of forty-nine American cities. The venues and receipts were smaller than during their earlier tours, but the band still went first class. They lived it up on the road, spending freely and gambling often, and returned home with jewelry and other expensive items they'd purchased. Most of the cash from this tour never made it back to the office. The Comets received some advances, but the big Decca checks came in only twice a year, and because the band's operations in the US needed cash every day to keep things running, they constantly borrowed from the Fidelity Trust Company.

For a long time after the South American tour, band staffer Sgro frequently butted heads with Johnny Grande, who was the main collector for the band on the road. "Where's the money?" Sgro would ask when Grande handed over only a few hundred dollars, or worse yet, returned empty handed from jobs. "Bill's got it," Grande would usually reply. Sgro would then go directly to Bill and Lord Jim, and they'd say, "Grande's got the money." That led Sgro to believe the Comets were spending all their income on the road but didn't want to tell him. The expectation was that Sgro would keep covering office and business expenses by borrowing against Decca royalty checks and spending the remaining residuals from the movies in which the band had participated.

The Comets' planned 1958 European tour marked the first time the partners had taken a booking of this magnitude without getting any money in advance. They were paid while on the tour, but they spent every penny they received staying in the best hotels and eating in the best restaurants. Sgro was miffed about the band's failure to send or bring any cash back from this European tour but made sure he borrowed enough from the bank to pay the band members' wives, who would come to the office to collect their husbands' checks.

Things got worse. When Bill and the Comets went on their next tour, to Mexico, they found that country so enjoyable they failed to wire any money home, and they stayed an extra ten days after the initial one-week engagement ended, spending all their earnings.

The organization's corporate income tax balance due on April 15, 1958, was $2,575, which Sgro paid. The Comets' accountant informed the partners, however, that some of the taxes that were supposed to have been deposited from monies collected on the road had never been paid. As a result, they were faced with a $59,000 bill for back taxes. Sgro was able to secure a $60,000 loan from the band's recording company, Decca Records, after driving to New York with Johnny Grande and Billy Williamson and obtaining a letter from the Decca treasurer stating that the Comets' next royalty check would cover that amount. Sgro believed the accountant knew the partners would have to borrow the money, and suspected that he'd split a $2,000 kickback on the interest fee with a bank vice president he was working with. The scheme later came to light when the executive was transferred to another branch.

Bill also had lost a big opportunity to mend the band's finances in 1957 when he turned down a potentially lucrative merchandising offer after being misguided once again by Lord Jim Ferguson. Lord Jim took a call one afternoon that year from Harlem Globetrotters' owner Hank "Abe" Saperstein, a seasoned merchandiser and shrewd businessman. He owned the marketing rights to the Lone Ranger, Wyatt Earp, and Lassie through his company Special Projects, Inc.

The previous August, Saperstein had cut a deal with Colonel Tom Parker to franchise the Elvis Presley name to merchandisers. He told Lord Jim on this call that within six months, merchants had paid him twenty-six million dollars for that privilege. According to Saperstein, Elvis and the Colonel's cut had ranged from 4 to 11 percent, depending on the merchandise. He offered Lord Jim a similar deal for Bill Haley.

Lord Jim looked over at Comets' drummer Ralph Jones, sitting nearby, and smirked. "I'll talk it over with Haley and get back to you," he said, hanging up and calling Bill in his upstairs office. Derisively describing Saperstein's proposal, he reminded Bill that they'd made similar merchandising deals in Australia and England and had been paid nothing. He then shouted, "Fuck that, Bill, we'll do it ourselves and make 100 percent." As usual, Bill let Lord Jim do what he wanted.

The next day, Lord Jim called Ward Advertising in Wilmington, Delaware, and ordered one thousand eight-inch square, clear glass ashtrays. "Bill Haley and His Comets" was to be embossed in yellow in the base of the tray, as well as four Comets song titles, one on each angled side: "Rock Around the Clock," "Shake, Rattle and Roll," "See You Later, Alligator," and "Crazy Man, Crazy." The ashtrays might have made great collectibles, but Lord Jim had no idea how to market them. Eventually the ashtrays were shipped free to disc jockeys across the country as a promotional gimmick, meaning that the cost of producing them, and any potential profits from selling them, were lost.

Other bad hires plagued the Comets' profits. The band's booking agent caused numerous problems because he refused to split commissions with other promoters who presented him with opportunities for band tours and engagements. He insisted on booking everything himself directly and earning 100 percent of the commissions. His greed almost prevented the Comets from taking a profitable tour of South America they were offered by Brazil's largest promoter, Paulinho Machado de Carvalho. De Carvalho's agent, Donald Ames, unable to book the Comets for a tour by working through the agent, showed up at a Comets appearance and talked directly with Bill's handlers. His offer—$75,000, including $35,000 up front, plus $14,000 worth of plane tickets and hotel rooms for a twenty-seven-day trip—was accepted, but the agent was infuriated that he didn't get his cut. His avarice undoubtedly caused the band to miss other opportunities.

The agent-client relationship was so bad that when promoter Walter Hofer called Sgro to try to arrange a Comets tour of Mexico, Sgro decided to avoid routing the request through the booking agent, which would have derailed the idea. Instead he drove up to New York to meet Hofer himself. He didn't tell the agent anything until the deal was signed, sealed, and almost delivered. Then Sgro went to him and successfully insisted that he write up a contract for the Mexican tour. This action by Sgro, and others by the Comets, infuriated the booking agent so much that when the Comets' four-year contract with his agency expired and they wouldn't re-sign with him, he filed suit against the band, seeking $100,000 in damages.

The suit was dismissed in early April 1958, but the agent cooked up a scheme with a friend of Bill's to get his old client back. The friend asked Bill to come up to New York to talk about doing some shows at Coney Island. Sgro went with him, and the three of them were having dinner in a restaurant when the booking agent walked in. Sgro said, "Come on Bill, let's get out of here. Quick."

Instead, Bill sat down with him and talked about the good old days and about letting bygones be bygones. The booking agent said he could get them TV commercials and lucrative gigs in Las Vegas and Hawaii. Bill believed every word, and he agreed to sign a new contract with the agency. Nothing had changed, however. Opportunities were missed again because he was not willing to share commissions with other agencies that offered jobs to the band, and the offering agencies refused to split their commissions with him.

Eventually, other band staffers caught on. According to a letter from Ferguson to the agent in September 1959:

> Although you have called us for many jobs, such as Chicago Theater, Asbury Park, Atlantic City, Jamaica, etc., you never came through with any work, even though you had us wire you acceptance. . . . You offered us Las Vegas, Moulin Rouge in California and also Honolulu. We accepted those places to work in but you never came back with a contract.

> . . . We could never locate you for days when you went
> to Canada, Washington and Chicago with your acts. The
> many times we phoned you all we got was a lot of double
> talk, stalling and lies.

Bill's generosity with band staffers and his refusal to fire people also hurt the band financially. At the height of the organization's popularity, there were seventy-five individuals on the payroll, many of whom contributed little or nothing of value. They'd been hired by Bill because he bought their sob story or liked something about them. Meeting payroll, however, was a matter of pride to Bill, and he made sure everyone else received their full salary before he was paid. Over the years, Sgro sometimes gave Bill a salary check for Bill himself that was so low Sgro didn't know how Bill ever paid his bills and bought groceries.

Because the Comets always had had a strong following in the Wildwoods area of New Jersey, in July 1959, Ferguson made a deal for the Comets to rent the Bayberry Room at Diamond Beach Lodge, work in it, and split the profits with the property owners.

On July 6, 1959, Bill's thirty-fourth birthday, he and Lord Jim drove Sgro down to see the place, and waited until they arrived to tell him that he was going to manage the enterprise. Taken by surprise, Sgro said, "Jim, what's going on here? I'm not going to run this place. I had enough of nightclubs. I don't want any part of it!"

Lord Jim ignored his response. They spent the entire afternoon in the vacant building with one of the property owners. Windows were broken and there was ankle-deep sand in the main room. Knowing their financial situation, Sgro was worried about how they were going to fix it up and where they were going to get chairs, tables, and liquor. The owner was giving Sgro evasive answers, but Bill and Lord Jim said, "That's okay, Sam. We'll do it. We'll take care of it."

Sgro had his hands full with the day-to-day headaches of running the organization from Chester, Pennsylvania. He said he could not afford to be away from the office, but Bill and Jim ignored his protests. Frustrated, Sgro went outside to wait while Bill, Jim, and the owner remained in the building, making plans, until dark. Finally they came out to Bill's pink Cadillac. Sgro was waiting for them in the front passenger seat. Right away, Bill started telling Sgro how he should run the club. Angrily, Sgro said, "Run what!?"

"We signed on," Bill said, as they started driving back to Chester. "We're going to come in here in five days. We're going to clean it all out

Bill Haley in his dressing
room on tour, 1956.
Photo Credit: Bill Haley Jr. Collection.

Bill relaxing at home, 1956.
Photo Credit: Bill Haley Jr. Collection.

Bill Haley polishing trophy case in basement den at Melody Manor, 1956.
Photo Credit: Bill Haley Jr. Collection.

Bill and Lord Jim Ferguson in the basement den at Melody Manor, 1956.
Photo Credit: Bill Haley Jr. Collection.

Lord Jim Ferguson with Joanie in the basement den at Melody Manor, 1956.
Photo Credit: Bill Haley Jr. Collection.

Bill with Joanie on the front steps at Melody Manor, 1956.
Photo Credit: Bill Haley Jr. Collection.

Bill throwing darts in the basement den at Melody Manor, 1956.
Photo Credit: Bill Haley Jr. Collection.

Bill polishing his Cadillac in front of Melody Manor
with Lord Jim Ferguson looking on, 1956.
Photo Credit: Bill Haley Jr. Collection.

The Comets at Steel Pier, Atlantic City, 1956.
Photo Credit: Bill Haley Jr. Collection.

The Comets at Steel Pier, Atlantic City, 1956.
Photo Credit: Bill Haley Jr. Collection.

A party in the basement den at Melody Manor, 1956. (l. to r.) Jolly Joyce, Bill Haley, Bob Hayes, Jimmy Lynn, Johnny Grande, Lord Jim Ferguson, Smiles Joyce.
Photo Credit: Bill Haley Jr. Collection.

Lord Jim Ferguson and Bill Haley in front of a theater in Australia, January 1957.
Photo Credit: Bill Haley Jr. Collection.

Bill on vacation, Skyline Drive in
North Carolina, September 1957.
Photo Credit: Bill Haley Jr. Collection.

Bill with Bill Jr., and Joanie at
Bill's office in Chester, PA, 1958.
Photo Credit: Bill Haley Jr. Collection.

Bill and Cuppy's bedroom
at Melody Manor, 1960.
*Photo Credit: Bill Haley Jr.
Collection.*

Bill (white jacket) in the reception line after his Royal Variety Performance for
Queen Elizabeth II at the Theatre Royal in London, November 22, 1979.
Photo Credit: PA Images via Getty Images.

and we're going to run the place. We're going to bring the band here and we're going play for the summer."

Sgro retorted defiantly, "You might play there, but I'm not going to run it!"

Bill said, "You're going to run it!"

This went on for the next ten minutes, with Bill getting more and more angry and demanding while Sgro answered back in a belligerent tone. Finally, Lord Jim attempted to intervene, and the first thing Sgro knew, Bill slammed on the brakes while driving at 80 m.p.h., and they all lunged forward as the car screeched to a halt on a desolate stretch of road.

"Get out!" Bill hollered. There was an awkward silence. Sgro, angry, defiant, and resolute, opened the door and got out, and Bill took off.

Sgro thought, "Now what do I do?" It was a dark, cloud-covered night. Standing about ten miles outside Rio Grande, New Jersey, on Route 47, on a narrow two-lane road with woods on both sides, Sgro didn't take a step. He remained calm. He'd been in tougher spots than this. He'd earned a Bronze Star and Purple Heart in World War II after surviving combat and a bout of malaria in the jungles of the South Pacific. Being alone in the woods of New Jersey on a pitch-dark night was not going to cause him to panic. He stayed right where he was and thought to himself, "Jim won't let him leave me here." Lord Jim was not a fighting fellow, Sgro told himself. Sgro knew him as well as anyone. They were great friends. And Sgro knew that in a nice, clean, clear way Lord Jim could talk Bill out of something, and he was Sgro's buddy. "They'll be back," he told himself.

Sure enough, a half hour later, Bill's Cadillac came roaring back down the road. Sgro was still standing right where they had left him. The car went *swoosh* right past him, spun around, came up, and stopped. Lord Jim opened the door. "Get in!" Bill said, clearly angry that Lord Jim had made him come back.

"No," Sgro said defiantly. "I think I'll stay right here the rest of the night. I'm not going to let you tell me I've got to run Diamond Beach!" Lord Jim hopped out and pushed Sgro into the car, into the back seat this time, and they drove home in awkward silence.

The next day Bill came into the office and apologized to Sgro. Sgro knew from experience that as bad as Bill was sometimes, later he was your friend. "Everything's going to be all right," Bill said with a smile, placing a hand on Sgro's shoulder. "We have to take a summer off, and that would be a good place for us to go," he reasoned. "And you always go down there anyway. You don't have to do anything. Just watch the money," Bill said. Sgro relented. He closed up the office in Chester, leaving only one employee there to take messages.

Diamond Beach was a working vacation for Bill and the band. Bill rented a house with a large screened porch where he and Cuppy and the children could relax and entertain guests.

Although the Comets were still a big name at the Jersey Shore, the length of their engagement and the isolated location, away from the more accessible clubs, worked against them. Even though room and board for the band members was taken care of, they still had salaries for the organization's other employees and other expenses to cover. Sgro would go in each night for dinner and collect money at the door. Initially the band would get free meals, but when they began eating like hogs, they were reeled in by the property owner, who told them to keep their bill below a certain amount. By Sgro's calculation, they lost about $17,000 that summer.

While the band's finances were tightening, Bill and Sgro had to spend the night in New York City on band business in fall 1959. Sgro called home to check in with his wife, Doris, who had invited Cuppy and her children over for dinner. When Bill got on the phone with Cuppy, he asked her "What are we going to do for Thanksgiving? Do you have enough money to buy a turkey?" and she said no. While Bill was talking to Cuppy, she was interrupted by the doorbell. Some men at the door had come to repossess Sgro's Pontiac, she told Bill over the phone. Doris tried to tell them the check was in the mail, but they took the car anyway.

32

The World Cracks Down . . . on Cuppy

When Bill had taken off to Mexico, he'd left Cuppy and his fellow business partners with nothing but debts. Soon Melody Manor was sold for $30,000 at a sheriff's sale after Bill and Cuppy defaulted on their outstanding $25,000 home equity loan. The IRS also attempted to seize all of Cuppy's personal property to satisfy the Haleys' outstanding tax obligations.

After Sgro intervened with the IRS on Cuppy's behalf, she was absolved from paying Bill's back taxes, as well as the heavy penalties that had accrued. Cuppy had gotten off easier than she'd thought she might. She walked out of the meeting, away from the men who had been threatening her, and felt relieved. It wasn't their fault, and she could see in their eyes that they were grateful their own wives and children weren't in her predicament.

When real estate agents representing the mortgage company came out to examine the property, Cuppy and the children were still living there, but the grounds looked terrible. Bill had always been particular about their appearance, making sure the lawn was cut and the trees and bushes properly trimmed. Now, however, the grass was so overgrown that you couldn't get a lawn mower through it.

While hovering on the brink of a nervous breakdown, Cuppy was given a deadline date to vacate the property. She started packing, and friends tried to help her, but some people were there for other reasons. One couple was more interested in what they could take than how they could help. "Can we have this?" they asked. "Can I have that?" Deflated and defeated, Cuppy simply said yes. She couldn't take everything anyway, she reasoned, and she watched vacantly as people dug up the azalea bushes in the front yard, removed the chandelier from the dining room, and took whatever else they could get their hands on.

Feeling helpless, Cuppy told herself she had to save her strength to do what she could do for her kids. After the IRS hearing, while Bill was on tour and before Cuppy vacated the house, she and the children, along with Cuppy's mother Sadie and Cuppy's Aunt Helen, shared a final defiant weekend at Melody Manor in July 1962. Cuppy tried to make light of their situation, even though it wasn't funny, but the children were simply confused.

As Cuppy pulled the front door closed for the final time, holding the key tightly in her shaking hand, a flood of memories came back to her. She thought of the large, beautiful dining room where she loved to entertain and serve experimental dinners for their friends; of watching the children playing on the swings and slides in the fenced-in area of the backyard; and of the huge Christmas tree that used to brush the ceiling in the living room, decorated each year by friends and family on Christmas Eve.

She knew she'd always remember the pink leather breakfast nook in the kitchen, where Jimmy once got his head stuck between the V-shaped chrome legs of the table. Cuppy had called in firefighters, who greased Jimmy's ears with Vaseline and pulled his head out as Joanie and Bill Jr. looked on and laughed uproariously.

There also was the dishwasher that no longer worked, and the rec room in the basement where Bill had stood behind the bar many nights making drinks for the band members and their wives. Plus the memory of little Joanie crawling from her bedroom to their bedroom and pounding on their door with her little fists until Bill opened the door, hugged and kissed her, and put her between them for the rest of the night.

In one final act of defiance, rather than lock the door, Cuppy turned and threw the key as far as she could. She watched it disappear into a thick thatch of grass in the once immaculately manicured front lawn. Her maroon T-bird was about to be repossessed, but she still had her kids and her memories of Melody Manor, many of them good. Pulling out of the driveway, she muttered under her breath, "There's no turning back now, kids," and then started singing, "We're off to see the Wizard, the wonderful Wizard of Oz," off-key.

Friends tried to help Cuppy find an apartment in the Wilmington, Delaware, area, but with four children and no job, it was impossible. Then someone told her about a house for rent in a quiet, newly built residential neighborhood in Barrington, New Jersey. The rent was $135 per month. Cuppy got the first month's rent and security deposit by selling her old furniture, and her father lent her the money for the moving van. Her Aunt Helen, battling an alcohol problem of her own, came to live with the family and help take care of the kids so Cuppy could find work.

Helen tried to abstain from alcohol and watched the children for a while, but when she started drinking again, Cuppy had to ask her to leave.

While Cuppy and the kids were moving out of Melody Manor, the Comets played in Caracas, Venezuela. They then headed north for a few weeks of performances in Quebec before leaving on an extended tour of US military bases in Germany in September and October. On October 1, 1962, Bill and the Comets appeared at the now-famous Star Club in Hamburg, West Germany, on a side street off the Reeperbahn. That club, which had recently opened, had featured the Beatles as its first act.

While in Germany that fall, Bill became aware of the new sound emerging from England in the 1960s that was becoming popular in Germany. In an interview in the British music magazine *Melody Maker* some two years later, talking about various groups playing the new sound, he said that between shows, the Comets "used to go and just watch and listen to them." When Bill returned to Mexico, he promoted the new English beat sound to no avail, recording a song called "The Liverpool" for Orfeon that was never released.

33

Cuppy Prays for Help and Her Prayer Is Answered

By November 1962, Cuppy and the children were starting to build a new life in their rented house in Barrington, New Jersey. Cuppy found work at the nearby Bobette Motel as a receptionist/cashier at the minimum wage. Befriending an older woman who worked there, she began occasionally meeting her and her husband for a drink at a local restaurant. At the woman's urging, Cuppy began dating their son.

Bill was back in Pennsylvania on November 20, appearing at Pushnik's Waterfall Room Theater Restaurant in Lebanon, the town where he'd once hosted a radio program in the 1940s. He called Cuppy, asking her to meet him in New York to talk about their situation, and offered to pay for her hotel room. She agreed and asked her friend's son to drive her to the train station in Philadelphia. Anxious and uneasy during the trip, she wasn't exactly sure what Bill wanted to talk about, and she also had mixed feelings. A part of her still loved him and hoped that he felt the same. Aside from thinking about a possible reconciliation, she was hoping he was going to give her some money to support his children.

Arriving in New York, Cuppy took a cab to her hotel, where Bill picked her up the next afternoon. He took her out to dinner at a nice restaurant, and then to a club, where the meeting's purpose became clear. Without mentioning Martha, Bill said he wanted Cuppy to agree to a divorce. Disappointed but not surprised, she stood her ground, feeling as though she had nothing to lose at this point. "Until you come up with money for child support, I'm not signing anything," she said firmly.

Bill said he was trying his best. It was hard to get paid for concerts in Mexico, he said, but as soon as things were better and he got his tax situation straightened out, he was going to do right by her and the kids.

The act was becoming a big hit down there. Skeptical, Cuppy repeated her earlier answer: no divorce until he paid child support.

Bill asked Cuppy to think about it, and they parted amicably. He drove her to the train station, gave her a polite kiss, and hugged her goodbye. As her train pulled into 30th Street Station in Philadelphia, the crushing weight of trying to feed her family and stay out of debt returned.

About a month later, when Bill was back in Mexico making records and starting his new family, his American family was forced to move out of the house in Barrington. Despite her best efforts, Cuppy had fallen behind on the rent and been evicted. Fortunately, she found another rental house in Gloucester, New Jersey, just south of Camden, with the help of her new boyfriend, William "Bud" Gargano.

Bud, a construction supervisor, had met Cuppy at Al-Jo's, a restaurant bar where she socialized with her coworkers from the Bobette Motel. He was attracted to her, and when she was forced out of the Barrington home, he suggested they rent a house together. Bud also suggested they trade in Cuppy's Thunderbird before it got repossessed and use the money to make a down payment on a second-hand Cadillac they'd share. The car would be in Bud's name, because he, not Cuppy, had the income to qualify for the loan to cover the rest of the purchase price of the car.

Bud truly wanted to be with Cuppy, but he didn't want to be a father figure for her four kids. He simply was unprepared to deal with the chaos and commotion involved. Not long after Bud moved in with Cuppy, his disinterest in the children turned into emotional abuse. He regularly reprimanded the boys and punished them for even imagined indiscretions. On weekends when he was recovering from one of his hangovers, they had to do homework, go to bed early, and be quiet in the morning. On Christmas morning, when the kids came downstairs full of anticipation, there was nothing: no tree and no gifts. Bud told them they wouldn't get any presents because they'd misbehaved. After enjoying their disappointment for a few minutes, he relented, however, and let Cuppy give them some things she'd bought for them with her parents' help.

Shortly afterward, in January 1963, it was announced that "Florida Twist" had been Mexico's best-selling record of 1962. And on January 14, 1963, thirty-seven-year-old Bill married his now-pregnant mistress, Martha. Without Cuppy's knowledge or consent, he'd obtained a Mexican divorce in January 1963 in Ciudad Juarez. The divorce decree named "tres hijos de nombres Joan, William y James Haley" as Cuppy's children, with no mention of nearly three-year-old Scott.

Before resorting to a Mexican divorce, Bill had called Lord Jim Ferguson and asked him to press Cuppy one more time for a divorce in the US. Jim obediently went to see Cuppy, who was still struggling to accept everything that had happened to her. She'd told Bill to his face that she wouldn't agree to a divorce if he wouldn't support his children. Now she told Lord Jim that if Bill wanted her consent, he'd have to come there and ask her himself. "Tell him not to think that I'm so stupid that I don't know there is someone else," she said. "And she's probably pregnant, because I know him!"

Although his mother had raised him as a Methodist, Bill had converted to Catholicism before marrying Martha. According to record producer Sam Charters, Martha came from Mexican family that was strong and close knit but had its own troubles. "She knew about drinking," Charters said, and "how to keep Bill close."

Later that spring, Bill and Martha's first daughter, Martha Maria Haley, was born. Two more children followed: Pedro Antonio Haley in 1971 and Georgina Haley in 1975. Years later, Pedro Haley told author Otto Fuchs that his maternal grandfather and several other members of his mother's immediate family had been alcoholics, and that as a result, Martha had grown up "in an abusive home."

Bill's new family moved around a lot, living first in Del Rio and Houston, Texas, then on the Gulf Coast of Florida, returning to Houston again, and then relocating to Juarez, Mexico. In 1974, they moved to a two-story villa overlooking the ocean in Veracruz, Mexico.

Martha decorated the twenty-four rooms in the Veracruz house with Mexican artwork, but she wasn't enthusiastic about being in Veracruz. "He [Bill] kept talking about fishing. He wanted to be near the ocean," Martha told an interviewer who'd asked her why they'd moved there. "He kept saying, 'Come on, baby, let's go to Veracruz.' I didn't want to. It was hot, humid, and ugly. Finally, I said okay."

In Veracruz, Bill got into fishing with a vengeance. He bought a twenty-one-foot boat that he named Martita ("Little Martha"), and with three local men, embarked on fishing trips in the Gulf of Mexico that lasted from five in the morning until seven at night. He also wanted to go into the hotel business, so he bought a half-built hotel in Donna, Texas, and started working on it. He and Martha also bought a three-hundred-acre mango farm and a ranch thirty miles south of their house where they raised horses.

After Georgina was born, Martha insisted on moving to the US. Bill still wanted to live near the ocean, so they bought a big white house with eighteen rooms in Harlingen, at the southern tip of Texas not far from the holiday resort of South Padre Island.

One reason Bill agreed to the move was that Texas reminded him of his early days as a country and western singer. He'd often take long drives along the Mexican border in his white Lincoln Continental, listening to Willie Nelson and Hank Williams on his tape deck. One day he drove past a trailer park for sale near Val Verde, Texas, and bought it. Soon Bill was spending much of his time maintaining the trailer park and collecting rent from the vacationers who populated it every season.

Perhaps to make up for deserting his two previous families, Bill matured into something like a good father to the children from his third marriage, going to his kids' school plays and baseball games and driving to Houston to buy them Christmas toys. When Martha Maria became a high school senior he bought her a car, and every year he took the whole family on long vacations in his Lincoln Continental.

Gina Haley, who became a singer-songwriter, told author Otto Fuchs years later that her father had encouraged her to be a performer when she was a little girl. Throughout her life, Gina said, her longing for a relationship with her dad, who died when she was only six, has been a major theme in her songs. "For a really long time," she said, "music has been such a bittersweet theme for me, possibly filling that dad-shaped hole in me." Although she sings different kinds of music, when she performs rockabilly, it's her way of trying to keep her dad's music alive, and a way of "bonding together."

Bill's youngest son, Pedro Haley, told Fuchs that Bill "spoiled me rotten . . . I was the 'apple of his eye.' He would buy anything I wanted; take me anywhere I wanted; let me do anything I wanted." Pedro said, "I don't remember ever getting a spanking or being scolded for misbehaving. Mom did that." He added, however, that there were times when "like Dr. Jekyll and Mr. Hyde, he [Bill] would change. I could tell that he was acting strangely, speaking strangely, and smelled strangely. Later I realized this was when he had been drinking."

Bill would occasionally go on two-week drinking binges, Pedro said. "He couldn't stop drinking around those periods, and he was rarely around the family. Either he didn't want us to see him like that or Mom forced him to stay away, to protect us." But during his nondrinking periods, Pedro remembered, Bill would often take him fishing, enjoying "the serenity, the peacefulness, and the solitude."

Meanwhile, back in Gloucester, New Jersey, Cuppy's relationship with Bud wasn't working out. One afternoon in February, after she dropped Bud off at work, Cuppy went to Camden to see her parents, who gave her thirty dollars for groceries because she didn't have any food in the house and the kids were hungry. When she pulled into the driveway an hour or so later, with the badly needed groceries in the trunk, she noticed that the living room drapes were drawn shut. "That's odd," she thought. "I didn't leave those drapes drawn when we left this morning."

Leaving the groceries in the car, Cuppy cautiously went inside to look around, and suddenly she heard the used Cadillac, which they'd put in Bud's name and which she'd parked in front of the house, start up and pull off. She opened the drapes, looked at the now-empty driveway, ran upstairs to the bedroom, and saw that Bud's clothes were gone. Cuppy had driven Bud to his job site in the morning, but apparently someone had given him a ride back to the house, where he'd hidden until she got home. He left her a note saying he couldn't take their domestic arrangement anymore.

The children weren't sorry to see Bud go, because his attempts to control them had become extreme. Billy and Jimmy had been forced to stay in the bedroom they shared, except to go to school, for a week before Bud left. He'd called them down to the living room, said there was an oil stain on a pair of pajamas, and wanted to know where it came from. Until they could explain it, they had to stay in their room all the time they were home.

Once again, Cuppy found herself in a desperate situation. She'd wasted time and money running up phone bills, placing calls to wherever she heard Bill's band was playing, and trying to track him down for support money. She'd leave messages, and Bill would call her back occasionally. "I'll make everything up to you and the kids," he would say. "I just need one more hit record and you and the kids will be set for life."

"It's always promises and no money," Cuppy thought to herself. Nevertheless, she encouraged Bill and told herself to be patient, because a part of her wanted to believe he would actually follow through. She couldn't believe that he'd just turn his back on his children.

With no money coming from Bill and Bud now gone, Cuppy thought to herself, "Now what am I going to do?" Bud had been helping with the rent and the food. Cuppy was making barely thirty dollars a week at the Bobette Motel's front desk, and a bit more working as a weekend hostess at an Italian restaurant. She was two months behind in her rent and the landlord was telling her she'd have to move out.

All Cuppy had left were a few remaining pieces of furniture from Melody Manor. She had nothing else, not even a car. She called her sister Catherine, who told her the only thing she could do now was apply for help from the federal government program Aid to Families with Dependent Children, known as AFDC.

With things about as bad as they could possibly get, a sympathetic neighbor loaned Cuppy her car for the morning. She drove to the local AFDC office in Camden. As she drove, she felt totally alone and helpless. Her parents had been hard workers and had taught her to be the same and never to ask for a handout. Now, at the age of thirty-one, she was pulling into a parking spot in Camden, where she had grown up, to seek public assistance. She got out of the car and put the last two dimes from her purse into the parking meter.

At the AFDC office, a kind woman named Sadie, the same name as Cuppy's mother, told her she needed to apply for welfare before applying for ADC. Cuppy walked to the welfare office. Shortly before noon, she took her place in line there, trying to avoid eye contact with others waiting in line. Some of the people there, mostly women, were hugging their coats protectively and clutching handbags to their chests. The room smelled of damp coats, stale cigarettes, and coffee. "Oh God, I just want to get out of here," Cuppy thought to herself.

Finally Cuppy made it to the front of the line. She walked up to the desk and sat down on a metal folding chair, across from a stern-looking woman behind a nameplate that read Mrs. Lincoln. For several minutes, Mrs. Lincoln shuffled papers. When she finally looked up, Cuppy, giving her name, said that her husband had left her, she had four children, and she wasn't receiving child support. Glancing at her watch, Mrs. Lincoln said, "I'm sorry, we're going to lunch." She gathered her belongings, stood up to leave, and told Cuppy to come back at 2 p.m.

Cuppy didn't have any money to buy lunch and wasn't hungry. The day was bitterly cold and it began to snow. She started walking around to kill time, saw the Catholic church on the corner she'd walked by so many times as a child, and went inside. Just as before, rows of candles that she remembered from her childhood flickered in front of the vestibule. A few people were lighting candles for loved ones, and other men and women knelt in the pews, saying the Rosary. Cuppy felt strange and uneasy, but she also felt some comfort.

Sitting down in a pew at the very back of the church, Cuppy began silently asking the Lord if she could stay for a while. She didn't seem to have the right words for a real prayer, but as she sat there alone and desperate, her mind became quiet, and the words she'd been searching for came pouring out. "Please help me, dear God, and forgive me for being so stupid," she said. "Help me let go of the bitterness I feel in my heart."

Cuppy also prayed for good health, strength, and an opportunity to work, not for herself but for her children. When she finished her prayer, something happened that she couldn't explain. It wasn't a vision, and she didn't hear any words. She just felt that the heaviness had been lifted, and she experienced an incredible wave of warmth and calmness. She got up off her knees and walked out of the church. She felt stronger, and feisty. Instead of turning toward the welfare office, she went in the other direction, got into her neighbor's car, and drove back home.

With new-found inner strength, Cuppy redoubled her efforts to find an alternative to welfare and made some calls. One was to her friend Helen Grande, Comet Johnny Grande's wife, whom she talked with regularly. "Helen, I'm at the end of my rope," Cuppy said. "I just don't know what to do. Can I bring the kids and come up?" Helen invited her to move in.

Cuppy's father loaned her money to rent a car, and he and Sadie agreed to take care of Jimmy and Scottie until Cuppy could get on her feet again. Cuppy took Joanie, Billy, and the few belongings she had left to Helen's home. She and the children had roofs over their heads now, and food. Cuppy started answering help-wanted ads, and soon found a job as a hostess in a popular smorgasbord restaurant called the Collegeville Inn.

34

Bill Pays
for a Divorce

You made a vow, that you, would ever be true.
But somehow, that vow, meant nothing to you.
–FROM THE 1957 HIT "LOVE LETTERS IN THE SAND,"
WRITTEN BY J. FRED COOTS, NICK KENNY,
AND CHARLES KENNY AND SUNG BY PAT BOONE

B ill and the band worked steadily in the US in the spring of 1963, and in May, they performed once again at American Armed Forces bases in West Germany. That summer, concerned about a potential bigamy charge and aware of his family's desperate situation, Bill arranged another meeting with Cuppy. Constantly worried about feeding the kids while paying rent to Helen, she'd already sent Jimmy and Scottie to live with her parents. Now she was considering taking the additional step of sending Bill Jr. to live with her sister Catherine's family. While her family was falling apart, she'd been straining her friendship with Helen by requesting daily rides to work.

Bill told Cuppy he'd pick her up at Helen's and they'd go for coffee and talk. He arrived with his pal Rudy, who knocked on the door and asked Cuppy to come out to the car. When she asked Bill if he wanted to see the children, he looked away from her and said, "I can't. If I do, I won't be able to go on."

They went to a nearby diner, where Bill once again told Cuppy everything was going to improve and he'd be able to help her. He said he'd made some new records in January, was going to tour Canada next, and had more work lined up after that. Then he asked Cuppy to sign an agreement not to contest the Mexican divorce that he'd brought with him. In return, he promised to give her $500 a month in child support, as well as $300 in cash right away to buy a used car he'd found for her. Bill insisted that although he was willing to pay Cuppy to sign the agreement, it meant nothing to him, and as soon as he began making big money again, they were going to have everything, and he was going to come back and see the kids.

Now Cuppy knew what Bill really wanted from their meeting: he wanted to be able to work in the States without a child support or bigamy charge hanging over his head that might get him arrested. Sitting in a cramped little booth in the dingy diner, with Bill holding out three hundred badly needed US dollars, Cuppy swallowed her pride, stifled her anger, and signed the paper. "The radio in the car doesn't work," Bill said apologetically, as he handed her the money along with the car dealer's name and address. "That's okay. I'll just sing," Cuppy answered.

In August, the Comets were back in Las Vegas again, earning union scale at the Showboat, still working off the mob debt incurred by Lord Jim Ferguson in 1958. In September, they appeared in Quebec. That same month, Elvis Presley accepted an invitation to join the Bill Haley Fan Club. On his completed application, he called Bill Haley his favorite singer and said he loved everything Bill did.

35

Cuppy Tries to Enter the Music Business While Bill Makes Drunken Calls

On February 7, 1964, the Beatles landed at New York's Kennedy Airport, touching off a wave of Beatlemania in America. By April, they occupied the top five positions on the US pop charts. Bill and his band were also internationally popular, with fans in the UK, Europe, Mexico, and Central and South America.

Bill made sporadic partial child support payments, but he failed to meet his obligations under the agreement with Cuppy. In May 1964, while Bill was in Europe, Cuppy consulted a lawyer, and a warrant was issued for Bill's arrest in Pennsylvania for nonpayment of child support. It set off a fruitless and expensive game of cat and mouse. Cuppy and her lawyer tried to have a subpoena served every time Bill came to Pennsylvania, but they were always too late. Once they almost had him, but it turned out that in the county where he was performing, a local law prohibited serving child support papers. Bill had learned this before he played there, and he knew Cuppy couldn't touch him. Occasionally he would write and apologize, making excuses and offering more empty promises. Half the time Cuppy would believe him, just because she wanted to.

By now, Cuppy was moving forward without Bill's support. In early 1964, she took a job with the Bell Telephone Company, parlaying her switchboard experience with the Comets' organization into a possible career. Although she was still low on the pay scale, she thought she could make ends meet. More importantly, she hoped eventually to move into a management position with the growing company.

By July, however, cold, hard reality had set in once again. Cuppy's pay from the Bell Telephone job wasn't big enough to support her family, and Helen Grande asked her to leave the house they shared. Living at Helen's hadn't been a pleasant experience for Joanie because Helen's daughter Linda had been mean to her, and she was happy to move. Linda never let Joanie forget for a minute that her family had nothing. She seemed to enjoy the fact that the Haleys had been riding so high for so long, and now Linda had a house and Cuppy didn't. Linda would torment Joanie and try to make a fool of her in front of all the kids in the neighborhood. They were Linda's friends, and she'd tell them not to play with Joanie.

If Bill was troubled by his problems in the US at this point, he still enjoyed his European tours. In June 1964 the band had drawn a crowd of thirty thousand in Berlin before making a triumphant return to England, where Bill was dubbed the Father of Rock 'n' Roll by the British press. The Comets returned to Great Britain in September. During an interview published in the September 19, 1964, issue of *Melody Maker*, Bill crowed that the Comets liked "to play in places where we feel the music is dying and needs someone to stir up the interest once again."

While Bill was in Europe, Cuppy moved the family to King of Prussia, Pennsylvania. She shared a rented house there with a friend and coworker at the Collegeville Inn who was also a single mother, raising three children of her own. A diary entry Cuppy made that September 23 said she'd seen Bill in July and he owed her two months' support.

By October 22, four days after the Comets had returned to New York from their highly successful UK tour, she'd received a little help. "Helen called," Cuppy wrote in her diary. "Rudy [Rudy Pompilli of the Comets] had called her. The band is home except for Bill—who's in Mexico" and he'd given Rudy $250 to give to Cuppy. "That's nice of him." Cuppy wrote, "since he owes me three months."

On November 1, Cuppy tried to enter the music business herself in partnership with a boyfriend. Her new man was Earle Hahn, owner of the Collegeville Inn. Hahn was married but had begun a romantic relationship with Cuppy before she'd quit her hostess job. Using his own money, Hahn formed a company called Cuppy Records in Folcroft, Pennsylvania. It was to be run by Bill's ex-bandmate and business partner Johnny Grande, who had recently quit the Comets, and ex-manager Jack Howard. For his investment, Hahn retained a 40 percent share of the company, and Cuppy was given a 25 percent share for the use of her name, with Grande and Howard splitting the remaining 35 percent share. Cuppy Records promptly recorded a song called "The Loner" by an up-and-coming local group, the Delights. It was later bootlegged, and it became a minor hit in England in the late '70s. Unfortunately, Cuppy Records folded six months after it opened without producing any hits, and without the shareholders earning any money from the venture. Cuppy didn't receive a penny for "The Loner" or any money from the company that bore her name.

On his next tour of Europe, in 1965, Bill was accompanied by Martha. Cuppy wrote to Bill several times seeking support money. In a long-delayed response, Bill said he couldn't pay her because of his IRS problems, which he blamed on the band's accountant. The next year, however, Bill and the Comets' recording contract with Orfeon was extended. Bill's good friend Big Joe Turner cut twelve sides for Orfeon in January 1966, with the Comets as the backing band.

Later that year, from August to October, the band toured Europe and again lost money. With rock 'n' roll out of fashion, Bill was reduced to playing small clubs and Army bases, and he reached an all-time low point in both his popularity and his spirits. The beginning ripples of a rock 'n' roll revival began to emerge, however: the band was booked to play the Alhambra Theater in Paris on September 24, 1966, opening for the Spencer Davis Group and the Pretty Things.

The engagement didn't start well when a girlfriend of one of the members of the British bands asked forty-two-year-old Bill, rhetorically, "Are you still alive?" Bill took it like a sock on the jaw. When the Comets took the stage that night, however, they received an unexpected rousing ovation. His old fans were there, *en masse*, with banners reading "Welcome Back Bill Haley." Much like the British, the French music fans were more impressed by Bill Haley and the Comets' role in creating rock 'n' roll than their American counterparts.

At this point, Cuppy didn't believe any of Bill's empty promises. She never discussed him with the children or mentioned anything to them about writing to their father. At Christmas time, however, she remembered that Bill always sent her a little money for holiday gifts for the children. When he didn't send anything at all to his family for Christmas, 1966, she knew he was doing exceptionally badly.

Cuppy had always thought that if Bill's fortunes revived, he'd make some kind of settlement, but she hadn't wanted any personal correspondence or phone conversations with him. Still, he'd call her occasionally. On one occasion around the holidays, when he went on and on, Cuppy could hear Martha in the background saying, "Bill, your dinner's on the table," and she mumbled to herself "He's your problem now!"

Bill had developed a propensity for extended drunken telephone diatribes that continued throughout the '60s. Cuppy would hear from him every couple of months and always at Christmas time, particularly on Christmas Eve. He'd be pretty drunk then, but if he remembered, he'd call back the next day and apologize. When he did so, Bill would keep Cuppy on the phone for hours, repeating himself over and over. Sometimes the calls amounted to more than a nuisance: he'd keep calling Cuppy all night long, and she'd keep hanging up on him, eventually just taking the phone off the hook. Sometimes, he would call her at work. When he found out she worked for the Bell Telephone Company in Ardmore, Pennsylvania, he called there one evening and said, "My wife works for Bell Telephone!" She wasn't there, but Bill kept calling back, driving the all-night supervisor half crazy. When Cuppy arrived at work the next morning, her boss gave Cuppy the number Bill had left and told her to use the conference room. Cuppy called the number, but by that time Bill was dead drunk and passed out. She was embarrassed, but her boss understood.

Many times when Bill called her, Cuppy would hear his drunken, slurred voice and just hang up. He'd call back, and then she'd leave the phone off the hook because he didn't make any sense. She kept saying, "Look, if you want to talk to me, call me when you're sober," but he'd ramble on about how the band's problems were everyone's except his own.

36

Bill's Career Starts to Revive and He Tours London . . . with Martha

They tell me a revival is only temporary.
So is a bath, but it does you good.
–BILLY SUNDAY

Throughout 1967, the Comets played in dozens of American towns, large and small. Instead of performing in arenas and other established music venues however, they played at an endless string of nondescript lounges.

At this point, the band had been traveling for forty-five straight weeks in the US, Europe, and South America. "We'll tour as long as we're popular," Bill told an interviewer between sets.

Although the Comets had no recording contracts, Bill was still trying to continue his own recording career. That August, he made a pair of demos at a Phoenix studio, while the band was appearing at JD's Lounge in Tempe, Arizona. One demo was a weepy country and western song, "Jealous Heart," backed by Trio Los Panchos, a local mariachi band. The other was a '60s rock tune called "Rock on Baby," backed by a band called Superfine Dandelion and featuring guitarist Mike McFadden. Disappointingly, club owner J. D. Musil, who paid for the session, waffled over the decision of whether to add backing voices to the tracks and never released these records.

Although a planned June 1967 tour to the UK had been cancelled when the promoter failed to come up with the advance money, the band kept plugging away for the rest of that year. They appeared mostly at military bases in Europe and small venues in Louisiana, Texas, and Florida, as well as on the US West Coast.

On April 6, 1968, while the Comets were appearing at the LongHorn Steak House in Portland, Oregon, the recording industry's equivalent of a lightning strike occurred. Music Corporation of America (MCA)'s reissue of the timeless recording "Rock Around the Clock" reentered the UK charts for one week, in the No. 20 spot. MCA had acquired the Decca catalog on January 1, 1968, and was reissuing many of that company's classic hits. Bill and the Comets were soon able to arrange a UK tour.

Earlier that year, a rock 'n' roll revival had ignited in London. On April 28, a contingent of the Wild Angels Rock 'n' Roll Society, which included original rockers, women with ponytails and bobby sox, and men with ducktail haircuts and leather jackets, were at the airport to greet Bill when he arrived there for a three-week tour of the UK and Scandinavia. He was wreathed with flowers and presented with a placard that read, "Welcome Back to Britain Bill Haley, King of Rock 'n' Roll Forever Home."

When Bill and the Comets appeared at the Royal Albert Hall in London on May 1, they packed the seven-thousand-seat theater. Enthusiastic Teds and young rockers booed the opening act, the Quotations, but the Wild Angels and Duane Eddy, who followed, were politely received. Still, Eddy had to ask people dancing in the aisles to return to their seats twice during his performance.

When the Comets' turn came, the crowd went crazy. After half an hour, the audience rushed the stage and a mock mini-riot ensued. John Lennon, who attended the concert, wrote, "To Bill, you started it all" on a photo he gave Bill. Paul McCartney, Cat Stevens, and Ringo Starr also showed up to watch the Comets perform.

Bill had brought Martha along on this trip, and as they dined at the Kensington Palace Hotel, he was reminded of the overwhelming reception he'd received during his first tour of England in '57 with Cuppy. "No one else is left playing rock 'n' roll the way it was originated," Bill told reporters, explaining the resurgent popularity of his sound.

In May 1968, the Comets drew twenty-one thousand fans to shows in Sweden and Denmark, and Bill signed a long-term, worldwide deal with the Swedish record label Sonet.

Meanwhile, back in Salem, New Jersey, Dottie's father passed away and Bill's first family had to leave their home. Sharyn, who had a troubled marriage, had already moved out, but Jack, now a senior in high school, and his half-brother, Lloyd, were reduced to sleeping in cars. Dottie kept their clothes in boxes in the back room of the bar where she worked. Eventually an older couple felt sorry for the boys and took them in until Dottie could find a place for them to live.

The Comets' first LP for Sonet, "Rockin'," included a new version of "Rock the Joint" and was recorded before a live studio audience. It was released in the US on the Pickwick label. A second Sonet LP that emerged out of that first session was titled "Just Rock 'n' Roll Music."

In September, however, Bill's reviving career suffered a setback. He and the band were back in the States, appearing at the Newport Beach Club in Miami, Florida, when the IRS caught up with him and seized his performance contract. At this point, the agency had been confiscating Bill's Decca record royalties for several years in an effort to collect his allegedly unpaid income taxes. The tax case that had originally begun in Chester, Pennsylvania, had moved to Philadelphia, Baltimore, and Washington, DC, and finally to the IRS International Operations branch. With his back to the wall, Bill returned to Chester and began working with Andrew P. Hoesch of H&R Block to resolve the outstanding tax matter once and for all. From that point on, the IRS followed Bill and took whatever money they could get wherever he played.

On February 3, 1969, two singles by Bill were released on the United Artists label: "That's How I Got to Memphis," a country and western tune composed by Tom T. Hall, and "Ain't Love Funny, Ha Ha Ha," produced by Henry Jerome and arranged by Hutch Davie. Cuppy bought a copy of each. As she listened to Bill pouring his heart into the "Memphis" vocal," she could hear what she thought was guilt, regret, and sadness in his voice.

37

As the Revival Continues, the Tax Men Retreat

If you drive a car, I'll tax the street, If you try to sit,
I'll tax your seat.
—FROM THE 1966 SONG "TAX MAN,"
WRITTEN BY GEORGE HARRISON AND
PERFORMED BY THE BEATLES

Proving that its 1968 British chart reentry hadn't been a fluke, the resurrected "Rock Around the Clock" reached No. 1 in 1969 on the Australian and Italian record charts. That spring, the Comets played a series of well-attended shows in Florida and the American Midwest, and on June 30 they flew to Oslo, Norway, for the start of another European tour. The UK leg of that tour opened in August at the Fiesta nightclub in Stockton, England.

"'I thought it would be good but it's better than good,'" Bill told an interviewer, referring to the UK tour the Comets were just beginning. "I'm quite surprised. It looks like we're really going to have a success. The major part of the audience seems to be the fans of the '50s, and they've given us a very warm reception."

That September, the Comets toured New York State and Canada. On October 18, 1969, Bill made his first New York City appearance in eight years, playing at the Felt Forum at Madison Square Garden as the headliner of impresario Richard Nader's "Rock 'n' Roll Revival" show. The show, which attracted an audience of twenty-seven thousand, also featured Sha Na Na, the Coasters, the Shirelles, Jimmy Clanton, the Platters, and Chuck Berry. After their set, Bill and the Comets received an eight-and-a-half minute standing ovation. "That ovation was one of the greatest moments of my life," Bill told the audience. "I'll never forget it. New York, I love you."

Rolling Stone gave that Comets' performance a rave review, saying that "they bounced out on stage with the *elan* of a winning bowling team: paunchy, perspiring in their watered silk jackets but, after two years of touring in Britain, Scandinavia, Australia and South America, in shape. Champions."

"That gas station guitar, just like you remember it," the article continued. "The soaring riffs of the tenor sax just as they should have been. The bass player balancing himself in the curve of the instrument while playing it, one leg thrashing in the air, showing that Hendrix fella a thing or two about musical gymnastics.

"The Comets wallowed their way through 'Shake, Rattle and Roll,' 'Thirteen Women,' 'See You Later, Alligator,' and, of course, 'Rock Around the Clock,' Haley's spit curl in place all the while. Beautiful.'"

On Saturday, December 6, 1969, a little less than two months after their successful Madison Square Garden appearance, Bill and the Comets recorded a live album at the Bitter End Club in Greenwich Village. They called it "Bill Haley's Scrapbook—Live at the Bitter End." In an interview after that show, Comets Nick Masters and Bill Nolte said they were "stunned" by how great their reception was. "There was a room full of hippies. We expected to die out there on the stage. But they dug it, just like the kids did in the '50s," Masters said. "They came up to us after the show and said, 'Man, there's no message there. We can just sit back and enjoy it, groove on it.'"

During the show, forty-four-year-old Bill repeated a quote of his that had appeared in that morning's edition of the *New York Post*: "When I'm 75, if you can still clap your hands, and I can still hold a guitar, we'll still have rock 'n' roll," he said. The album they recorded at the Bitter End was produced by Richard Nader in association with Lewis Merenstein, and released in February 1970 on Buddah Records' Kamasutra label.

Early in February, the Comets also scored a win on the tax front. After nearly three years of arguing with the government while the IRS collected about $21,000 by attaching royalties and seizing personal appearance fees, Bill ended up getting a refund of $8,000. With his tax troubles behind him, Bill appeared on the *Andy Williams* and *Dick Cavett* television shows. The Comets also picked up a contract to perform in Playboy clubs across the country. At long last, their prospects in the US seemed to be brightening.

38

Cuppy and Joanie's Florida Visit

In late February 1970, Bill and the Comets appeared at the Rooster-tail club in Detroit, one of scores of small clubs and hotel lounges the Comets would play that year. Although the band still would have been able to fill large halls in Europe, it remained a lounge act in the United States.

Bill was doing well financially, however, thanks to the rock 'n' roll revival and the reemergence of "Rock Around the Clock" on the music charts. He was free-spending and generous, just like he'd been in the old days. Once, during a break between shows on a California tour, Bill flew the band over to Japan for a steak dinner. He often bought toys and gifts for the children of his band members. Meanwhile, he still failed to make any restitution to Cuppy for the years of missed child support payments.

After playing in small clubs all over the US during the spring and summer of 1970, Bill and the Comets went back to New York City, where in September and October they played at the Electric Circus on St. Mark's Place. They then went to Nashville to record the LP *Rock Around the Country* for the Chess/Janus label (Sonet's American distributor). Curly Chalker played steel guitar on this album, which was reissued later on UK Sonet. Other musicians on the album, which featured rock 'n' roll songs along with some country and western material, included Jimmie Riddle, Hargus "Pig" Robbins, and Nick Masters, who played lead guitar and was lead vocalist on the song "Travelin' Band."

Sam Charters produced *Rock Around the Country*, his first assignment after signing on with Sonet. Charters was a musicologist who specialized in Memphis-based blues, as well as a producer. A month earlier, he'd gone to New York to meet Bill and catch his act at the Electric Circus. Charters was favorably impressed, and he was initially excited about the recording project. At this point, Bill was convinced that he could revive his career by reverting to his country and western roots and singing ballads. However, although this album may have been the best thing musically he'd done in a decade and a half, it was a commercial flop.

On October 25, 1970, the Comets appeared at the 651 Musical Lounge in York, Pennsylvania, not far from Bill's old stomping grounds around Chester. Nowhere near as popular in that area as he'd been in his glory days, he *still* must have been surprised when the house was only half-full at midnight even though the four-dollar cover charge for the second show had been lifted.

An article by Walter F. Naedele, who covered the event for the *Philadelphia Bulletin*, described the show in detail:

> Haley was hanging back. He had done the lead on the first couple of songs, but dropped back in the group as first one, then another of his men took a solo. They kept encouraging someone to dance. No one was taking up the dare.
>
> After a while, one couple came out and jitterbugged. They played "Guitar Boogie" and another couple jitterbugged— the girl in a full skirt that billowed when she twirled, the boy in a short sleeve white shirt and a tie held in place by a clip.
>
> The other Comets were doing their parts, but it was Haley who kept bobbing back and forth in time to the music, keeping the tempo with his body. And when the drummer went into a dirty song, it was Haley who played the role the heaviest, being surprised at each new line, laughing along with the audience.

Bill still refused to pay child support to Cuppy, but when he appeared in Miami during this tour, he told the *Miami Herald* he didn't really need to work. "'It's just a thing I'd rather do," Bill said. "When I stay home too long I start to get restless. . . . And besides, I like to do it."

Cuppy decided to take Joanie down to Florida to see her father during this Miami engagement. Bill had called and suggested the trip, which was supposed to be a high school graduation present. Now eighteen, Joanie was afraid and nervous at first, but she wanted to see her father because she felt there was something unfinished between them. After all, the last time they'd met, she'd been nine. She suppressed her nerves until they were on the plane, but then developed a bad headache. When they arrived in Miami that evening, it was late at night and Bill was playing in a club nearby. He was drunk and wanted to see Joanie, but she couldn't do it: she was sick and ready to throw up.

The next morning, father and daughter arranged to meet. When Bill came into the coffee shop at the Moulin Rouge Hotel where Cuppy and Joanie were staying, he was still drunk and Joanie was appalled. It was before noon. She whispered to her mother, "Oh God, he's drunk!"

When he saw Joanie, Bill just cried and cried, hugging and kissing her. Although Joanie was screaming inside with all the things she wanted to say, the only words she could utter were "Oh, hi Dad," like nothing had ever happened. She was in shock.

That night, Cuppy and Joanie went to the club to see the Comets perform, and Joanie started feeling better. She was surprised to see all these people who still liked Bill so much. Cuppy had bought her a new black-and-white polka-dot silk skirt with a halter top that tied, and Joanie thought she looked really nice.

Over the next few days, Bill had guys in the band bring Cuppy and Joanie to the show and took them all out to dinner afterward. He always had the band with him. Wherever he went in Florida, including attractions such as Sea World, everyone else went too.

Joanie never was entirely comfortable with her father during her stay. At one point, he actually made her squeamish. She'd been tanning outside by the pool in a lounge chair, saw him coming, and thought he might be admiring her figure. That made her very uncomfortable.

The nearest thing to a "special moment" between father and daughter was when Bill shared his visions of future success with her. They were in his hotel room, and at this point she was starting to feel a little more relaxed. She was still afraid of him, but she was always afraid of men, especially those who were her father's age; because she was essentially a fatherless daughter, she had no idea how men his age behaved. While they sat together, Bill told Joanie how he was going to do this and that, and he played her some tapes he'd made. One of the songs was "Me and Bobby McGee," and Bill said proudly to his daughter, "I really think I'm going to make it with this song."

Still, the situation was difficult, since Bill continued his life-long habit of surrounding and shielding himself with associates. Joanie wanted to have a meaningful relationship with her father, but apparently, he didn't quite know how to relate to her. Joanie figured Bill had a lot of guilt. She befriended Bill's pal Rudy Pompilli because she was comfortable with him. Pompilli was always trying to fix everything, and she thought he took more responsibility for her and her brothers than her father did. Compared to her father, he seemed to be stable and dependable.

By now, Bill was just too strongly in the grip of alcohol to confront and address his failures as a father. When he told Joanie that Martha was pregnant with a boy, Joanie didn't know how to react. He had three sons in Pennsylvania and one in New Jersey he'd walked away from and ignored, and now he was proud he was going to have another? She was in a state of mild shock the whole time she was there.

At one point Bill and Cuppy had a serious discussion. Some band members were talking with Joanie, and Bill and Cuppy were standing away from them, next to the road. They were so intent on their discussion, Joanie noticed, that a bus came by on the highway so fast that if they'd been standing any nearer to the road, they'd have been killed.

It seemed to be very difficult for Bill to see Joanie grown up after everything that had happened. Forced by their proximity into dealing with long-suppressed feelings, he and Cuppy tried to explain to each other how they felt. Cuppy, now thirty-eight, aired grievances she'd thought about for a long time, and Bill realized that he'd have to live for the rest of his life with the hurt he'd caused his family by deserting them. Cuppy saw him as a man who just couldn't face things that went wrong. Bill told her how proud of her he was for the way she was raising their children and said he was surprised she was able to do it.

Joanie's impressions of her visit with her father remained with her long afterwards. For years, shish kabob with Spanish rice was her favorite meal because Bill had ordered it for her at a restaurant during this trip.

Her father obviously retained power over her. She'd become engaged on Christmas 1969, and she was wearing an engagement ring in Florida. Cuppy had disapproved of the match—she felt that Joanie could do much better and did not want her to make a mistake that she would later regret. But she hadn't been able to talk her daughter out of it, even though she'd raised Joanie all these years. But now, after a couple of words from her dad, Joanie came home and broke off the engagement.

When Cuppy and Joanie returned to Pennsylvania, Bill called to see if they'd got home safely. They didn't hear from him again for six months. Joanie had hoped they'd end up building some sort of a relationship, but much to her disappointment, they never did.

39

Hail Hail Alcohol

By 1971, Bill was having a difficult time. He'd been trying to finish building a hotel he wanted to open in Donna, Texas, late that year, but he couldn't do so, partly because of financial problems. (On several occasions, he'd appealed to Sonet Records for advances to continue construction on the project.) Later, Bill claimed he'd found out that a Mexican syndicate wanted the building's site too and had been trying to muscle him out.

Meanwhile, the mango operation at his ranch in Mexico wasn't making a profit. Bill believed he had a right to fence off his property and plant mangoes there, but local cattle ranchers insisted they had a right to drive their herds through his acreage. Haley told friends and associates he was having trouble with *pistoleros* (gun fighters), who'd presumably been hired by the ranchers to keep him from completing the fencing. Once again, his affairs were in general disarray. Compounding matters, Bill's alcoholism was consuming him. By now, he was drinking practically around the clock.

In early 1972, Bill and the Comets played at the Hollywood Bowl in Los Angeles as part of Richard Nader's Legends of Rock 'n' Roll show. They also appeared in Hayward, California, near San Francisco, where former Comet Marshall Lytle was in the audience. They hadn't seen Lytle since September 1955, when he and some other band members had split from the Comets and formed the Jodimars. Bill told the audience Lytle was the original bass player on "Rock Around the Clock," invited him back to his dressing room, and introduced him to Martha. During their conversation, Bill casually told Lytle that he was drinking a fifth of tequila every day.

In September 1972, Bill and the Comets rejoined the Legends of Rock 'n' Roll show and were scheduled to appear in Philadelphia. Bill Jr. and his half-brother Jack were both in the audience that night hoping to see their father perform, although neither of Bill's sons was aware of the other's presence. Cuppy had predicted that Bill wouldn't show, and she was right. Instead of appearing onstage, Bill spent the evening in a Howard Johnson's motel room on the Jersey Turnpike, drinking until he passed out.

When Jack went backstage to see what had happened, performer and vocalist Chuck Berry, who was legendary for his vulgarity as well as his duck-walk guitar solos, didn't help matters by letting Jack know just what he thought of Bill. Crushed and crying, Jack hitched a ride with Rudy Pompilli to Bill's hotel room and confronted his father, who had passed out on the bed with two empty bottles of Jack Daniels beside him on the nightstand.

Aroused from his drunken stupor, Bill took a wild swing at Jack, missing badly, before gathering his wits and fumbling for an explanation. First, he claimed a couple of mob enforcers had roughed him up and warned him not to show up for the show. Then he said he was refusing to perform because Nader hadn't paid him for the Nassau Coliseum performance the previous night.

The Nader show moved on, with more bumps in the road for Bill. His binge drinking and general ill health, exacerbated by chain-smoking, had worn him down. When the tour hit Chicago on May 26, 1973, Bill lost his prized black Gibson L-7 guitar when someone stole an equipment truck he'd left it in overnight. Later that year, he was arrested twice in one week in Iowa on charges of public intoxication. Finally, he managed to pull himself together to record another album for Sonet, *Just Rock 'n' Roll Music*, with the Comets.

Bill created tremendous difficulties for everyone involved in making that record, especially producer Sam Charters. He was constantly drunk, staggering, hard to get to the studio, and hard to handle once he got there. He complained of severe headaches and told Charters he feared for his life. He said he and his family had been threatened repeatedly by Mexican mobsters. By the end of the recording session, Bill was so drunk he couldn't even find the microphone without assistance. After engaging in several destructive, drunken escapades in the hotel corridors while the other band members locked themselves in their hotel rooms, Bill was drummed out of Nashville as soon as the *Just Rock 'n' Roll Music* album was completed.

Bill made a temporary recovery, however, and after touring Australia and New Zealand during December, he and the Comets once again appeared on *The Andy Williams Show* in the US on January 2, 1974. In March and April, they went back to London and made several other stops in Europe, as well as numerous television and radio appearances. This successful tour refilled Bill's coffers. He bought an eighteen-room house at 1902 South First Street in Harlingen, Texas, complete with swimming pool, and filled the three-car garage with two Lincoln Continentals and a Trans-Am, a graduation gift for his daughter Martha Maria.

In March 1974, "Rock Around the Clock" reentered the UK Top 20 for the fifth time and climbed to No. 12. In May, "Rock" reached No. 39 on the US charts on the strength of its inclusion on the soundtrack of the popular movie *American Graffiti*, starring Richard Dreyfus and Ron Howard. The song stayed popular when it also was played repeatedly on the soundtrack of a hit television series that movie inspired, *Happy Days*, which also starred Ron Howard.

Released in 1973, *American Graffiti* chronicles the adventures of some teenagers cruising around downtown Modesto, California, on a single night in 1962 while listening to rock 'n' roll music on their car radios. Produced by Francis Ford Coppola, it was the first movie since 1969's *Easy Rider* to replace a traditional film score with a musical sound track consisting entirely of popular songs, including the Comets' "Rock Around the Clock." (One of the proposed titles for the film was *Rock Around the Block*, which later became the title of a failed TV show that wasn't about the Comets or Haley.)

American Graffiti Director and Screenwriter George Lucas wrote each scene in that movie with a particular song in mind as its musical backdrop. "Rock Around the Clock" plays on the soundtrack as the credits roll and the opening scene begins, the same way the song had been utilized in *Blackboard Jungle*. Although numerous other rock 'n' roll tunes are heard in the film, none are sung by Bill's arch rival Elvis Presley. Elvis's record company, RCA, had demanded more money for his songs than Lucas wanted to pay.

Considering the moralizing brickbats that had been thrown at Haley and his fellow rock 'n' rollers, it's striking that *American Graffiti*, far from being a sex-filled gangland thriller, was a funny, nostalgic, and bittersweet look at a group of recent high school grads' last days of innocence. The movie received widespread critical acclaim and became one of the most profitable films of all time, garnering an estimated return of well over two hundred million dollars in box office and home video sales, not including merchandising. In 1995, the United States Library of Congress deemed the film "culturally, historically, or aesthetically significant" and selected it for preservation in the National Film Registry, where it joined *Blackboard Jungle*, the first film that had used Bill's music.

American Graffiti inspired the TV show *Happy Days,* which in its first two seasons focused on "innocent teenager" Richie Cunningham, played by Ron Howard, his family, and his high school friends. The show took a wistful look at adolescence. Locking in the connection with the movie, the first two seasons of *Happy Days* also used "Rock Around the Clock" as the show's opening theme song (although the *Happy Days* version was a slightly shorter version of the song recorded by the Comets in the fall of 1973). Broadcast from 1974 through 1984, *Happy Days* became one of the biggest hits in television history.

In addition to its usage in *Happy Days* and *American Graffiti,* "Rock Around the Clock" also had been played on the soundtracks of three other Hollywood movies: *Blackboard Jungle* and *Rock Around the Clock* (discussed earlier in this book) and the 1958 Hollywood film *The Reluctant Debutante,* making it one of the most popular rock 'n' roll soundtrack selections of all time.

In July 1974—featuring newcomer William Trimarco, also known as Bill Turner, on lead guitar—the Comets toured the Western US and western Canada. In November and December of that year, the band went to Europe again, performing in Switzerland, Germany, Sweden, Norway, and France.

On one of their tours in Germany, the band was snowed in at their hotel, and Bill spent three hours talking with Bill Turner, whom he called "Billy T," in his hotel room. After chatting about guitars and cars (Bill had just treated himself to a brand-new white Mercury Ford station wagon), the conversation took an unexpected turn when Bill started talking about his relationship with the Mafia.

In a rambling fashion, Bill told Billy T about his friendship with mob associate and go-between Ralph Carluca, who was involved in peddling bogus name-brand watches and other "hot" items hijacked from trucks and ships. Bill met Carluca during one of his periodic appearances at a gangster-owned supper club in Rhode Island. To pay down the 1958 mob loan taken out by Lord Jim Ferguson in Bill's name, Bill and the band had worked throughout the early '60s for union scale at a variety of mob-controlled establishments throughout the country, including the Roundtable in NYC and the El Cortez, the Nevada Club, and the Showboat in Las Vegas.

Bill confided to Billy T that he had developed a friendship over the years with Carluca, who would take him to all-night cards games and hangouts frequented by underworld associates. Gradually the 1958 debt, plus the interest, was paid off, and toward the end of the process,

Bill was "invited" to a meeting. Bill asked Ralph Carluca to make the preliminary arrangements, as a go-between and to "break the ice."

Bill described to Bill Turner how he was led through the corridors of a Las Vegas hotel to a private area and into a boardroom, describing the scene as something straight out of *The Godfather*. Seated around the board table were several smart-suited "businessmen" who proposed to Bill that they would open a nationwide chain of Supper Clubs under the general name of the Rock Around the Clock Lounge. Bill and the Comets would work the circuit on a year-round basis, and they would get a share of the action. Bill was given some time to consider his answer and led back out of the room. Bill was worried sick, fearful of the consequences of either getting in deeper with the mob or incurring their wrath by declining their offer.

After discussing the situation with Rudy Pompilli, his right-hand man and business partner, Bill came up with a plan to deflect the offer without causing offense. When he was taken into the same boardroom the following week to give his answer, he said, "Look, this sounds like a great deal to me . . . and I thank you for considering me in this. But I have to be 100 percent honest here. I'm being investigated by the federal government—the IRS is watching every cent I make, and I just can't be seen with you guys. It would bring the FBI down on *all* of us, and none of us need that!"

This appears to have convinced the "Chairman of the Board," who, after a moment of silence, replied, "Okay, I see. If you ever change your mind . . . you know where to find us!" Relieved, Bill completed the contract in Vegas and parted company with the Mob for good, although Morris Levy would occasionally send his regards to Bill through one of his European associates.

40

The Comets
Fade Away

You are damaged and broken and unhinged.
But so are . . . comets.
–Nikita Gill

On April 23, 1975, just a few days before the end of the first season of *Happy Days* featuring "Rock Around the Clock" on its
soundtrack, Bill and Martha's second daughter and third and final
child, Linda Georgina Velia "Gina" Haley, was born. Gina says Bill
was a kind and loving father. But in February 1976, Rudy Pompilli, the
longtime Comet who was Bill's best friend, died of cancer at the age of
51. Bill couldn't bring himself to attend Pompilli's funeral. He'd relied
heavily on him for emotional support, and his death undermined any
attempts Bill may have been making to stay sober, or to right the financial and emotional wrongs he'd inflicted on Cuppy and her children.

Nine months after Pompilli died, Bill formally abandoned Cuppy
and the kids. On November 3, 1976, he filed a last will and testament
in Harlingen, Texas. Paragraph 2 of the document reads, "I am pres-
ently married to Martha V. de Haley. I have been married twice before.
It is my intention that neither my former wives nor any of my children
by my former wives receive any benefits under this Will." The will left
his estate to Martha if alive, or to his children with her if they were
alive. His sister-in-law Antonia V. de Armas of Houston, Texas, was the
next person in line, and the last was his brother-in-law "Gustavo Velasco
A." of Houston.

Soon Bill and the Comets recorded another album for Sonet, at Fame
Studios in Muscle Shoals, Alabama: *R-O-C-K*, produced again by Sam
Charters. Unable to come up with new material suited to his unique but
limited style, Bill reached back once again into his store of tunes from
his Decca and Essex days, throwing in a Ray Charles cover of "I Got a
Woman" for good measure. Having hit rock bottom with his drinking,

Bill brought Martha and his son Pedro along with him to help him stay sober during the recording session. Subdued and humbled, he had a hard time connecting with the musicians Charters had assembled.

Bill and the latest incarnation of the Comets then set out on yet another British tour. The agreement was that if Bill took a drink, everybody would get on a plane and fly home. Whether he was drinking or not, the sixty-minute shows received consistently bad reviews, and Bill was heavily criticized for singing only five songs himself. A scathing review by Brian Harrigan in the December 11, 1976, issue of the British music magazine *Melody Maker* said, "Seeing him on stage was like watching your granddad embarrassing everyone by doing a rock 'n' roll routine at the local British Legion. . . . The movements were those of a pensioner, the voice that of a retired greengrocer, the stage act that of a group of overweight Rotarians at a fancy-dress party. Haley seemed intent on getting through the set as quickly as possible and doing as little as he could." The tour hit a final low point when a show at London's Victoria Theater ended abruptly in a spontaneous, half-hearted brawl that resulted in several arrests.

Bill, aged fifty-one, then retired from the music business and stayed retired until early 1979. Refusing to give interviews, he divided his time between deep-sea fishing and his Mexican business ventures. In late 1978, he started drinking again and making late-night calls. On one call to Rudy Pompilli's widow Ann, whom he'd never met in person, he criticized the new Comets, saying "I can't play with these clowns."

Bill made infrequent drunken calls to Cuppy as well, usually looking for sympathy. He liked to tell elaborate tales, repeating himself over and over. Many were hard to believe. In one of his drunken conversations, he said he was in the hospital because he'd had a fight with Martha's two brothers, who'd beaten him and broken his leg in retaliation for mistreatment of Martha. The next time he called, he said he had cancer. After that, he reported that he'd had a heart attack, or was going to blow his brains out. Cuppy thought he was trying to get attention and sympathy. When Elvis died on August 16, 1977, Bill called Cuppy just to let her know he was still alive, thinking she might have been fooled by headlines proclaiming that "The King of Rock 'n' Roll" was dead.

Nearly one and a half years later, in March 1979, Bill came out of retirement. He sold his trailer park and toured England, again receiving mixed reviews. Bill said he was performing again partly because after Elvis died, there was no one else left to carry the banner of 1950s rock 'n' roll.

(Elvis beat Bill again, however, after both men had died. When the Rock and Roll Hall of Fame inducted its first class in 1986, Elvis was among the inductees, as were Chuck Berry, James Brown, Ray Charles, Sam Cooke, Fats Domino, the Everly Brothers, Buddy Holly, Jerry Lee Lewis, and Little Richard. Bill had to wait until 1987, when he was inducted along with the Coasters, Eddie Cochran, Bo Diddley, Aretha Franklin, Marvin Gaye, B. B. King, Clyde McPhatter, Ricky Nelson, Roy Orbison, Carl Perkins, Smokey Robinson, Big Joe Turner, Muddy Waters, and Jackie Wilson.)

Later in 1979, Bill made another album, *Everyone Can Rock 'n' Roll*, that mixed rock 'n' roll and country songs. It was similar to the trick he'd been pulling off all his life: combining these two styles of music into individual songs. Now, however, he simply alternated country and western songs with rock 'n' roll songs on the same album. It failed.

He kept trying. From November 7-9, 1979, Haley and a new group of musicians, the Likeable English Comets, played the Starlight Club in Plettenberg, West Germany. On November 10, they appeared at the Bachmair club in Rottach-Egern. And on November 22, 1979, in recognition of Bill's past services to music, Bill and the Likeable English Comets did a Command Performance for Queen Elizabeth II of England at Buckingham Palace. The Queen told Bill it brought back memories for her, and he replied, "It reminds me of when I was young too, Ma'am!"

Gina Haley remembers Bill's Command Performance at Buckingham Palace very well, although she wasn't there. When Bill returned home to Texas, he'd encourage her to sing at home by announcing that the very young Gina had been selected to appear "before her majesty Queen Elizabeth the Second of England." Bill would say, "Tonight we have Georgina Haley at a Royal Command Performance." Gina said she'd come "onstage," make up a silly song, and Bill would interview her afterwards.

Gina grew up to become a professional musician and now performs in Texas with the Gina Haley band. One of the songs she wrote and still performs, called "Mountain Top," is about Bill, and at the very end of the song she sings about when her Dad shook the hand of the Queen of England.

Completely contrary to the image of the British leg of the tour that he'd evoked for his young daughter, it was rumored among Haley fans that Bill went off the deep end at a show in Germany later that year, tearing his clothes off, kicking fans, and throwing a microphone stand into the crowd. And in a comeback performance and interview taped in Sweden a bit later, Bill looked a little worse for wear. He was missing several upper teeth, showing gaps when he smiled, and his face was bloated. He sang "Hail Hail Rock 'n' Roll" with a tired but proud confidence and a slight smile on his face.

This was not Chuck Berry's version of this song, which was titled "School Days" when it was released in 1957. As the title indicates, Berry's song was almost entirely about a student's rough day at school. Berry didn't sing the now iconic phrase "Hail hail rock 'n' roll" until the next-to-the-last line of the song, which is followed by the line, "Deliver me from days of old," and then the song ends.

Bill's version of the song, now titled "Hail Hail Rock 'n' Roll," was a musical valedictory speech in which he lyrically reviewed the birth and revival of rock 'n' roll, the music he'd made prominent. The song reached its peroration when Bill sang, " . . . take the dance floor with your girl, rock 'n' roll is here and here to stay." He sang the song with a tired but proud confidence, as if he'd finally found a new song that really fit his old style.

No matter how bruised and battered, Bill was saying, he was still out there fighting. The Swedish audience ate it up as though it were 1956 all over again.

41

The End of the Road

At the end of the road is a mirror.
–Nick Waingrow, played by Danny Huston,
on the *Paranoid* TV series

In early November 1979, Scott, Bill's youngest son with Cuppy, was playing tight end for the Temple University Owls football team and Bill Jr. was a journalism major at Temple. Both boys were living in King of Prussia, Pennsylvania, with Cuppy, who was now forty-seven years old. When Scott played in a regionally televised football game featuring Temple versus the University of Hawaii and caught two passes, ABC announcer Keith Jackson noted that Scott was the son of rock 'n' roll star Bill Haley.

Temple's public relations director called the Philadelphia press. On November 8 and 9, several articles appeared in the Philadelphia newspapers featuring interviews with Scott. Rex Zario, an associate of Jack Howard, saw the telecast and sent the clippings to Bill Sr., and he, in turn, reestablished contact with Scott and Bill Jr. Bill Sr. began a series of late-night telephone calls to his sons that continued until his death a year and a half later. He was very proud that Scott was a football player. Bill Sr. loved football, and Earl Campbell and the Houston Oilers were his favorites.

During the late-night calls, in rambling, disjointed stream-of-consciousness fashion, Bill Sr. told Scott and Bill Jr. that he'd been a Marine, which they knew was not true. He also told them, falsely, that he was working with the US Drug Enforcement Administration as a "deputy sheriff." Telling Bill Jr. he'd read he was a musician who played several instruments, he challenged his son's ability, saying, "You'll never be as good a picker as me."

He then told an elaborate tale about how he'd recently gone into a bar when he noticed, "Now Appearing— Bill Haley Jr." on its marquee. He said he went in and listened, and thought the kid did all right "doing the country music thing." So after the set, he said, he'd called the kid over to his table and let him know that he sure wasn't Bill Haley Jr., because he, himself, was Bill Haley Sr. The shocked kid then continued to hang out and drink with him. In a drunken, rambling fashion, Bill Sr. then conveyed to the real Bill Jr. what he said was the fatherly advice he'd given this presumably imaginary kid.

Bill Jr. told Bill Sr. that he'd liked his latest album, *Everyone Can Rock 'n' Roll.* Bill Sr. chuckled and said, "Oh, so you're a fan!"

"I'm more than a fan. I'm your son!" Bill Jr. said, and Bill Sr. asked, "What do you want from me, Bill. Do you want money?"

"No dad. I want a father," Bill Jr. replied.

Bill Sr. was silent for a moment, took another drink of whiskey, and in an angry voice said, "Do you know what you being my son means to me?"

"No," Bill Jr. answered.

Gulping another drink, Bill Sr. said, "I stuck my dick in your mother and you came out." Bill Jr. realized it was the whiskey talking, but it still hurt.

In other phone calls, Bill Sr. talked about his current accomplishments, telling both Scott and Bill Jr. numerous times that he'd played for the Queen of England, as if he'd never mentioned that to them before. He also talked quite a bit about his manager Patrick Malynn, and about his own business dealings and legal entanglements at home involving his mango ranch and Donna, Texas, hotel. He also often hinted at something even more sinister, implying there was underworld involvement and that it was a dangerous situation. He warned Bill Jr. not to get involved with "the people in Philadelphia," and when Bill Jr. asked him why, he wouldn't or couldn't elaborate.

During almost all these conversations, Bill Sr. sounded as if he were blind drunk. Often there would be interruptions in his litany—thirty seconds or a minute or more while he poured himself another glass of Johnny Walker and gulped it down, or stumbled off to the bathroom to take a pee. "Beer?" he laughed, on one occasion, when Bill Jr. asked what he was drinking. "Beer, ha, ha, ha, no, I don't drink beer Billy. I never drink that." He then took another gulp of whiskey.

One night it was very late—as most of these phone calls were, about 3 a.m.—and Bill Sr. and Bill Jr. were having a particularly good conversation. Bill Jr. was feeling close to Bill Sr. "It was beautiful to me," Bill Jr. said. His father was a little drunk, but not out of control or slurring his speech or losing his train of thought, which he did often enough.

On this particular night, things were going really well, and before his father hung up, he said, "I'll call you in the morning, Bill."

Bill Jr. said "Okay, dad," and hung up, not really believing his father would call or that he would even remember the conversation. The next morning, a Saturday, Bill Jr.'s phone rang, and it was his father, but his voice was different. It was clear, direct, very restrained, and humble. The moment he heard it, he knew his dad was completely sober. This was probably the first time he'd heard his father like that since he was a child.

"Hello," Bill Jr. said. "How are you doin'?"

"Good," his father replied.

"I said I would call you this morning," Bill Sr. said.

"Yeah," Bill Jr. responded. He was nervous. This was his real father, not some half-crazed drunk babbling on the other end of the phone, but a real, clear-minded, sober parent. There was a long pause that seemed like an eternity of total silence.

"Well," Bill Sr. said, "I'll give you a call later in the week."

And that was it. They hung up, and Bill Jr. knew right then and there that he would never work things out with his father. There were many more calls after this one, but never again was his father completely sober in any of them.

From late May into June 1980, Bill Sr. went to South Africa for what proved to be his final tour. The band was a hit in Johannesburg but received mixed to poor reviews elsewhere. Bill cancelled tours to England and Europe scheduled for later that year.

Bill's oldest son, Jack, went to visit Bill Sr. at the house in Harlingen, Texas, in October 1980. His father had asked him to come, but provided only a one-way ticket. Bill Sr. and his friend Buddy Larimore, the Harlingen Police Chief, picked up Jack at the airport, and the first day, everything went well. Father and son had dinner and stayed out until 2 a.m.

The following day they didn't go out of the house or eat all day. Around dinnertime, Jack asked Bill if they could go get some food to eat, and they went to Sambo's, a local diner-type restaurant. Before they went in, Bill told Jack not to tell anybody who he was, but as soon as they got inside, Bill said to the hostess, "Hey, you know who I am? I'm Bill Haley."

Bill kept repeating this statement to the waitress, the busboy, and anyone else who might listen. When they went back home, Jack noticed about fifteen copies of the LP *Everyone Can Rock 'n' Roll* on a table. He asked if he could have one, and Bill freaked out. Throwing the records across the room, he shouted, "All you Haleys are alike! That's all you want!" Jack backed off and went to bed.

The next morning, Jack came downstairs and Bill was still up, sitting in the living room and drinking coffee, staring at Jack with his one good eye. They went to Sambo's again for breakfast. Bill didn't eat, but after breakfast, they stopped at the liquor store. Bill asked Jack what he drank. "Budweiser," Jack said, and they went into the store, where the clerk knew Bill well. Bill purchased a six-pack for Jack and three bottles of liquor for himself. They went back to the house, where Bill quickly got drunk and told Jack to call Pedro.

Jack tried, but Martha wouldn't let Jack talk to Pedro and asked him if Bill was drinking. Bill was furious that Martha wouldn't let Jack talk to his half-brother, and another freak-out ensued. Scared, Jack ran out of the house, found a pay phone, and called Larimore. The police chief took Jack back to the house to get his things and then drove him to the airport. Out of cash, Jack had to charge a plane ticket to Philadelphia as well as a hotel room for the night, because there were no flights that day. That was the last time Jack saw his Dad.

When Bill cancelled another scheduled tour of England and Europe in October 1980, Patrick Malynn, one of his managers, circulated rumors that Bill was near death from an alleged brain tumor. Bill's German manager, Wolfgang Burch, was quoted in the October 25 edition of *Bild*, a German tabloid, as saying Bill "can never play his guitar again. Never again will he be able to sing his wild songs." Haley had never mentioned anything about having a brain tumor in his talks with Scott and Bill Jr., however, and in fact denied it when Bill Jr. asked him about it.

Malynn's attempt at a cover-up was badly damaged shortly thereafter by the respectable German newspaper *Berliner Zeitung*, which reported that Bill was undergoing a "cold turkey" alcoholism cure. The *Zeitung* story stated that Bill had collapsed after a concert in Texas and been taken to a hospital, where it was determined that the cause was "the huge consumption of alcohol by the singer."

Around Thanksgiving 1980, when Martha took the additional step of attempting to have Bill committed to the Rio Grande Center, a Texas state facility for the mentally disturbed, Bill used the tumor story to block this move. He called his lawyer, who alleged to the appropriate court that Bill's mental infirmities were the result of a "physical ailment, brain cancer." Whatever the exact cause of his mental problems, Bill's last few months were spent fading in and out of psychosis. Due to his alleged brain cancer or simply chronic alcoholism, he was now half out of his mind, as evidenced by the countless rambling phone calls he made to his sons and others during these months.

The US supermarket tabloid, the *Star*, reported on March 3, 1981, that by now, "The man who topped the charts in the '50s would often shun the lime-light completely." But at other times, Bill's friends said, he seemed to live in the past, and he regaled anyone within earshot with stories about his life as a superstar.

Barbara Billnitzer, a waitress at Sambo's restaurant in Harlingen, told the *Star* that Haley would visit there two or three times a week when he was in the mood to mix with the townsfolk. "He always seemed real lonely," Billnitzer said. "Sometimes he would walk in and tell us he was Bill Haley and then show us his driver's license, as if to prove it. . . . Sometimes he would walk up to different customers and introduce himself. When he'd tell you who he was, he'd act like it was a big secret he was giving away."

During one visit to Sambo's, Billnitzer said, Bill simply "would sit at the counter and start singing. Then he'd talk to people, like he wanted them to figure out who he was without him having to tell them."

Carl Strong, a regular customer at that restaurant, said he'd known Haley for about two and a half years. "He was quite likeable," Strong said. "Sometimes he would sit at the counter and look at nothing. Sometimes he'd order a meal and not even eat it. . . . But when he did feel like talking, he would say, 'I'm the guy who made 'Rock Around the Clock.' Then he'd show me his driver's license."

The *Star* reported that Bill also would drive his Lincoln Continental to the Hop Shop bar in Harlingen. "There were times when he seemed very lonely and very unhappy with life," said Jim Freeman, a friend of Haley's and deputy manager of the Hop Shop. "He was in here about three or four times a week. Sometimes he would sing a few of his old songs and once he even brought his guitar with him." Freeman told the *Star* that Harlingen Police had found Haley wandering late at night several times and dropped him off at his home.

42

The Day the Music Died

The death of one million people is a statistic.
The death of one person is a tragedy.
—JOSEPH STALIN

On February 8, 1981, the day before Bill Haley died, he called his son Bill Jr. two nights in a row. Bill Sr. was very distressed. Martha had kicked him out and and wouldn't let him talk to the children, he told his son. Bill Jr. later learned that his father was staying in a little room in the pool house near the garage. Its windows had been spray-painted black. Each time Bill Sr. called Bill Jr. that week, he was beside himself because Martha would not respond to him.

According to Gina Haley, Bill's youngest daughter with Martha, Bill had moved to the pool house voluntarily. He hadn't wanted his kids to see him when he was drunk or having neurological problems that likely had been caused or exacerbated by his drinking, Gina said. Martha told *Texas Monthly* that when Jack Haley had visited in October, she, Pedro and Gina stayed at her sister's house south of Houston; Martha Maria, Bill's oldest child with Martha, stayed elsewhere; and all of them returned before Christmas.

By the afternoon of February 8, Bill Jr. said, he was tired of hearing about Bill Sr.'s problems with his new family, including Martha's and his children's absences. He told his father so, but that didn't deter him. Bill Jr. continued to listen to his father's complaints and tried to offer some words of encouragement, to no effect.

"Give it some time, dad," Bill Jr. said. "Maybe she (Martha) just needs a break." But Bill Sr. continued to ramble on and on, begging and pleading with Bill Jr. to call Martha for him and ask her to take him back.

"'No,' Bill Jr. finally said. '"I won't do that. I've never spoken to Martha. She doesn't know me.'" Bill Jr. said he didn't have a tremendous amount of compassion for his father at that moment. He didn't feel any sense of filial obligation to the father who abandoned his family, talked to him rudely so often, and been absent for so much of his life. He also thought his father was just being overly dramatic, as usual.

Bill Sr. was relentless, however. "Please, please. Pleeeeaaaase!" he said. Finally, Bill Jr. lost patience and hung up the phone.

On February 9, 1981, Bill Haley's long odyssey came to an unceremonious end. At 12:35 p.m., the man who'd sold more than seventy-five million records and had created forty Top 40 hits was found dead in his bed at the pool house at his home at 1902 South 1st Street in Harlingen, Texas, at the age of 55. He was wearing pajamas. His friend Buddy Larimore found him. Haley had been dead no longer than six hours; Larimore had spoken with him at 6:30 that morning.

Tommy Thompson, Justice of the Peace in Harlingen, ruled that Bill had died of natural causes. He said Bill Sr. had been found lying in a "normal fashion, as though he were asleep." Haley was pronounced dead at 12:44 p.m., and his death certificate listed a heart attack as the probable cause of his demise. No autopsy was conducted.

A funeral service was held two days later at the Immaculate Heart of Mary Catholic Church in Harlingen. About seventy-five people attended. Later, Bill's body was cremated at a Brownsville Crematorium and his ashes taken to a church in Mexico. Its location was not disclosed.

Cuppy heard the news while at work in her management position at AT&T. She was surprised how sad it made her. That evening at home she sat down and cried, remembering the good times, the bad times, and the dreams she and Bill had once shared. The next day she sent Bill's mother's favorite flowers, "Sweet Williams," to the funeral home in Texas. Her card simply read, "See Ya Later, Alligator. Cuppy."

On February 19, 1981, Martha Haley filed a deposition to probate Bill's will. It was approved on March 2. The estate was assessed as follows: "real and personal property described generally as home, cash, securities, automobiles, household goods and personal effects of probable value in excess of $25,000."

Cuppy hired an attorney to investigate Bill's estate. That lawyer received a letter from Harlingen attorney Karl M. Gibbon discussing conversations Gibbon had had with Bill's attorney, Lee Wiley. Gibbon's letter reads: "With respect to the assets of the estate of Bill Haley, [Wiley] is pessimistic, stating that Mr. Haley began to deteriorate some two years ago and had been drinking very heavily. He said that his office had represented Bill Haley for several years but about two years ago, he ceased paying his bills and they did very little for him over the last two years of his life."

The letter went on to state that as far as Wiley knew, about the only assets Bill Sr. had had were two Lincoln automobiles, one of which was repossessed at about the time of his death, and the house. Wiley also said his investigation at the County Clerk's office "shows the deed to the house to be in Martha Haley's name."

Gibbon's response indicated that Bill had spent all his royalties from his musical career before he died, including, apparently, his recent royalties from the use of "Rock Around the Clock" in the *American Graffiti* movie and the *Happy Days* TV series. He probably used the money to pay living expenses for himself, his third wife, and their three children, and to finance his numerous failed Mexican business ventures.

A few years later, Cuppy married her long-time companion Earle Hahn, who had lost his wife to breast cancer. Hahn passed away in 2008, but Cuppy remains in good health and lives comfortably in Montgomery County, Pennsylvania.

The day Bill Sr. died, Bill Jr. had been at work and heard his father's voice, singing 'Shake, Rattle and Roll' on the radio. He thought it was strange because he wasn't listening to an "oldies" station. When the song ended, he heard the news of his father's death. After an initial jolt, he thought to himself, how ironic that in the end, the man who brought so much joy to so many people through his music died alone and broken-hearted

Bill Jr. went on to say that he harbored some measure of anger, bitterness, and resentment toward his father at that time, and for some time thereafter. When newspaper reporters from all over the country contacted him, looking for a statement from the family, his constant response was "No comment."

Moving on, he said he tried to suppress thoughts about his relationship with his father, but those thoughts were always there, lingering, lurking, nagging—unfinished business, seeking resolution. He felt a dichotomous mixture of pride and shame about his father.

For many years, Bill Jr. refused invitations to attend tributes or events celebrating Bill Sr.'s accomplishments. Gradually, however, that began to change. The original Comets reformed in 1987, and over the next few years they occasionally played in the Philadelphia area and on the Jersey Shore. They were still friends with Cuppy, and when Bill Jr. accompanied her to some of their shows, he accepted their invitation to appear with them and sing a few of his father's hit songs from time to time.

Bill Jr.'s interest in playing and writing music was rekindled. Forming a garage band called Bill Haley and the Satellites, he wrote a half-dozen new songs and recorded them on a CD entitled *Already Here*. He has described them as "heavy on 1970s-style guitars and exploring the themes of love, alien time travel, imminent nuclear environmental disaster, and the mysteries of life and death."

When friends of Bill Jr. hosted a CD release party for him in their retail store in Phoenixville, Pennsylvania, they asked Bill Haley and the Satellites to perform a few of his dad's tunes as well, which they did "rather poorly," Bill Jr. said. As it turns out, a Haley fan at that party, Wayne Young, posted a cell phone video on YouTube of the group singing its spontaneous version of "Rock Around the Clock." This resulted in a request from a booking agent to Bill Jr. to put together a professional band that would play Bill Sr.'s music authentically.

Bill Jr. seized that opportunity. He assembled a new band and created a "Rock and Roll History Show" using songs from the Comets' beginning days up through their familiar Decca hits. In between the numbers, Bill Jr. tells a variety of stories, supplementing the experience with a simultaneous slide show of about two hundred mostly rare photos. That show was the beginning of Bill Jr.'s finding a way to exorcise his negative feelings for his father. He began to vicariously experience what a small part of his father's life must have been like.

Over the last few years, Bill Jr. has performed in the UK at the Hemsby Rock 'n' Roll Weekender, the Shake Rattle and Roll Weekender, and Rocker's Reunion festivals, and made a guest appearance on a German television show to talk about his father. He and his band have played music together throughout the US and on cruise ships, and in 2014, they traveled to New Zealand for a three-and-a-half-week, thirteen-city tour.

Bill Jr. explained that his father was on the road forty-plus weeks per year for most of his childhood. His own experience traveling and performing made him realize how impossible it would be to maintain your connection and affection for home when you're almost never there. But understanding that was not enough.

In August 2016, Bill Jr. came down with a mysterious ailment that started out as stomach discomfort that progressively got worse for about three weeks. He lost twenty pounds, went to a doctor who diagnosed an ulcer, and scheduled a follow-up appointment the following Monday. But that Sunday he found himself in the hospital emergency room. After three days of testing, doctors said the cause was "most likely" some type of bone marrow virus.

Bill Jr.'s white blood cell counts were all out of whack, his spleen and liver had enlarged, and his gall bladder wall had thickened. He said the

doctors began treating him with high doses of Prednisone while they tried
to locate and identify the virus. On the fourth night in the hospital, he
was told that they'd eliminated practically every known virus and were
waiting for results of a test for leukemia.

Bill Jr. heard the word, but intuitively dismissed that possibility. He
told himself it was nothing serious. He lay awake all that night, unable
to sleep, yet he was calm and relaxed. He was absolutely certain that
whatever he had was treatable and he was going to walk out of there
just fine. Bill Jr. tried to quiet his mind by shuffling the playlist on his
iPhone and popping in the ear buds.

He became even more introspective than he'd already been in trying to comprehend the essence of what he really was. As he quieted
the chatter of his inner voice, he focused on the likelihood that his life
journey must have a purpose, and that he must have played some role
in creating that purpose. And although he'd chosen to put himself in a
situation where he'd be regarded as someone who lived in the shadow
of someone larger than himself, he was being challenged to evolve
without the guidance and protection of that parental figure. He also
realized that his effort to learn as much as possible about his father and
share that knowledge with the world was a journey of self-discovery. By
coming to that conclusion, he turned the tables on what had plagued
him his whole life—seeing himself as a victim and resenting his circumstances.

Bill Jr. said his revelation in the hospital also required the acceptance of his own responsibility for his circumstances. As much as
possible, he said, he's been able to let go of any lingering resentment
toward his father. Now he looks at his father in an empathetic and
admiring light, and understands that his father's drinking was a disease
that ultimately destroyed him.

Bill Jr.'s mystery illness soon resolved itself. He was released from
the hospital and his blood counts eventually returned to normal. "So
here's the ironic part," Bill Jr. said. All his life he longed for the love
and recognition of his father, which he could never get. Now, through
circumstance, he's telling his father's story. He's out on the road, singing
his father's songs and telling stories about his father's musical accomplishments, presenting an energetic, visually entertaining representation of his father's band, making an effort to preserve his father's legacy
in a positive way—and there's an unexpected bonus to all that.

After each show he gets to meet his father's fans. He's met thousands
of his father's fans through the years who love to tell him how happy his

father's music made them, how much they enjoyed Bill Jr.'s show and how it brought back some of the happiest memories of their lives. Many bubble with excitement as they share their stories of where they were when they first saw Bill Sr. or what they were doing when they heard their first Bill Haley record.

Some of these fans say to Bill Jr., "Your father must be looking down from heaven and be so proud of you!" and Bill Jr. thinks to himself, "Either that or he's rolling over in his grave!" But Bill Jr. said he does hope and chooses to believe it may well be the former. And he thinks of it as his father's indirect way of loving his son.

Nobody can be everything to everybody, Bill Jr. said. We all have our faults and shortcomings as well as our own unique gifts and abilities. From the very beginning, whether it originated in the support and encouragement he received from his parents, or rose from a source deep inside himself, Bill Sr. believed with every ounce of his being that he was destined to become a successful and famous musician, Bill Jr. explained. He never wavered in his pursuit of that destiny, even though it ultimately cost him the opportunity to have meaningful relationships with significant people in his life and probably contributed to his chronic alcoholism.

Nevertheless, Bill Jr. said, his father followed his calling, which was to make millions of people happy through his music, and he succeeded beyond his wildest dreams. "He continues to succeed," Bill Jr. concluded. "Every time I listen to his music, I can feel the love pouring out of him. And even though I am only one of millions, I'm okay with that. So thank you, Dad. I accept and appreciate your love from afar, and I love you back."

Bill Haley Jr.'s Acknowledgements and Thanks

I WOULD LIKE TO THANK my literary agent, Lee Sobel, for contacting me and taking the steps necessary to get this book into print, and for connecting me with my coauthor, Peter Benjaminson. I owe a great debt of gratitude to Peter, who took my originally unwieldy one-hundred-fifty-thousand-word monster of a manuscript, removed much of the extraneous detail that bogged it down, and skillfully added transitions and elaboration where appropriate.

I am also deeply indebted to those individuals acknowledged in the "Note to Readers" at the beginning of this book, especially my mother Cuppy and Sam Sgro, who patiently sat for numerous lengthy interviews over an extended period of time and freely shared their intimate knowledge of my father. I'd also like to thank the untold number of original Haley fans who shared their recollections of attending Comet performances in the 1950s and '60s.

Finally, I'd like to thank Chris Gardner, recognized as the world's leading Haley expert, and other members of a Bill Haley Yahoo discussion group moderated by Alex Frazer-Harrison who contributed quotes and information to this book. Known as the International Razor Bunnies, they also directed me to an enormous amount of relevant information, including newspaper clippings, photos, video links, audio links, and opinions posted online by the world's most ardent and knowledgeable Haley fans, including Dave Hirschberg, Klaus Kettner, Paul Bye, Wayne Young, Carl Savich, Piet Steens, Tore Christensen, Jens Boening, Robert McLeod, and ex-Comet Johnny Kay.

Peter Benjaminson's Acknowledgements and Thanks

MY THANKS to my wife, Susan Harrigan, for supporting me in writing yet another book about rock 'n' roll and for brilliantly editing several drafts of this book; to Mark Thompson and his staff at Harlem Coffee, where she did most of the editing; to my agent, Lee Sobel, who came up with the brilliant idea of uniting me with Bill Haley Jr. to help him write the story of his father; to Bill Jr. for accepting me as his coauthor; to Damien Tillman and the members of his New York Writers' Club; to my daughter Anne, her husband Greg Naarden, and my two grandchildren, Leo and Abby, for cheering me on as always; and to the FBI and the National Archives for answering my Freedom of Information Act inquiries about Bill Haley Sr.

And both authors would like to thank the editorial staff at Backbeat Books, Rowman & Littlefield, and Hal Leonard Books, including John Cerullo, Clare Cerullo and Bernadette Malavarca, for their skilled editorial suggestions and guidance.

Bibliography

The Beatles Anthology. San Francisco Chronicle Books, 2000.

Benjaminson, Peter. *The Story of Motown*. New York: Grove Press, 1979; Los Angeles: Rare Bird Books, 2018.

Birmingham Evening Dispatch, February 12, 1957.

Berliner Zeitung, Berlin, 1980.

Bild, Berlin, 1980.

Billboard Magazine, New York, NY. Numerous articles from 1949 to 1981.

Bill Haley and His Comets in Great Britain 1957, Volumes 1-3. Complete Press Cuttings Compiled by Press Representatives Suzanne Warner, Ltd., 45, Lowndes Sq. London, SWI.

Cohn, Nik. *Rock from the Beginning*. New York: Stein and Day, 1969.

Daily Mirror, London. February 7, 1957.

Dawson, Jim. *Rock Around the Clock: The Record That Started the Rock Revolution*. San Francisco: Backbeat Books, 2005.

Delaware County Times, Wilmington, DE. Numerous articles.

Fuchs, Otto. *Bill Haley: The Father of Rock 'n' Roll*. Bks. 1 and 2. Norderstedt, Germany: Herstellung und Verlag Books on Demand, 2016.

George-Warren, Holly and Patricia Romanowski (eds.). *The Rolling Stone Encyclopedia of Rock and Roll*. New York: Fireside, 2001.

Glasgow Daily Herald, February 9, 1957.

Glasgow Daily Record, February 19, 1957.

Greenville News, Greenville, SC. May 23, 1956.

Hadju, David. *Love for Sale: Pop Music in America*. New York: Farrar, Straus and Giroux, 2016.

Haley, John W. and John von Hoelle. *Sound and Glory: The Incredible Story of Bill Haley, the Father of Rock 'n' Roll and the Music that Shook the World*. Wilmington, Delaware: Dyne-American Publications, 1990.

Hall, Michael. "Fading Comets." *Texas Monthly*, June 2011.

Hearn, Marcus. The Cinema of George Lucas. New York: Abrams Books, 2005.

www.history.com, 11/13/09, "The American Invasion Begins as Bill Haley and the Comets Storm Britain," published by A&E TV Network.

Honolulu Advertiser, August 14, 1960.

Kirby, David. *Crossroad: Artist, Audience, and the Making of American Music*. Milwaukee: New American Press, 2015.

www.legacy.com, November 2011, "Bill Haley: The Father of Rock and Roll" by Legacy Staff.

London Daily Mail, February 6, 1957.

London Daily Mirror, February 7, 1957.

London Daily Sketch, London. February 7, 1957.

London Morning Advertiser, London. February 6, 1957.

London Observer. February 10, 1957.

Manchester Evening News, February 22, 1957.

Melody Maker, London, September 16, 1964; December 11, 1976.

Miami Herald, April 23, 1971.

Nash, Graham. *Wild Tales.* New York: Three Rivers Press, 2013.

Newsweek, New York, NY. October 1956.

New York Age, New York, NY. November 19, 1955.

New York American Journal, New York, NY. November 16, 1956.

New York Times, New York, NY. November 1955.

North Wales Pioneer. February 15, 1957.

Now Dig This, Ford, Peter. "Rock Around the Clock and Me,"
     June 2004 (#255).

Now Dig This, Gardner, Chris. "Taking Care of Bill."

Philadelphia Bulletin, October 25, 1970.

Rolling Stone, August 1968.

Shaw, Arnold. *The Rockin' '50s.* New York: Da Capo Press, 1974.

Stanley, Bob. *Yeah! Yeah! Yeah!: The Story of Pop Music from Bill Haley to Beyonce.*
     New York: W. W. Norton and Company, 2014.

Star, March 3, 1981.

Swenson, John. *Bill Haley: The Daddy of Rock and Roll.* Briarcliff Manor, NY:
     Stein and Day, 1982.

The Terre Haute Indiana Star, October 30, 1958.

Texas Monthly, Austin, Texas. June 2011. Hall, Michael. "Falling Comet."

Variety Magazine, New York, NY. October 1955.

Warwick, Neil, Jon Kutner, and Tony Brown. *The Complete Book of the British
     Charts, Singles and Albums.* London: Omnibus Press, 2004.

Whitburn, Joel. *Billboard Book of Top 40 Hits, 1955-2009.* 9th ed.
     New York: Billboard Books, 2010.

Whitburn, Joel. *Joel Whitburn's Top Pop Singles, Billboard,
     1955-2006.* Menomonee Falls, WI: Record Research, 2007.

Whitburn, Joel. *Joel Whitburn's Top R&B Singles, 1942-1988.* Menomonee Falls,
     WI: Record Research, 1985.

Whitburn, Joel. *Joel Whitburn's Top Pop Albums, 1955-1985.* Menomonee Falls,
     WI: Record Research, 2001.

Bill Haley Discography

(Note: Parentheses after some listings contains the name of the songwriter(s), the name of the company holding the copyright, the number assigned to the record on which the song was released, and the months and/or dates on which the record was released and recorded)

Songs recorded with Four Aces of Western Swing, at WPWA Chester in 1948 but unreleased

"Easy Rockin' Chair"

"I Love You So Much"

"Honestly"

"I Dream of an Old Love Affair"

1948 Cowboy Records Releases with the Four Aces of Western Swing

"Too Many Parties, Too Many Pals" (Hank Williams) b/w "Four Leaf Clover Blues" (Bill Haley and Shorty Long) (1700) (July)

1949 Cowboy Record Releases with the Four Aces of Western Swing

"Candy Kisses" (George Morgan) b/w "Tennessee Border" (Red Foley) (1701) (February)

Songs recorded with the Saddlemen at WPWA Chester in 1949 but unreleased

"Are You Teasin' Me?"

"Ages and Ages Ago"

"Little Rock, A-R-K"

"Behind the Eight Ball"

1950 Center Records Releases with the Saddlemen

"Stand Up and Be Counted" b/w "Loveless Blues" (102)

1950 Atlantic Records Releases with the Saddlemen

"Why Do I Cry Over You?" b/w "I'm Gonna Dry Every Tear with a Kiss" (727) (September)

1950 Keystone Records Releases with the Saddlemen

"Deal Me a Hand (I Play the Game Anyway)" b/w "Ten Gallon Stetson (With a Hole in the Crown)" (5101) (January)

"I'm Not to Blame" b/w "Susan Van Dusen" (5102) (March)

1950 Cowboy Records Release as Reno Browne and her Buckaroos with Bill Haley on Vocal

"My Palomino and I" b/w "Sweet Little Gal from Nevada"
    (October) (1705)

1950 Unreleased Cowboy Records Tracks with the Saddlemen

"Yodel Your Blues Away" (Bill Haley and Jack Howard)

"Rovin' Eyes" (Dr. Louis Menaker)

"Rose of My Heart" (Bill Haley and Jack Howard)

"A Yodeler's Lullaby" (Slim Stuart)

"Candy and Women" (Bill Haley and Eddie Mallie)

"Foolish Questions" (Writer Unknown)

"The Covered Wagon Rolled Right Along" (Britt Wood and Hy Heath)

"Wreck on the Highway" (Roy Acuff)

"Behind the Eight Ball" (Writer Unknown)

"My Mom Heard Me Crying" (Bill Haley)

"Within This Broken Heart of Mine" (Slim Stuart, Elmer Newman and Jimmy
    Walker, Jack Howard Publishing [B.M.I.])

"Cotton-Haired Gal" (Bill Haley and Eddie Mallie)

Holiday Record Releases (Mid to Late 1951)

"Rocket 88" (Jackie Brenston) b/w "Tearstains on My Heart" (Bill Haley and Harry
    Broomall) (105) (July)

"Green Tree Boogie" (Bill Haley) b/w "Down Deep in My Heart" (Bill Haley)
    (108) (August)

"Pretty Baby" (Griffin Bros.) b/w "I'm Crying" (Memphis Slim). Both recorded
    with Loretta Glendenning and the Saddlemen (110) (November)

"A Year Ago This Christmas" (Haley) b/w" I Don't Want to Be Alone This Christ-
    mas" (Haley) (111) (November)

Holiday Records Releases (Early 1952)

"Jukebox Cannonball" (Jesse Rogers, Borrie, and Rusty Keefer) b/w "Sundown
    Boogie" (Bill Haley and Jesse Rogers) (113) (January)

1952 Essex Records Releases as the Saddlemen

"Icy Heart" (Berk-Berk) b/w "Rock the Joint" (H. Crafton, D. Keene, and Doc
    Bagby) (303) (March)

"Rocking Chair on the Moon" (Bill Haley and Harry Broomall) b/w "Dance with
    the Dolly with a Hole in Her Stocking" (J. Hand, J. Eaton, and H. Leader)
    (305) (June)

1953 Essex Records Releases as Bill Haley and the Comets

"Stop Beatin' 'Round the Mulberry Bush" (B. Reichner and C. Boland) b/w "Real
    Rock Drive" (Bill Haley) (310) (January)

"Crazy Man, Crazy" (Bill Haley) b/w "Watcha Gonna Do?"
(Bill Haley) (321) (April)

"Pat-A-Cake" (Bill Haley and Billy Williamson)/"Fractured"
(Bill Haley and Marshall Lytle) (327)

"Live it Up" (Bill Haley) b/w "Farewell, So Long, Goodbye" (Bill Haley) (332)

"I'll Be True to You" (W. McLemore)/"Ten Little Indians" (Bill Haley) (340)

"Straight Jacket" (Bill Haley) b/w "Chattanooga Choo Choo"
(Gordon N. Warren) (348)

"Jukebox Cannonball" (Rusty Keefer, Jesse Rogers, and Borrie) b/w "Sundown
Boogie" (Bill Haley) (374)

"Rocket 88" (Jackie Brenston) b/w "Green Tree Boogie" (Bill Haley) (381)

1953 Transworld Essex Records Releases

"Rocket 88" (Jackie Brenston) b/w "Green Tree Boogie" (Bill Haley) (381)

"Yes Indeed" b/w "Real Rock Drive" (718)

1954 Decca Records Releases

"Thirteen Women (And Only One Man in Town)" (Dickie Thompson) b/w
"Rock Around the Clock" (Jimmy DeKnight and Max C. Freedman)
(29124) (April; Recorded April 12, 1954)

"Shake, Rattle and Roll" (Charles E. Calhoun) b/w "ABC Boogie"
(Al Russell and Max Spickol) (29204) (June; Recorded June 7, 1954)

"Dim, Dim, the Lights" (Beverly Ross and Julius Dixon) b/w "Happy Baby"
(Frank Pingatore) (29317) (October; Recorded September 21, 1954)

1955 Essex Records Re-Releases

"Rock the Joint" (H. Crafton, D. Keene and Doc Bagby) b/w
"Farewell, So Long, Goodbye" (Bill Haley) (399) (June)

1955 Decca Records Releases

"Mambo Rock" (Bickley Reichner, Mildred Phillips, and Jimmy Ayre) b/w
"Birth of the Boogie" (Bill Haley, Billy Williamson, and Johnny Grande)
(29418) (January; Recorded January 5, 1955)

"Two Hound Dogs" (Bill Haley-Frank Pingatore)/Razzle Dazzle" (Charles E. Calhoun) (29552) (June; Recorded May 10, 1955)

"Rock-A-Beatin' Boogie" (Bill Haley)/"Burn That Candle" (Winfield Scott) (29713)
(October; Recorded 9/22/55)

"See You Later Alligator" (Robert Charles Guidry) b/w "Paper Boy (On Main Street
USA)" (Bill Haley-Catherine Cafra) (29791) (December; Recorded 12/12/55)

1956 Decca Releases

"R-O-C-K" (Bill Haley, Rusty Keefer, and Ruth Keefer) b/w
"Saints' Rock 'n Roll" (Arrangement by Bill Haley and Milt Gabler)
(29870) (March; Recorded 9/22/55)

"Rockin' Through the Rye" (Bill Haley, Rusty Keefer, Catherine Cafra, and Milt Gabler) b/w "Hot Dog Buddy Buddy" (Bill Haley) (29948) (May; Recorded 3/30/56)

"Rip It Up" (Robert A. Blackwell and John S. Marascalco) b/w "Teenager's Mother (Are You Right?)" (30028) (July; Recorded 7/12/56)

"Rudy's Rock" (Bill Haley and Rudy Pompilli) b/w "Blue Comet Blues" (30085) (September; Recorded 3/23/56)

"Don't Knock the Rock" (Fred Karger and Robert E. Kent) b/w "Choo Choo Ch' Boogie" (Vaughn Horton, Denver Darling, and Milt Gabler) (30148) (November; Recorded 10/4/56)

LP: "Rock 'n' Roll Stage Show" (8345)

"Calling All Comets"

"Rockin' Through the Rye"

"Rudy's Rock"

"Hook, Line and Sinker"

"A Rockin' Little Tune"

"Choo Choo Ch' Boogie"

"Hide and Seek"

"Blue Comet Blues"

"Hey Then, There, Now"

"Goofin' Around"

"Hot Dog Buddy Buddy"

"Tonight's the Night"

1957 Decca Releases

"Forty Cups of Coffee" (Danny Overbea) b/w "Hook, Line and Sinker" (30214)

"Rockin' Rollin' Rover" b/w "(You Hit the Wrong Note) Billy Goat" (J. Leslie McFarland) (30314)

"The Dipsy Doodle" b/w "Miss You" (30394)

"Rock the Joint" b/w "How Many?" (Blaire-Barnes) (30461)

"Mary, Mary Lou" b/w "It's a Sin" (Eddie Arnold) (30530)

1958 Decca Releases

"Skinny Minnie" (Bill Haley, Rusty Keefer, Milt Gabler, and Catherine Cafra) b/w "Sway with Me" (same writers) (30592)

"Lean Jean" b/w "Don't Nobody Move" (30681)

"Chiquita Linda (Un Poquito De Tu Amor?)" b/w "Whoa Mabel" (Bill Haley, Rusty Keefer, Milt Gabler, and Catherine Cafra) (30741)

"Corrine, Corrina" (J.M. Williams, Bo Chatman, and Mitchell Parish) b/w "B. B. Betty" (30781)

1959 Decca Releases

"Charmaine" b/w "I Got a Woman" (Ray Charles) (30844)

"(Now and Then There's) a Fool Such as I" b/w "Where'd You Go Last Night"
(30873)

"Caldonia" b/w "Shaky" (30926)

"Joey's Song" (Joe Reisman) b/w "Ooh! Look-A-There, Ain't She Pretty!"
(Todd-Lombardo) (30956)

"Skokiaan" b/w "Puerto Rican Peddler" (31030)

"(Put Another Nickle In) Music, Music, Music!" b/w "Strictly Instrumental" (31080)

Other Decca Releases

"Ida, Sweet as Apple Cider" (Eddie Leonard)

"Eloise" (Bill Haley, Rusty Keefer, Milt Gabler, and Catherine Cafra)

"Dinah" (Harry Akst, M. Lewis, and Joe Young)

"Hide and Seek" with Billy Williamson on lead vocal (Paul Winley and Ethel Byrd)

"Tonight's the Night" (Bill Haley and Catherine Cafra)

"Move It on Over" (Hank Williams)

"The Beak Speaks" (1958)

"Rock Lomand" (1957)

"Walkin' Beat" (1958)

"Drowsy Waters" (1958)

"Summer Souvenir" (1958)

"Goofin' Around" (1958)

"Dragon Rock" (1958)

"ABC Boogie" with Billy Williamson on lead vocal
(Bill Haley and Fern Dougherty) (1958)

"Calling All Comets" (Bill Haley, Milt Gabler, and Rudy Pompilli) (1958)

"Rockin' Little Tune" (Johnny Grande and Billy Williamson) (1958)

"Pretty Alouette" (1958)

"Piccadilly Rock" (1958)

"Rockin' Rollin' Schnitzlebank" (1958)

"Vive La Rock 'n' Roll" (1958)

"Come Rock with Me" (1958)

"Wooden Shoe Rock" (1958)

"Me Rock-A-Hula" (1958)

"Oriental Rock" (1958)

"Rockin' Matilda" (1958)

"El Rocko" (1958)

"Rockin' Rita" (1958)

"Jamaica Deejay" (1958)

Unreleased Decca Tracks

"All I Need is Some More Lovin'"

"Trouble in Mind"

"Life of the Party" with Billy Williamson on lead vocal

"I Should Write a Song About You"

"Be By Me"

"Football Rock 'n' Roll" (Not a studio tape)

1960 Warner Bros. Records Releases

"Candy Kisses" b/w "Tamiami" (5145)

"Chick Safari" b/w "Hawk" (5145)

"So Right Tonight" (Bill Haley and Bob Hayes) b/w "Let the Good Times Roll, Creole" (5151)

"Flip, Flop and Fly" (Charles Calhoun and L.W. Turner) b/w "Honky Tonk" (5228)

LP: "Haley's Jukebox" (W 1391) (1960)

"Singing the Blues"

"Candy Kisses" (George Morgan)

"No Letter Today" (Frankie Brown)

"This Is the Thanks I Get"

"Bouquet of Roses"

"There's a New Moon Over My Shoulder"

"Cold, Cold Heart" (Hank Williams)

"The Wild Side of Life"

"Any Time"

"Afraid"

"I Don't Hurt Anymore"

"Detour"

LP: "Bill Haley and His Comets"

"Crazy Man, Crazy" (Bill Haley)

"Kansas City"

"Love Letters in the Sand"

"Shake, Rattle and Roll" (Charles Calhoun)

"I'm in Love Again"

"Stagger Lee"

"Rock Around the Clock" (Jimmy DeKnight and Max C. Freedman)

"I Almost Lost My Mind"

"Blue Suede Shoes"

"My Special Angel"

"Blueberry Hill" (Al Lewis)

"Whole Lotta Shakin' Goin' On"

1961 Gone Records Releases

"The Spanish Twist" b/w "My Kind of Woman" (5111)

"Riviera" b/w "War Paint" (5116)

Early 1962 Roulette Records LP ("Twistin' Knights—Live at the Round Table" N.Y.C.) (R25174)

"Lullaby of Birdland Twist" (George Shearing)

"Twist Marie" (Roy Alfred)

"One-Two-Three Twist" (Sid Wyche)

"Down by the Riverside Twist" (Wally Schuster)

"Queen of the Twisters" (Doc Pumas-Mort Shuman)

"Caravan Twist" (Mills-Ellington-Tizol)

"I Want a Little Girl" (Mol Mencher)

"Whistlin' and Walkin' Twist" (Franny Beecher-Billy Williamson)

"Florida Twist" (Caruso-Rudy Pompilli)

"Eight More Miles to Louisville" (Grandpa Jones)

November 1961-January 1966 Orfeon Records Releases

"Florida Twist" b/w "Negra Consentida" (1047) (1961)

"Pure De Papas" b/w "Anoche" (1195) (1962)

Released as Singles or on One of Two LPs Released in 1965: "Bill Haley Y Sus Cometas" (1037); "Discos Del Millon De Rock 'n' Roll & Twist" (2084)

"Estomago Caliente"/"La Tierra"

"De Las Mil Danzas"

"Silbando Y Caminando"

"Twist Español"

"Tampico Twist"

"La Paloma"

"Caravana Twist"

"Tren Nocturno"

"Actopan"

"Mas Twist"

"Al Compas Del Reloj"

"Baja California Sun"

"Cerca Del Mar"

"Comet Boogie"

"El Madison"

"El Expresso"

"Jarrito Twist"

"Mish Mash"

"No Te Pueblito Español"

"Hay Nos Vemos Cocodrilo" (1965)

"ABC Boogie" (1965)

"Nueva Orleans" (1965)

"Nocturno De Harlem" (1965)

"Rip It Up" (1965)

"Skokiaan a Go Go"

"La Cucaracha"

"El Blues De Los Cometas"

"Caravana"

"How Many"

"Shake, Rattle and Roll"

"Skinny Minnie"

"High Heel Sneakers"

"Hambone"

"Corrine Corrina" (Joe Turner on lead vocal)

"La Marcha De Los Santos" (1965)

"Martha"

"La Tierra De Las Mils Danzas" b/w "Estomago Caliente" (6060/6061)

1963 Newtown Records Releases under the name "B. H. Sees Combo: (Arranger Bobby Martin. Harold B. Robinson Publishing Company, ASCAP)

"Tenor Man" b/w "Up Goes My Love" (5013)

"White Parakeet" (M. Levinson) b/w "Midnight in Washington" (M. Levinson) (5014) (Also released on NEW-HITS in Philadelphia)

"Dance Around the Clock" (M. Levinson) b/w "What Can I Say After I Say I'm Sorry?" (5024)

1963 Nicetown Records Releases under the name "Bill Haley and The Comets" (Arranger Bobby Martin; Harold B. Robinson Publishing Company, ASCAP)

"Tandy" (M. Levinson-R. DiCicco) b/w "You Call Everybody Darling" (Clem Watts-Sam Martin-Ben Trace) (NT5025)

Logo Records Releases (1962-1963)

"Yakety Sax" b/w "Boots Randolph's Boots' Blues" (7005)

1964 Decca Release

"The Green Door" b/w Yeah! She's Evil!" (31650)

1965 Apt Records Releases

"Burn That Candle" b/w "Stop, Look and Listen" (25081)

"Haley A Go Go" b/w "Tongue Tied Tony" (25087)

1968 Sonet LP "Biggest Hits" (GP9945). (Released in US in 1970 as "Rockin'")

"Rock Around the Clock"

"Skinny Minnie"

"Ling Ting Tong" (M. Godwin)

"Rock the Joint"

"Rock-A-Beatin' Boogie"

"See You Later Alligator"

"Flip, Flop and Fly"

"Saints' Rock 'n Roll"

"Shake, Rattle and Roll"

1969 Sonet Records LP (released in US on Janus): "Razzle Dazzle" or "Bill Haley on Stage" (Live in Stockholm Studio) (GPD9989)

"Rip It Up"

"Rudy's Rock"

"Lucille" (Al Rappa, vocal)

"Whole Lotta Shakin' Goin' On" (Nick Nastos, vocal)

"Caravan"

"Kansas City"

"What'd I Say?" (Gert Lengstrand, vocal [Swedish singer])

"Razzle Dazzle"

"Crying Time"

"Yakety Sax"

"Jenny, Jenny"

"Johnny B. Goode"

"Malaguena"

"Guitar Boogie"

"New Orleans"

February 3, 1969, United Artists Single Release

"That's How I Got to Memphis" (Tom T. Hall) b/w "'Ain't Love Funny, Ha, Ha, Ha" (F. Burch) (50483) (Produced by Henry Jerome, Arranged by Hutch Davie, BMI)

1969 Kama-Sutra-Janus Release
LP "Bill Haley's Scrapbook—Live at the Bitter End:" (BSBS20114)
"Rock the Joint"
"Rock-A-Beatin' Boogie"
"Rip It Up"
"Razzle Dazzle"
"Framed" (G. Lelber and M. Stoller)
"Rock Around the Clock"
"Crazy Man, Crazy"
"Saints' Rock 'n' Roll"
"Shake, Rattle and Roll"
"Skinnie Minnie"
"Rudy's Rock"
"See You Later Alligator"

1970 Bell Records LP "Let the Good Times Roll" (Soundtrack)
"Rock Around the Clock"
"Shake, Rattle and Roll"

1971 Sonet Records LP "Rock Around the Country" (Released on Janus in the US in 1972 as "Travelin Band") (GP100040)
"Me and Bobby McGee" (Kris Kristoferson-Fred Foster)
"How Many" (Blaire-Barnes)
"Who's Been Stopping the Rain" (J. C. Fogerty)
"Pink Eyed Pussycat" (Neal Merritt)
"Travelin' Band" (J. C. Fogerty)
"No Letter Today" (Frankie Brown)
"Dance Around the Clock" (M. Levinson)
"Games People Play" (Joe South)
"A Little Piece at a Time" (Neal Merritt and Shorty Hall)
"I Wouldn't Have Missed It for the World" (Charley Williams and Carl Walden)
"Boney Maroney" (Larry Williams)
"There's a New Moon Over My Shoulder"

1973 Sonet Records LP "Just Rock 'n' Roll Music" (SNTF645)
"High Heel Sneakers"
"Blue Suede Shoes"
"Tossin' and Turnin'"
"Flip, Flop and Fly"
"Whole Lotta Shakin' Goin' On"
"C. C. Rider"

"Lawdy Miss Clawdy"

"Bring It On Home to Me"

"Personality"

"Crazy Man, Crazy"

"Rock 'n' Roll Music"

1976 Sonet Records LP *R-O-C-K*, recorded in Muscle Shoals, Alabama (SNTF710)

"Ooh, Look-A-There Ain't She Pretty" (Todd and Lombardo)

"Dim, Dim the Lights" (Beverly Ross and Julius Dixson)

"Burn That Candle" (Winfield Scott)

"I Got A Woman" (Ray Charles)

"R-O-C-K" (Haley and Keefer)

"Farewell, So Long, Goodbye" (Haley)

"ABC Boogie" (Russel and Spikol)

"Dance with the Dolly" (Shand, Eaton, and Leader)

"I'll Be True to You" (McLemore)

"Mohair Sam" (Dallas Frazier)

June 25, 1979, Sonet Records LP *Everyone Can Rock 'n' Roll* (SNTF808): (Recorded at Fame Studios in Muscle Shoals, Alabama, with the "Fame Gang" from Jackson, Mississippi as supporting musicians.)

"Hail, Hail Rock 'n' Roll" (S. Murray)

"Jim Dandy Got Married" (Lincoln Chase, Tyrone Carlo, Alonzo Tucker, and Al Green

"That's How I Got to Memphis" (Tom T. Hall)

"Juke Box Cannonball" (A. Keefer, J. Rogers and W. Barrie)

"Let the Good Times Roll Again" (Bill Haley)

"God Bless Rock 'n' Roll" (R. Harwood and N. Jenkins)

"Everyone Can Rock 'n' Roll" (Teddy Wilson)

"The Battle of New Orleans" (J. Driftwood)

"Heartaches by the Number" (Jack Howard)

"Tweedle Dee" (Winfield Scott)

"So Right Tonight" (Bill Haley and Bob Hayes)

Index

Index